YEATS AND THE NOH: A COMPARATIVE STUDY

THE IRISH LITERARY STUDIES SERIES
ISSN 0140–895X

1 *Place, Personality & the Irish Writer*. A. Carpenter (ed.)
2 *Yeats and Magic*. M. C. Flannery
3 *A Study of the Novels of George Moore*. R. A. Cave
4 *J. M. Synge & the Western Mind*. W. Thornton
5 *Irish Poetry from Moore to Yeats*. R. Welch
6 *Yeats, Sligo, & Ireland*. A. N. Jeffares (ed.)
7 *Sean O'Casey, Centenary Essays*. D. Krause & R. G. Lowery (eds)
8 *Denis Johnston: A Retrospective*. J. Ronsley (ed.)
9 *Literature & the Changing Ireland*. P. Connolly (ed.)
10 *James Joyce: An International Perspective*. S. B. Bushrui & B. Benstock (eds)
11 *Synge: the Medieval & the Grotesque*. T. O'B. Johnson
12 *Carleton's* Traits and Stories *& the Nineteenth Century Anglo-Irish Tradition*. B. Hayley
13 *Lady Gregory, Fifty Years After*. A Saddlemyer & C. Smythe (eds)
14 *Woman in Irish Legend, Life & Literature*. S. F. Gallagher (ed.)
15 *'Since O'Casey' & Other Essays on Irish Drama*. R. Hogan
16 *George Moore in Perspective*. J. Egleson Dunleavy (ed.)
17 *W. B. Yeats, Dramatist of Vision*. A. S. Knowland
18 *The Irish Writer & the City*. M. Harmon (ed.)
19 *O'Casey the Dramatist*. H. Kosok
20 *The Double Perspective of Yeats's Aesthetic*. O. Komesu
21 *The Pioneers of Anglo-Irish Fiction, 1800–1850*. B. Sloan
22 *Irish Writers & Society at Large*. M. Sekine (ed.)
23 *Irish Writers & the Theatre*. M. Sekine (ed.)
24 *A History of Verse Translation from the Irish 1789–1897*. R. Welch
25 *Kate O'Brien, A Literary Portrait*. L. Reynolds
26 *Portraying the Self: Sean O'Casey & the Art of Autobiography*. M. Kenneally
27 *W. B. Yeats & the Tribes of Danu*. P. Alderson Smith
28 *Theatre of Shadows: Samuel Beckett's Drama 1956–76*. R. Pountney
29 *Critical Approaches to Anglo-Irish Literature*. M. Allen & A. Wilcox (eds)
30 *'Make Sense Who May': Essays on Samuel Beckett's Later Works*. R. J. Davis & L. St J. Butler (eds)
31 *Cultural Contexts & Literary Idioms in Contemporary Irish Literature* M. Kenneally (ed.)
32 *Builders of My Soul: Greek & Roman Themes in Yeats*. B. Arkins
33 *Perspectives on Irish Drama & Theatre*. J. Genet & R. A. Cave (eds)
34 *The Great Queens: Irish Goddesses from the Morrigu to Cathleen ni Houlihan*. R. Clark
35 *Irish Literature and Culture*. M. Kenneally (ed.)
36 *Irish Writers & Politics*. O. Komesu & M. Sekine (eds)
37 *Irish Writers & Religion*. R. Welch (ed.)
38 *Yeats & the Noh*. M. Sekine & C. Murray

YEATS AND THE NOH:
A COMPARATIVE STUDY

MASARU SEKINE
CHRISTOPHER MURRAY

with contributions by
AUGUSTINE MARTIN
PETER DAVIDSON
COLLEEN HANRAHAN
KATHARINE WORTH

Irish Literary Studies: 38

COLIN SMYTHE
Gerrards Cross, 1990

First published in 1990 by Colin Smythe Ltd
Gerrards Cross, Buckinghamshire

British Library Cataloguing in Publication Data

Sekine, Masaru, *1945*–
    Yeats and the Noh : a comparative study. – (Irish
literary studies series; ISSN 0140–895X; 38).
    1. Drama in English. Yeats, W. B. – Critical studies
I. Title. II. Murray, Christopher, *1940*–   III.
Series
822'.8

ISBN 0–86140–258–8

Produced in Great Britain
and printed and bound by Billing & Sons Limited,
Worcester

CONTENTS

ILLUSTRATIONS

PREFACE

This is the first joint comparative study of Yeats's unique dramatic works, *Four Plays for Dancers* (1921), and the Japanese Noh theatre which inspired them. It is also unique in having been chiefly produced by an Irish academic, Dr. Christopher Murray, and a Noh actor.

I should like to thank the Japan Foundation for a Visiting Professorship of Japanese Culture at University College, Dublin, and the British Council for a Fellowship at St. Andrews University. The former provided the first link between Waseda University, Tokyo and University College, Dublin. Professor Augustine Martin, who courteously arranged this invitation, also encouraged the production of two plays: the Noh play, *Nishikigi*, and Yeats's *The Dreaming of the Bones*; Christopher Murray acted in both pieces. It was in producing these two, very different, plays that I first conceived the idea of a book comparing the Noh theatre and Yeats's drama, to explore further these telling examples of Eastern and Western creativity.

Ironically, Yeats wrote plays which were quite close to Noh plays before he became consciously involved with this aspect of the Japanese heritage. However, when he developed his interest in Noh his sources of information were confused, because Ezra Pound, who edited the Fenollosa translations of Noh plays, did not always fully understand these works in context. Similarly, Michio Ito, the 'Noh actor' Yeats worked with, was without any real knowledge of this art form. Therefore Yeats, who never actually saw a Noh play properly performed, had no real way of understanding the Noh and its religious profundity. Accuracy, however, was not of the first importance as Yeats was a romantic poet, intent on expressing his own subjective vision.

This study shows the kind of differences which exist between the Noh, a highly aesthetic and sophisticated art form performed by actors disciplined in an arduous, esoteric tradition, and Yeats's plays, which tended to be performed occasionally in drawing rooms before a small invited audience. The stage directions, the format of each play, the imagery, and the underlying statement as to man's place, and destiny, are compared so that readers can discover the exact scope of this cultural transfusion. Plays which influenced Yeats's *Four Plays for Dancers* are analysed here; their form and techniques are examined, and also the extent to which Yeats decided on rejection, adaptation or assimilation.

Valuable contributions to this comparative study have been made by Professors Augustine Martin, Katharine Worth, Dr. Peter Davidson, and Colleen Hanrahan whose most varied expertise and practical experience have all helped further to define these differences.

Many scholars and institutions have extremely kindly and thoughtfully helped to make this book possible. I gratefully single out Waseda University, in particular, without whose varied aid, including a substantial publishing grant, this whole research programme could not have taken place, and Professor Augustine Martin, for his generous support. Many thanks also go to everyone else who has encouraged this international enterprise.

Tokyo, Japan   MASARU SEKINE
January, 1989

ACKNOWLEDGEMENTS

In writing this book, we have received helpful suggestions, as well as research material and illustrations, from A. N. Jeffares, Hiroshi Suzuki and Koichi Sekine. Our thanks are due to Tatsuo Yoshikoshi, Ken Yoshikoshi and Fergus Bourke and the Peacock Theatre for their illustrations. Grateful acknowledgement is also made to Waseda University who supported the publication of this work of international scholarship. To avoid confusion over the frequent use of italics, we used italics only for unfamiliar words (not names) and titles of works.

INTRODUCTION

YEATS'S NOH: THE DANCER AND THE DANCE

AUGUSTINE MARTIN

When I saw my first real Noh play in Kyoto I understood something that my Japanese friends had been telling me for years: that
Yeats either did not understand the Noh conventions or chose to
evade or transcend them. One has only to look at the surviving
photographs of Michio Ito who played the Guardian in the first
production of *At the Hawk's Well* in Lady Cunard's drawing room,
and compare his posture to that of a typical Noh dancer, to sense
the enormous gap between the two modes. Ito was not a Noh
dancer, had in fact come to Europe to study modern dance and
choreography. His posture, flexed, demonstrative and athletic, is in
the sharpest contrast to that of a Noh dancer. There the body is
tightly swathed in ceremonial costume, the face inset, as it were,
with an impersonal, symbolic mask, the body held in a rigid
crouch.

The tradition of the Noh is unbroken for 600 years. No editing
or adaptation is permitted with the hundreds of scripts in its repertoire. The dialogue is virtually incomprehensible to a modern
Japanese audience. The movement of the actors is confined to
short, shuffling steps. Their speech is weirdly, thrillingly artificial, moving from a plaintive falsetto in the female characters to
the most profound bass resonances. The most assertive gesture that
I observed was the stamping of a slippered foot, denoting an
extremity of rage.

The life so short, the art so long to learn: Masaru Sekine in his
definitive book on Ze-Ami has explained the elaborate and
punishing training that the Noh actor must undergo. It has no
parallel in the western theatre except, perhaps, in the ballet schools.
It differs however from western dance in being so esoteric that even
in Japan it has only a handful of connoisseurs. Even with a good

xiii

translation, as I had, and the help of a learned commentator, Sekine himself, I got no more than the general idea of the genre at a single performance. And one cannot go back the next day because the religious nature of the Noh forbids a second showing.

When I saw my Noh play in Kyoto I asked: 'Where's the Folding of the Cloth?' I was recalling Yeats's stage direction at the opening of the *Hawk's Well* where two musicians come onstage and 'slowly unfold the cloth, singing as they do so'. This I had always taken as a deeply symbolic action — involving the passing of time, the unfolding of destiny, the lord knows what. It took a while for the question to register, and then I was told: 'Yeats must have meant the cloth going up.' Then I recalled that the *shite* had entered at the left before doing his shuffle along the ramp towards the main stage; and that a small curtain had gone up, folding up itself, to allow his entrance. It has no more symbolic significance than the rise of a western theatre curtain, and is far more swift and perfunctory.

So what do we say of Yeats's momentous folding and unfolding of the cloth? Do we regret it as an embarrassing misreading of Pound's misreading of Fenollosa? Or chalk it up as a proto-Bloomian example of creative misprision, if the misunderstanding is deliberate, of clinamen if casual? It is surely more sensible to accept that Yeats saw in the cloth a valuable histrionic resource; a device new to western theatre which would achieve his object of drawing his small audience into ritual sympathy. It may be significant that in his last play for dancers, *The Death of Cuchulain*, Yeats dispensed with the device in favour of a valedictory prologue. He may have learned in the interim that he had misconstrued his initial sources; more probably he acted in the interest of the play in hand.

What is certain therefore is that Yeats knew what he was doing. He had a radical vision of theatrical possibility and the Noh was his inspiration. From it he took all the elements he needed for his new genre — the sense of religion and ritual, the sacredness of place, the omnipresence of the supernatural, custom and ceremony, the eloquence of gesture, mime, dance, the dramatic power of silence and stillness; above all, perhaps, an impersonality which would replace the modern naturalistic preoccupation with character and personal idiosyncrasy. He virtually withdrew from the Abbey workshop 'in scorn of this audience', and of these artistic proclivities, after the death of Synge. In the Noh Yeats found the inspiration to rediscover in theatre those qualities that he had always sought in the lyric and defined most sharply in such an early essay as 'Symbolism in Poetry' (1899):

All sounds, all colours, all forms, either because of their preordained energies or because of long association, evoke indefinable and yet precise emotions, or, as I prefer to think, call down among us certain disembodied powers, whose footsteps over our hearts we call emotions; and when sound, and colour, and form are in a musical relation to one another, they become, as it were, one sound, one colour, one form, and evoke an emotion that is made out of their distinct evocations and yet is one emotion.

Western directors have almost universally sought to create that sense of symbolic action. It would be a fascinating exercise to collect and compare those modern productions preserved on video over the past decade or so throughout the world to observe the energy and ingenuity with which so many gifted directors have sought to achieve it — Tomás Mac Anna, Joe Dowling, James Flannery, Katharine Worth, Raymond Yeates, Naomi Ashe. The variety of masks and costume, the range and effect of musical instruments, from the French horn to the tin whistle — 'the music of the beggar-man' — the tomtom to the bodhrán; the diversity of dance and gesture from the 'tinker shuffle / Picked up in the street' to those elaborate choreographies in the tradition of Ninette de Valois. If we are to credit the Old Man in the prologue to *The Death of Cuchulain* Yeats would have accepted either insofar as they were not the dancers painted by Degas, with their 'short bodices, their stiff stays, their toes whereon they spin like pegtops'. It is hard to know, in the matter of costume, whether he would have warmed to a famous production of Flannery's in which Cuchulain appeared in the accoutrement of an American footballer. But I've seen a lovely production of *At the Hawk's Well* by Raymond Yeates at the Abbey in which the musicians wore swimming-helmets — suitably disguised — and another of *Cathleen Ni Houlihan* by the same director in which the actors used hand-held masks before their faces.

The options to us in the west are legitimately legion. But the questions still remained: what would it be like if an English translation of a Noh play, for instance *Nishikigi*, were performed under the auspices of a professional Noh director: and what would be the effect of the same Noh director producing on the same night its Yeatsian equivalent, *The Dreaming of the Bones*, according to the Noh convention? The opportunity for such an experiment presented itself to us in 1986 at University College Dublin when we had Professor Masaru Sekine as Visiting Professor for our graduate programme in Anglo-Irish Literature and Drama. The experiment has proved so stimulating, not least in retrospect and 'excited reverie', that it made the present book a virtual necessity.

The spirit in which we entered upon the adventure was so un-calculating that it occurred to no-one to have the performances recorded. For a sense of them we must rely on the few colour photographs taken on the night, the Noh masks which Sekine fashioned from wire, paper and paint — I have them on the wall of my office — the symbolic pine branch made of wire and cloth, and the short dissertations written by the student actors which formed part of their academic assessment. The most extended of these by Colleen Hanrahan is the basis of her article in the present book. There was no hope that the director could, in the couple of months available to him, train his players in the intricate mysteries of Noh performance. But I have seldom seen a troupe of actors work so hard, or strive so bravely to apprehend the inner strangeness of so unfamiliar a form.

They often sat into the small hours in my house listening to the *sensei* explain the nuances of the Japanese convention, the Buddhist world view that stood behind it, the religious connotations which gave weight to this or that inflection of voice or nuance of gesture. Sometimes the house would echo to Sekine's bass cutting loose with an unearthly Noh incantation. There were moments of unnerving silence which I dared to interpret as meditation and the gathering of psychic force. There were interludes of levity and laughter. There were certainly times when the Thespians of the west wished they had never embarked on such an exotic journey and pined for the luxury of practical criticism, textual commentary, the sane delights of the catalogue and the footnote.

Two performances of the double bill were planned. It was decided to stage them in the seminar room, with flat lighting, a white sheet for background, a tiny humped tent to represent a mountain and a cave, and an invited audience of about thirty on each occasion — no more in number 'than those who listened on the first occasion to Milton's *Comus'*. Both occasions were charged with ex-citement unusual even for a theatrical first night. It took the steadying presence of Professor Sekine and Dr Christopher Murray — who was cast in the role of *waki* in *Nishikigi*, Diarmuid in *The Dreaming of the Bones* — to ensure that all performed their tragic plays without failure of nerve or concentration. It turned out deeply satisfying.

When in 'L'Allegro' Milton wrote of music such as 'the meeting soul may pierce' he was assuming a more than sympathetic rela-tionship between the art and the listener; an audience that did not have to have its attention bribed by the stratagems of show-biz. Likewise with his *Comus*, Yeats's named exemplar whose great occasion emboldened Yeats's prologue to tell the audience 'not to shuffle their feet or talk while the actors are speaking'. We had such audiences at UCD for the two performances, the first night mostly students and academics, the second mostly invited guests from the town. On both nights a brief introduction to the drama's conventions settled them in their seats, their sense of curiosity, civility and expectation carried them into the first overtures of speech and music, and then came that live silence that marks real theatre in action. They were a perfect audience, and it was clear that such a perfect audience is necessary for such an occasion in the west. The players were word perfect so that their ritual delivery cast its strange spell without faltering for a moment; the stylized dances and gestures carried a little of the awe of a religious ceremony. Masaru Sekine's powerful rendering of the Noh chant in Japanese in the intervals of speech and movement was mysteriously touching.

The spell held firm through the two plays; the applause, after a short hushed silence, was sustained and animated. Yet while rejoicing in the palpable success of the evening one had to acknowledge that it was a privileged form of theatre. The meeting soul of the auditors was so guaranteed that even a less accomplished performance might have had the same reverent response. Maybe this is why theatre people of the west regard these plays of Yeats with suspicion, if not resentment. In demanding a religious response to what has so long been for them a profane medium the poet is perhaps seen as evading the challenge of living drama, the challenge of the market-place. I also recalled that in Kyoto I had been a little shocked to notice that members of the audience came and went during the production, which took place in plain white light. But their movement seemed to have no effect on the actors who performed almost within a closed circuit of their own stage fire. The analogy with a religious ceremony in the west was almost complete, as for instance the indifference of the priest during the consecration of the Mass to the shufflings of his congregation. This recollected impression was reinforced when I recalled the preparation of the *shite* in his dressing room — for I had had the privilege of observing it — before the performance where he sits for twenty minutes looking intently in a mirror before putting on his mask. It brought me back to my days as an altar boy watching the priest vesting.

What our performances yielded was something between the

closed circuit of the Japanese Noh and the more democratic and profane experience of contemporary theatre; something nearer the rarefied atmosphere of the Cunard drawing-room than the normal theatre feeling created by professional renderings of the dance plays. In the latter case the use of stage lighting and the routine audience-actor relationship provides its own aura of invulnerability for the performance. But the potential fragility of that relationship in our experiment seemed to create a sort of precarious suspense that threw the dialogue into a new clarity, giving the poetry enhanced resonance, and making the predicament of the characters simpler and more poignant. This quality could not have been caught in any recording, however sensitively done.

What the two back-to-back performances told us about the nature of the two traditions and the links and differences between them would be harder still to define. One difference that struck me forcibly may be worth mentioning. It has to do with our western sense of time. With Yeats's lovers and their potential deliverer, the Young Man, time was painfully at issue. In the manner well defined by Northrop Frye in *Fools of Time* all three were caught in the tragic web of their history. What had been done could not be undone. Theirs was the tragic rhythm without cathartic release. The pain of that predicament was intimate and eloquent in the performance. Out of Ireland they had not come, nor would they ever. Though *Nishikigi* had abundant dialogue with time, the temporal element did not tend to press on the characters or on us. Instead there was a sense of the miraculous, an expectancy that guilt could be redeemed and existence blessed. Apparently most Noh plays end in a blessing. It took Yeats another twenty years or so to express his sense that tragedy is a uniquely western mode; in his great poem, 'Lapis Lazuli', and in his letter about it to Dorothy Wellesley:

Ascetic, pupil, hard stone, eternal theme of the sensual east. The heroic cry in the midst of despair. But no, I am wrong, the east has its solutions always, and therefore knows nothing of tragedy. It is we, not the east, that must raise the heroic cry.

Our modest experiment at UCD did not resolve these mighty antinomies. But it brought the two modes, for an evening, into an agreeable and illuminating propinquity, and in the process gave us a great reckoning in a little room.

AUGUSTINE MARTIN
Professor of Anglo-Irish Literature and Drama
University College Dublin

I. 'LIKE AN OLD TALE STILL':
YEATS'S *FOUR PLAYS FOR DANCERS*

Among the formal tendencies which Yeats developed as a playwright were two which underly his *Four Plays for Dancers* (1921) and allow them to be viewed as part of his whole dramatic output. These are his concepts of literature as 'an old wives' tale'[1] and his interest in the dramatic cycle. The purpose of this chapter is to explore the relationship between Yeats's own dramaturgy and that of the Japanese model he discovered in late autumn 1913, through Ezra Pound. The argument will be that though Yeats imitated the Noh form with a great degree of sincerity, finding in its form, themes and conventions, correspondences with his own notions of dramatic art, he necessarily failed to make authentic Noh plays. By being true to himself and his tragic vision, he could do no other than write plays that were at variance with an alien tradition; yet by adopting the form as enthusiastically as he did, Yeats alienated himself from the Abbey Theatre. In the end, he had to modify the Noh form considerably in the 1920s in order to make his peace with the Abbey. A playwright is not a playwright without a theatre; a theatre exists on conventions built up from the manners and practices of local or ethnic or colonial influence; Yeats (assisted by Synge, Lady Gregory and others) had spent almost twenty years de-colonizing the Irish theatre so as to make it nationalist and truly expressive of individual Irish experience. It was folly to imagine that he could undo that venture by initiating what was virtually another form of cultural colonization.

From his very beginnings as a professional playwright, with the writing of *The Countess Cathleen* and the production in 1894 of *The Land of Heart's Desire*, Yeats showed his interest in fable, or dramatic parable. When *The Countess Cathleen* was eventually staged, and launched at the Irish Literary Theatre in Dublin, in May 1899, the explosive potential of the fable was emphatically demonstrated. The play caused a furore in Dublin, even prior to its production, and was given a riotous reception in the Antient

1

Concert Rooms, as James Joyce testified.[2] By telling a tale of an aristocratic lady who sold her soul to demons in order to buy back the souls of her starving tenants, Yeats was challenging orthodox Christian, or at any rate Roman Catholic, notions of altruism and salvation. Many regarded Yeats's conclusion as blasphemous, and it notoriously made Edward Martyn uneasy also, as the Countess is granted forgiveness by the Angel and welcomed into Paradise when she dies:

> The light beats down; the gates of pearl are wide;
> And she is passing to the floor of peace,
> And Mary of the seven times wounded heart
> Has kissed her lips, and the long blessed hair
> Has fallen on her face: The Light of Lights
> Looks always on the motive, not the deed,
> The Shadow of Shadows on the deed alone.[2a]

Contained in this play is a concept of self-sacrifice or heroism to which Yeats was to adhere throughout his career as playwright, though it became more complex when it was united with a contrary impulse within the heroine (as in Emer in *The Only Jealousy of Emer* discussed below) or hero (as in the Young Man in *The Dreaming of the Bones*, also discussed below). The fable in Yeats's early plays was usually drawn from folk-lore or Celtic saga, and its function was to clarify a paradoxical relationship between the material and the spiritual worlds. By damning herself, the Countess Cathleen actually saves the community, and hence herself also. In *The Land of Heart's Desire* Mary Bruin's departure with the Fairy Child stands as an inversion of the cultural values of the peasant household which she leaves (just as the crucifixes turned to the wall manifest the polarity of fairy world to Christian belief). The 'world elsewhere' invoked by the fairy presence is a poetic expression which is at once lyrical celebration of the invisible world and criticism of the ordinary world. The siren-song of the fairies may be standard romantic stuff, but dramatically the final exit of Mary Bruin is quite ambiguous: on the one hand, her going makes the solid peasant cottage seem tawdry and good to escape from, but on the other hand Mary is actually going to her death. Entry to the fairy world is only by way of death. The fable, for Yeats, negotiates a course between the mundane and the supernatural.

Following the completion of the Irish Literary Theatre experiment in 1901 and marking his involvement with the Fay brothers in 1902, Yeats developed a more concrete, assured set of attitudes towards theatre and drama. Writing on 'The Reform of the Theatre' in *Samhain*: 1903, the organ of the Irish National Theatre Society, he expounded quite radical ideas. The opening sentence issued a ringing challenge to the contemporary theatre: 'I think the theatre must be reformed in its plays, its speaking, its acting, and its scenery. That is to say, I think there is nothing good about it at present' (*Explorations*, p. 107). He went on to say that:

We have to write or find plays that will make the theatre a place of intellectual excitement. . . . If we are to do this we must learn that beauty and truth are always justified of themselves, and that their creation is a greater service to our country than writing that compromises either in the seeming service of a cause. (p. 107)

In short, he was determined to create a theatre of art and not of propaganda. Yeats realized that in the theatre nationalism makes an uneasy bedfellow and, no doubt, he already had reservations about the extraordinary effect created by his *Cathleen Ni Houlihan* in 1902. With its historical background of the 1798 rising that play was not so much fable as allegory, and in line with his programme of 'reforms' Yeats steered his art more towards 'beauty and truth', those Keatsian synonyms, than towards any kind of Shelleyan/Shavian utilitarianism.

With plays such as *The King's Threshold* (1903), *The Shadowy Waters* (1904), *On Baile's Strand* (1904) and *Deirdre* (1906), Yeats moved from history and folklore to myth as his subject matter. Yet he retained the notion of drama as fable or parable. At this stage in his career the fables had subjective application, since Yeats only wrote about what interested or, indeed, obsessed him. Thus *The Shadowy Waters*, which he revised constantly, was more a dramatization of his spiritual beliefs than it was a heroic play. Its vagueness, so irritating to Synge during its first production, was ominous. Unless Yeats could get beyond this tendency to embody his beliefs in a form that was unconventional and puzzling he was doomed never to get past what Roger McHugh has called 'allegorical, dreamily poetic fantasies, full of shadow and of the lure of the supernatural or of the ideal world'.[3] The heroic plays, from *The King's Threshold* to *Deirdre* were an advance, since the subject matter ensured a concreteness and clarity of outline in characterization and dramatic form. In particular, *On Baile's Strand*, Yeats's first Cuchulain play, and *Deirdre* achieved a happy equilibrium between saga material and personal, subjective passion. In both plays, in contrast with the allegorical *The King's Threshold* and the mystifying self-indulgence of *The Shadowy*

Waters, Yeats transcended his feelings of disappointment over Maud Gonne's marriage and made universal tragic statements concerning wisdom, loss and self-destruction. He now realized that 'the greatest art symbolises not those things that we have observed so much as those things that we have experienced'.⁴ With the writing of Deirdre, in which he used travelling musicians as chorus, Yeats clarified his dramatic ideas to the point where he was anticipating his discovery of the Noh form some seven years later. Besides the 'moment of intense life'⁵ which he had already found to be the focus of his plays, he now asserted that passion rather than character was better suited to the tragic form he favoured. The fable existed less to show character in action than 'character isolated by a deed'⁶ and the feelings inherent in such isolation. Mood, variety of feeling, the conflict of polarized attitudes to life, all made for a more complex dramatic form than the simple dichotomy between material and spiritual worlds which the earlier plays enacted. One has to agree, accordingly, with Leonard E. Nathan when he says that Yeats did not so much adopt Noh as discover in it 'a catalyst which brought his own experiments to their logical conclusion. The Yeatsian Nō was implicit in earlier plays and was, notably in Deirdre, becoming more and more explicit in his work.'⁷ By a strange process of evolution, Yeats was already moving towards the Noh form before even he knew of its conventions. The Noh taught him how to employ fable symbolically.

*

The notion of a dramatic cycle appealed to Yeats very early on in his career.⁸ He records in his essay 'At Stratford-on-Avon' (1901) how appealing Shakespeare's history plays (the cycle from Richard II to Richard III) were to him as model. Philip Edwards has shown, in Threshold of a Nation, the link between Yeats's cultural nationalism and that expressed by Shakespeare. He comments further:

Yeats's Shakespeare is an honorary Celt. Beginning a new literary movement and inspiring a new theatre in the burgeoning new life of an old nation, Yeats was replacing the Shakespeare who initiated the cultural greatness of England. And in the sense that Shakespeare's England stood for Britain, union, empire, and shared culture, Yeats was bound to undo his work.⁹

Inspired by Shakespeare's history plays Yeats wrote On Baile's Strand. He planned — or hoped for — a cycle of plays about Cuchulain, and eventually a cycle did emerge, of six plays: On Baile's Strand, The Green Helmet, At the Hawk's Well, The Only Jealousy of Emer and The Death of Cuchulain. These plays were written separately over a period of thirty-five years between 1904 and 1939. The manner of their writing cautions us against seeing them as a cycle in the same way as we regard Shakespeare's history plays, and we must constantly bear in mind that Yeats favoured the one-act, concentrated dramatic form beloved by all symbolists. At the same time his whole vision can be described as cyclical: *A Vision* dramatizes this cyclical diagram of human history with powerful, if eccentric, tenacity. It is the rhythm of Yeats's cyclic vision that is most significant for his plays: they form a dance of opposites, reconciled tragically but with the lyrical commentary that life goes on and the wheel will turn again elsewhere. Where Shakespeare may have expressed such continuity as a political idea, related to the divinity of kingship, Yeats understood the dynamic as organic, the pressure of natural energy against the limits of being, socially imposed.

Thus Yeats's plays tend to fall into cycles thematically unified, on love, or war, or death, or the hereafter. The use of Cuchulain in more than one play does not mean that such a group is *thematically* unified. The analogy with Noh is here very interesting. Just as in the Noh form there is a unity of belief rather than of episode or action in the six plays comprising a cycle, so too in Yeats's plays in general there are binding beliefs rather than continuities offering coherence.

Initially, Yeats intended *The Cat and the Moon* for inclusion in the *Four Plays for Dancers*, 'but did not do so as it was in a different mood' (*Variorum*, p. 805). His sense of inappropriateness here outweighed his knowledge that in the Noh cycle a *kyogen* or farce was usually included. 'I intended my play [*The Cat and the Moon*] to be what the Japanese call a "Kiogen", and to come as a relaxation of attention between, let us say "The Hawk's Well" and "The Dreaming of the Bones" ' (*Variorum*, p. 805). Presumably, Yeats inadvertently omitted mention here of *The Only Jealousy of Emer*, which would logically come before *The Dreaming of the Bones*: but the whole note is infuriatingly vague.

Ezra Pound described the Noh cycle as 'a complete service of life. We do not find, as we find in Hamlet, a certain situation or problem set out and analysed. The Noh service presents, or symbolizes, a complete diagram of life and recurrence.'[10] Similarly, in an article related to *Where There is Nothing* (1902), Yeats had said: 'Drama is a picture of the soul in man, and not of his exterior life. . . . Drama describes the adventures of men's souls rushing through the thoughts that are most interesting to his time.'[11] He followed this remark with a distinction between his drama and Shakespeare's: where Elizabethans had been interested in 'questions of policy and kingcraft' these questions were reflected in Shakespeare's plays. But Ireland was interested primarily in religion, morals, and personal emotion and so, 'I who have been bred and born here, can hardly write at all unless I write about religious ideas'.[12] His various plays are attempts to look at various manifestations, public and private, of this single religious impulse.

*

Four Plays for Dancers derived, then, from Yeats's own convictions as a playwright. From 1907 on, however, he experienced such a growing bitterness and disillusion with Irish middle-class society in general and with the Abbey audience in particular that he was quite ready by 1913 to move out and pursue his art in England. The riots over Synge's *Playboy* and the failure of the Dublin people to support Hugh Lane's appeal for a municipal gallery of art built up in Yeats this sense of repudiation. Moreover, his ideas on theatre were more and more opposed to the naturalism with which Abbey audiences seemed fixed in sympathy. Having worked off a certain amount of his spleen in the grotesque *The Green Helmet* (1910), Yeats concentrated on new productions of *The Hour Glass* and *Deirdre*, making use of the new ideas on staging gleaned from his admiration of Edward Gordon Craig. Essentially, these ideas, much written about in the last twelve years or so, paved the way further for Yeats's reception of the Noh conventions. Yeats fully agreed with Craig's repudiation of nineteenth-century illusionistic scenery, and welcomed his claim, made in the first issue of *The Mask* (1908): 'Once let the meaning of this word "Beauty" begin to be thoroughly felt once more in the theatre, and we may say that the awakening day of the theatre is near.'[13] This Oriental emphasis on beauty as the main purpose behind drama anticipated the *Yugen* which Yeats was to discover as central to Noh drama.[14] Further, as Yeats had for long hoped for a bare stage which might be used in a style reminiscent but not imitative of the Elizabethan and classical Greek stages, he found in Craig's emphasis on abstract design, use of lighting, and interest in masks, ideas which after 1910 came to seem indispensable to him. He persuaded Craig to make a set of screens for his use — 'those admirable ivory-coloured screens'[15] — and declared he now had 'a scene capable of endless transformation, of the expression of every mood that does not require a photographic realism'.[16] They made their debut at the

Abbey in the revised *Hour Glass* in January 1911. When the English director Nugent Monck came to the Abbey later that year Yeats briefly found a theatre man to whom he could communicate his new ideas. Monck had a particular interest in medieval theatre, to the conventions of which, in use of space and time, Yeats responded with enthusiasm. Later he was to exploit the resemblance between medieval, anti-illusionist staging and that of the Noh.

It was almost inevitable, therefore, that when Ezra Pound introduced Yeats to Japanese aristocratic drama, through the translations of Ernest Fenollosa which he was editing, Yeats should experience a shock of recognition. The non-naturalistic style, the symbolism, the masks, the costumes, the stylized action, the use of chorus and musicians, the stage bare except for a drawing of a huge pine tree on the wooden backwall, and the minimum of properties, all coincided with Yeats's own ideas on staging. He became involved in Pound's project, arranged for the publication of four of the Fenollosa translations by his sister's press, the Cuala Press, in September 1916, and wrote an Introduction himself. (The plays were: *Nishikigi, Hagoromo, Kumasaka* and *Kagekiyo*.) In the Introduction, dated April 1916, he declared that he had written a play inspired by these Noh plays, and thereby, 'I have invented a form of drama, distinguished, indirect and symbolic . . . an aristocratic form'.[17] This play was entitled *At the Hawk's Well*, the first of the *Four Plays for Dancers*. It was first staged not at the Abbey Theatre, nor indeed in any theatre, but in Lady Cunard's drawing room in London on 2 April 1916. It was directed and designed by Edmund Dulac, who also composed the music (for flute, harp, drum and gong), but the choreography was by the Japanese dancer Michio Ito,[17a] who played the part of the (female) Guardian of the Well. Yeats had entered upon a whole new phase of his playwriting career.

Theatrically, *At the Hawk's Well* departed radically from the conventions of the proscenium stage to which Yeats had been tied at the Abbey. No front curtain was called for, a matter which seems to have inspired Yeats to invent the ritual of unfolding and folding a large cloth (estimated at eight feet long by four feet wide) for the beginning and end of the play.[18] This ritual was accompanied by a song evoking the setting, for there was no scenery besides a small square of blue cloth to symbolize the well. A practical function of the unfolding of the cloth was to allow the Guardian to enter unnoticed by the audience (a scruple which indicates how bound Yeats actually was to naturalistic stage conditions, since nowadays the presence of the Guardian on a bare stage before the play begins would present no problem to audiences). The song (alternate rhyming trimeters) evoking the setting reveals Yeats's skill at generating a sense of place:

> I call to the eye of the mind
> A well long choked up and dry
> And boughs long stripped by the wind,
> And I call to the mind's eye
> . . . .
> . . . .
> A man climbing up to a place
> The salt sea wind has swept bare.[19]

The entrance of the Old Man through the audience was a novelty, defying convention and serving to identify the (select) audience with this dutiful, unadventurous, common man. In other respects, the play, being in verse, is no different from Yeats's earlier work (for example, *Deirdre*), until one comes to the dance. Here the essence of the Noh form is imitated, and the effect of the play depends largely on the skill of the dancer, for Yeats offers little help in his stage directions, beyond saying that 'the Guardian of the Well has begun to dance, moving like a hawk. . . . The dance goes on for some time' (p. 409). Since there is nothing in Irish culture to correspond to the kind of expressive dance called for, it is here, above all, that Yeats's new form of drama breaks with the Irish tradition (with which his *Four Plays for Dancers* may otherwise be accommodated) and demands the services of a modern dancer.[20]

Later, in 1927, Yeats attempted to bridge this gap between native Irish dancing and modern dance by persuading Ninette de Valois to head a School of Irish Ballet at the newly opened Peacock Theatre in Dublin. This was a courageous attempt, fruitful for Yeats's own continuing experiments, but it came too late to benefit *Four Plays for Dancers*. Indeed, it is significant that even with the talents of Vinette de Valois at his service, Yeats felt obliged to rewrite one of the *Four Plays* in prose, with modern music, as *Fighting the Waves*, before he could feel confident enough to present it before an Irish audience (Abbey Theatre, 13 August 1929).

At the Hawk's Well seems to correspond to the 'warrior play' in the Noh cycle. A Young Man comes to the location of a holy well, whose waters confer immortality. The well is dry, however, and flows only at rare intervals, marked by terrible supernatural events. The Young Man encounters an Old Man who has been waiting for fifty years for the waters to flow. There is also a Guardian of the well, a hawk-woman, who is inert when the Young Man arrives but subsequently dances before him, distracts his attention

from the well and eventually leads him away to be attacked by the
goddess Aoife, who becomes his lover and mother of the son he
will later kill in combat.
Although the trappings of Noh drama are present, this is not
really a Noh drama. Certainly, there is use of masks, symbolic
well, the Old Man as *waki* and the Young Man as *shite*, there are
musicians (who also act as Chorus) and above all there is a dance
at the climax of the play. What seems to be missing is a clear
recognition of the role of the supernatural. The Guardian becomes
possessed and therefore it is as a demon or witch she dances before
and seduces the Young Man; her motive seems negative, for she
wants to preserve the well unused and she wants the Young Man
not for herself but for the wild women of the mountains, led by
Aoife. What power the Young Man is serving is therefore left in
doubt. Instead, what is dramatized is the contrast between the terrified, passive response of the Old Man to the Guardian, and the
defiant, reckless response of the Young Man. In meeting the
challenge of her seductive dance he exits to his heroic destiny; he
is thus initiated into his fatal role, as is clear from his declaration
of his identity as he finally leaves in pursuit of the Guardian: 'He
comes! Cuchulain, son of Sualtim, comes!' (p. 412). The Old Man,
in contrast, has hidden himself from the terrible power of the Guardian, and in so doing has lost yet again the opportunity to drink
from the well, which flowed during that moment. The play thus
celebrates heroism over caution, since death is inescapable.
Cuchulain, initiated sexually, has chosen right, even though
fatally:

> He might have lived at his ease,
> An old dog's head on his knees,
> Among his children and friends.   (p. 411)

Such a safe, domestic life is not for the warrior. In contrast, the Old
Man, for all his advocacy of caution, fares worse, for he has wasted
his life in fruitless waiting:

> The accursed shadows have deluded me,
> The stones are dark and yet the well is empty;
> The water flowed and emptied while I slept.
> You have deluded me my whole life through,
> Accursed dancers, you have stolen my life.   (p. 411)

A new hardness has come into Yeats's drama, a combative
fatalism, replacing the romantic neuraesthenia of his earliest work.
It is but a short step from *At the Hawk's Well* to the stern *sprez-
zatura* of 'An Irish Airman Foresees His Death'.
Where *At the Hawk's Well* is a warrior play, celebrating in

haughty fashion the hero's indifference to security, *The Only Jealousy of Emer* is a 'woman' play, which comes next in the Noh cycle. (It corresponds to *Awoi No Uye*, to which it will be compared in the following chapters.) Unfortunately, of the *Four Plays for Dancers* only *At the Hawk's Well* was staged immediately; they would have made an effective programme if staged together (with *Calvary* first, as the 'God' play), but to finish the cycle Yeats would have had to include *The Resurrection*. Yet Yeats, after all, did not plan a cycle in this way,[21] and the writing of *The Only Jealousy of Emer* itself was frustrated by the unavailability of Michio Ito (who went to New York in 1916) and by Yeats's being diverted by the Irish rebellion into the writing of *The Dreaming of the Bones*.

In a production of *The Four Plays for Dancers* it would be necessary to include *On Baile's Strand*, in spite of its quite different dramatic style. The narrative gap between *At the Hawk's Well* and *The Only Jealousy* is simply too great for the latter play to make its full impact otherwise. Certainly Emer supplies the details of Cuchulain's death, but to those ignorant of *On Baile's Strand* her description carries none of the horror surrounding Cuchulain's madness after he recognizes that the opponent he has killed was his own son.

If we consider *The Only Jealousy of Emer*, however, as one of the *Four Plays for Dancers*, its relationship in style to *At the Hawk's Well* is obvious. Yeats emphasizes this point in his opening stage direction:

Enter Musicians, who are dressed and made up as in *'At the Hawk's Well'*. They have the same musical instruments, which can either be already upon the stage or be brought in by the First Musician before he stands in the centre with the cloth between his hands, or by a player when the cloth has been unfolded. The stage as before can be against the wall of any room, and the same black cloth can be used as in *'At the Hawk's Well'*.[22]

Again, there is a song for the unfolding and folding of the cloth, this time a lyric emphasizing the roots of beauty in moral discipline through time: a preliminary statement to the conflict in the play between beauty and service, which defines the nature of Emer's achievement. As at the start of *At the Hawk's Well* also, the location is defined linguistically, thus dispensing with the need for illusionistic scenery:

> I call before the eyes a roof
> With cross-beams darkened by smoke;
> A fisher's net hangs from a beam,
> A long oar lies against the wall.
> I call up a poor fisher's house;
> A man lies dead or swooning . . .   (p. 533)

What follows is an extremely neat and compact combination of Yeats's thoughts concerning the after-life and a love-story, indeed a melodrama of a conventional nature. (His source was mainly Lady Gregory's *Cuchulain of Muirthemne*, 1902.) The more conventional the love story is felt to be, the more easily Yeats's circumambient philosophy may be tolerated if not registered as dramatically comprehensible. The situation at the outset is this: Cuchulain lies suspended between life and death and may yet be reclaimed. His wife Emer and his mistress Eithne Inguba face each other across his body, and Emer puts aside her pride so far as to beg Eithne to call Cuchulain back with a kiss. When Eithne complies it is not Cuchulain but Bricriu, god of discord, who appears, causing Eithne to flee: 'I show my face, and everything he [Cuchulain] loves / Must fly away' (p. 543). The slight to Emer tests her fortitude. Bricriu explains that Cuchulain, seen crouching *'near the front'*, is in a dream and may either be awakened or be lost forever to the Sidhe or supernatural powers. To be awakened he must be released from the guilt or remorse caused by his infidelity to Emer, and such release is dependent on Emer's renouncing her love for Cuchulain forever. Otherwise, he will gain release another way, by falling victim to the Woman of the Sidhe, Fand, come to dance before him to seduce him. Such is the central conflict: between Emer and the Woman of the Sidhe. The Ghost of Cuchulain comes to life when the latter dances, and their exchange is observed by Emer as if it were a play within the play (a structure Yeats used again in *Words upon the Window-pane*). To give the inset emphasis, Yeats casts it in rhymed verse.

The Ghost of Cuchulain recognizes the Woman of the Sidhe as the Guardian of the Well whom he had encountered as a young man in *At the Hawk's Well*. A similar pattern is followed as was enacted there: she goes out, and he follows. What is at stake is once again Cuchulain's immortality, but now the terms of that immortality are much clearer: Cuchulain is to be used by the Woman of the Sidhe to attain her own perfection (or 'completion'), imprisoning him in an eternity where 'there shall be oblivion / Even to quench Cuchulain's drouth' (p. 555). Whereas such a state of oblivion might seem attractive, objectively considered, Emer fears it and Bricriu clearly regards it as utterly negative and undesirable. The audience is urged, accordingly, to sympathize with Emer as she faces her dilemma: to save Cuchulain from undesirable oblivion she must renounce his love forever. Her role is to intervene and break a spell, just as the Old Man in *Purgatory* later attempts to intervene and release his mother's soul from *her* dream. At the last second Emer does, of course, cry out to renounce Cuchulain's love forever and thereby gain her Pyrrhic victory. Eithne Inguba returns to gain the credit of his resurrection from Cuchulain. The final song is a lament for Emer, whose self-sacrifice, unlike that of the Countess Cathleen in Yeats's early play, goes unrewarded. The heroic act, Yeats is saying, is essentially ambiguous. If it is a service that confers or exhibits moral beauty, it is, like that brought forth by the patriots celebrated in 'Easter 1916', a terrible beauty.

Easter 1916, indeed, lies at the heart of the next play to be considered, *The Dreaming of the Bones*. The Young Man, the *waki* figure, who encounters the spirits of Diarmuid and Dervorgilla on the hills bordering Clare and Galway, is actually on the run from the rebellion: 'I was in the Post Office, and if taken / I shall be put against a wall and shot.'[23] Although the general outline of the play corresponds well enough to the form of the third or 'woman' play in a Noh cycle (such as *Nishikigi*, which he much admired), its concern with Irish history gives it an untypical particularity. Indeed, Yeats himself, fully aware of the political topicality, confessed to Lady Gregory that it might have been 'only too powerful politically';[24] and he cannot have been too surprised that it was not staged during the turbulent years following the 1916 rebellion. Liam Miller has said that its political overtones actually precluded its production for fourteen years:[25] its premiere was in 1931, at the Abbey Theatre, five years after the premiere of *The Only Jealousy of Emer*.

This public sensitivity to *The Dreaming of the Bones* because of its political implications may serve to distract attention from the lyric beauty of the play. It is, in fact, the most beautiful and most moving of the *Four Plays for Dancers* and among the best of all Yeats's plays. His imagination caught fire here when he set the play around the ruined Abbey of Corcomroe, in the west of Ireland, with all its associations of foreign domination. From the start, the play establishes a mood of lonely desolation in the opening song for folding and unfolding the cloth:

> Have not old writers said
> That dizzy dreams can spring
> From the dry bones of the dead?   (p. 763)

This is the keynote of the play which follows, this insistence that the dead live on among us, seeking to appease their remorse and grow into a purified state. There is continuity here with *The Only Jealousy of Emer*, where it is stated:

> The dead move ever towards a dreamless youth
> And when they dream no more return no more;   (p. 549)

and it was a belief (fully explicated in *A Vision*) which was to energize Yeats's drama to the very last, to *Purgatory* and *The Death of Cuchulain*. What he calls here 'the fantastic conscience' (p. 766) has become his enduring theme.

It is established, then, in the encounter between the *shite*, the Stranger, and the *waki*, the Young Man, that the dead suffer on and may be forced to 'live through their old lives again' (p. 766) in expiation. The fact that the Young Man is unmasked and in modern, peasant dress whereas the Stranger and the Young Girl, later to be revealed as the spirits of Diarmuid and Dervorgilla, are both masked and *'in the costume of a past time'* (p. 764) visually clarifies for the audience the gap between the living and the dead.

The First Musician, who acts as narrator, states that the three characters pursue their journey to the abbey, while Yeats's stage direction makes clear that no climbing is actually undertaken: *'They go round the stage once'* (p. 766). This theatrical convention, familiar to Yeats from medieval drama, allows the narrator to comment on the landscape so as to emphasize its antiquity:

> They've passed the shallow well and the flat stone
> Fouled by the drinking cattle, the narrow lane
> Where mourners for five centuries have carried
> Noble or peasant to his burial;   (p. 767)

This verbal scene-painting prepares for the exchange between the Stranger and the Young Man over the ruined abbey, when they reach the summit and can see it. The abbey evokes the theme of wilful destruction, and hence guilt, since it did not merely decay but was suppressed during the Reformation: it was 'killed' just as surely as the Big House was killed in *Purgatory* and prompts the Young Man's question:

> Is there no house
> Famous for sanctity or architectural beauty
> In Clare or Kerry, or in all wide Connacht,
> The enemy has not unroofed?   (p. 769)

The journey reaches its climax here, within sight of the abbey which symbolizes the Irish spiritual tradition and its betrayal. The tomb of a Munster king, Donough O'Brien, raises the question of loyalty, since he rebelled against 'his rightful master' and thereby 'made Ireland weak' (p. 769). It also raises the question whether the guilty spirits spoken of earlier as restlessly working out their 'penance' on the mountain were buried in the abbey graveyard.

For the first time, the Young Girl speaks, answering the Young Man's query about the ghosts who walk the mountain. She relates their predicament: lovers, they are doomed never to be at one and at peace until 'somebody of their race' (p. 773) can forgive them:

> Their manner of life were blessed could their lips
> A moment meet; but when he has bent his head
> Close to her head, or hand would slip in hand,
> The memory of their crime flows up between
> And drives them apart.   (pp. 771–72)

From her account of this 'crime', bringing the Normans to Ireland as conquerors, the Young Man recognizes the subjects of the narrative, although he does not yet recognize the company he is in. The play has shifted suddenly to a combat between his hard masculine rationalism and her feminine emphasis on feeling. His statement that Diarmuid and Dervorgilla will never be forgiven their crime brings to an end this central part of the play.

In the final part, the journey is continued to the summit (again, 'They go round the stage once'), on the other side of which lie safety and deliverance for the Young Man. From his first timid entry with a lantern he has now become self-reliant and utterly detached: no narrator is needed as he looks down from the summit and describes the Galway landscape. He has become authoritative. His relationship towards the lovers is as a priest towards suffering spirits. On the summit, therefore, the play's antitheses are starkly set out: the view of Galway raises by its poverty the moral issue of colonial degradation; the dance of the lovers, self-involved and seeking to shut out time, addresses the imagination with an aesthetic formulation which might obliterate the moral issue. The dance is display or image, its beauty riven by the pain of the lovers. As in the two earlier plays for dancers, the seduction of the hero is what the dance implies, but now the wider meaning of that seduction is far more powerfully expressed. The Young Man, far from being shut off in a dream like the Ghost of Cuchulain in *The Only Jealousy*, and far from being an arrogant collaborator with the dancer as Cuchulain is in *At the Hawk's Well*, here withstands the image of the dance on ideological grounds. To forgive would be to give assent to colonial domination and to deny the nationalist cause. Although his rejection of the lovers' appeal has caused dispute among critics of the play it cannot be called ambiguous. The Young Man is a republican, and he gives the republican answer to a call to forfeit his historical position, which is to say his integrity. As Yeats said elsewhere, 'The heroic act, as it descends through tradition, is an act done because a man is himself . . . a sacrifice of himself to himself, almost.'[26] The Young Man's refusal banishes the lovers to continuing suffering, which is a reversal of what happens at the end of *Nishikigi*, and yet his fidelity to tradition has to be regarded as admirable:

I has almost yielded and forgiven it all —
Terrible the temptation and the place!   (p. 775)

The 'terrible beauty' of the dance has succeeded in clarifying on stage the impasse reached when love of country resists love itself. The political impulse, the passionate interest in Irish history balanced against spiritual fulfilment seems also to have been at the root of *Calvary* in its earliest form. In a letter to Lady Gregory early in 1918 Yeats announced that he had finished *The Only Jealousy of Emer* and was 'hesitating on a new one, where a Sinn Feiner will have a conversation with Judas in the streets of Dublin. Judas is looking for somebody to whom he may betray Christ'.[27] The play, eventually published in *Four Plays for Dancers*, has neither a Dublin setting nor any member of the Sinn Fein among its characters, so the Muse did not let Yeats down on this occasion. Politics would have been the ruination of *Calvary*, which is perhaps Yeats's most purely spiritual play. As such, its coming last among the *Four Plays for Dancers* re-asserts what the political feeling of *The Dreaming of the Bones* ran the risk of obscuring: that these plays are essentially celebrations of existence, quality of life, in its god-like potential.

Yeats chooses the most sacred moment in Christian belief, the death of Christ, as his dramatic 'moment of intense life'. As Peter Ure has pointed out, what follows is a play of ideas. It is worth quoting Ure's summary account of Yeats's belief, as background both to *Calvary* and *The Resurrection*:

On Christianity, so far as they are relevant to his plays, his thoughts can be described briefly, without doing them very much injustice. He saw the pagan world, in particular the world of Greece and Rome, as a primary civilization; at the time of Christ's coming it was drawing to its pre-ordained end in the cyclical movement of history and was becoming subject to the loss of control which heralded the birth of the next age. This next, or Christian, age was antithetical to its predecessor. It begins with the Annunciation of a God who seeks to live like a man while teaching that man must seek to live like God. Yeats's favourite gnomic phrase for this, which he uses at the end of *The Resurrection* and elsewhere, was a saying borrowed from Heraclitus: 'God and man die each other's life, live each other's death.'[28]

What is summed up in Christ's suffering, accordingly, is a turning of the gyre, a failure of certain falcons to hear the great falconer, and,

in turn, his despair over the limits of his godhead. Christ is surrounded by the indifferent, the natural, and the recusant, none of
whom he can save. (The situation is vastly more complex, accordingly, than the Countess Cathleen's otherwise similar self-sacrifice.)
Christ's passivity high-lights their activity, their gestures of rejection, betrayal, and (in the case of the three Roman Soldiers)
physical performance: dicing and dancing.

If it is a play of ideas, however, *Calvary* is also a dream play.
This is what allies it to the Noh form, to which it adheres quite
closely. Indeed, Richard Taylor says: 'As a dramatic ritual, the
play is by far the boldest and most interesting experiment in the
new dance form.'[29] This will not be apparent unless the setting,
the characters and the main property, the cross, are seen not as
illustrations of scriptural narrative or left-overs from a medieval
mystery or passion play but as unreal evocations of the mind of
Christ, whom Yeats once described as 'no more than the supreme
symbol of the artistic imagination'.[30] The First Musician, following the song for the folding and unfolding of the cloth, makes clear
that what happens in the play takes place within the mind of
Christ:

> The road to Calvary, and I beside it
> Upon an ancient stone. Good Friday's come,
> The day wheron Christ dreams His passion through.
> He climbs up hither but as a dreamer climbs.
> The cross that but exists because He dreams it
> Shortens His breath and wears away His strength.[31]

Thereafter the play falls into three parts, as is customary. The divisions come with the entrances of Lazarus, Judas and the Three
Roman Soldiers; each marks a stage in the experience of Christ.
The play culminates in the dance of the soldiers around the cross,
when Christ asks in despair, 'My Father, why has thou forsaken
Me?' (p. 787), and the play ends with the song for the folding and
unfolding of the cloth. We are to imagine that Christ is reliving his
frustration at the limitations of his godhead.

Calvary is unlike religious Noh plays about gods, with which it
should be contrasted rather than compared. Moreover, it does not
seem to have been noticed by critics that in this play, as distinct
from its three predecessors, Yeats chose material not from myth or
from history but from scripture. The crucifixion of the man Chris-
tians believe was the son of God is attested by the four Evangelists
and therefore has a textual character quite different from the stories
of Cuchulain or of Diarmuid and Dervorgilla. What makes Yeats's

play a 'fable' is the introduction of Lazarus and Judas, neither of
whom was present at Calvary. Yeats imagines what might have
gone through Christ's mind prior to and justifying his cry of
despair, 'My father, why hast thou forsaken Me?', which is a
modification of the line in the Bible: 'My God, my God, why hast
thou forsaken me?' (Matthew: 27.46). In working up to this moment of isolation Yeats fabricates the visits of Lazarus and Judas,
taking his cue from Oscar Wilde's brief prose poem, 'The Doer of
Good', in which Jesus meets in turn the leper he had cured, the
blind man, the woman forgiven and finally Lazarus:

> And He went towards him and touched the long locks of his hair and
> said to him, 'Why are you weeping?'
> And the young man looked up and recognized Him and made answer,
> 'But I was dead once and you raised me from the dead. What else should
> I do but weep?'[32]

Yeats's recusants are frankly blasphemous. The drama derives,
indeed, from the *frisson* of their unorthodoxy. Lazarus resents his
resurrection, recognizing quite clearly that it implied a calling to
love Christ and be his ancillary. His attitude is entirely negative:

> But death is what I ask.
> Alive I never could escape your love,
> And when I sickened towards my death I thought,
> 'I'll to the desert, or chuckle in a corner,
> Mere ghost, a solitary thing.' I died
> And saw no more until I saw you stand
> In the opening of the tomb; 'Come out!' you called;
> You dragged me to the light as boys drag out
> A rabbit when they have dug its hole away;
> And now with all the shouting at your heels
> You travel towards the death I am denied.
> And that is why I have hurried to this road
> And claimed your death.   (pp. 782–83)

Lazarus is a type: a nihilist. The irony is that God is inescapable
and he does not know this. He says he will go search for death
'Among the desert places where there is nothing/But howling wind
and solitary birds' (p. 783). Yeats had called an early play *Where
There is Nothing* (1902) and in its course the predicate is supplied:
'where there is nothing, there is God'.[33] Lazarus will come full circle and find God in the desert. Judas is another type: the anarchist,
philosophical and Satanic:

> I could not bear to think you had but to whistle
> And I must do; but after that I thought,

'Whatever man betrays Him will be free';
And life grew bearable again. And now
Is there a secret left I do not know,
Knowing that if a man betrays a God
He is the stronger of the two?   (p. 785)

The portrait seems Russian, as if Yeats had been reading *The Possessed*. Judas is a crazed being, whose selfhood he elevates like an assassin who thirsts for notoriety. Both he and Lazarus mistake will for liberation.

So far as the drama is concerned these characters are Christ's opposites, his 'masks', in Yeatsian parlance. Those whom the Bible records as being at Calvary — besides the Roman Soldiers — John and the three Maries, reflect Christ's own love and commitment: there's no room for drama there. By imagining the appearance of Lazarus and Judas, Yeats accentuates the meaning of Christ's love for mankind. It exists in spite of the Lazarus-principle or the Judas figure. And the cross he dies on, or dreams on here, is the only true means of liberation, according to Christian interpretation. It is ironic — and quite effective — that Judas should be chosen by the soldiers to 'hold up the cross' (p. 785) while Christ submits to his crucifixion. He is chosen because he wants nothing from Christ, whereas the crowd is kept back: 'They are always wanting something' (p. 786). Yet it was for the crowd that Christ died. Judas ensures that the ritual is completed.

Likewise, the Three Roman Soldiers realize Christ's destiny by being detached from its meaning. They, too, 'have asked for nothing' (p. 786). They are like the birds in the Musician's song, self-contained and unredeemed. To be redeemed, the play states, is to abandon the casualness of chance signified by the dice of the soldiers. The dice is next found in *The Words upon the Window-pane*, where Vanessa tries to persuade Swift to accept the body, sex, and procreation:

Look at me, Jonathan, your arrogant intellect separates us. Give me both your hands. I will put them upon my breast . . . O, it is white — white as the gambler's dice — white ivory dice. Think of the uncertainty. Perhaps a mad child — perhaps a rascal — perhaps a knave — perhaps not, Jonathan. The dice of the intellect are loaded, but I am the common ivory dice.[34]

Yet it is Swift who resembles the Three Soldiers, while Vanessa resembles Christ: such is the nature of Yeats's antitheses. Vanessa despairs and dies, having failed to 'save' Swift. In *Calvary*, what is imagined is the apparent victory of chance, cloaking the real triumph of sacrificial power or godliness.

*

Two points need to be stressed, in summing up Yeats's achievement in writing *Four Plays for Dancers*. In the first place, the charge that the plays are untheatrical carries no basis whatsoever. Sean O'Casey was among those to make this charge, in his autobiography, referring to the production of *At the Hawk's Well* at Yeats's home in Merrion Square, Dublin, at the end of March, 1924. O'Casey's conclusion to a scathing account was: 'There was grace and a slender charm in what had been done, now that he had had a long time to look back at it; but it wasn't even the ghost of the theatre.'[35] Such a view, even from a fountain of good sense like O'Casey, leads quickly to the belief that Yeats was no more than a dilettante in the theatre. Such a view is untenable. It has to be accepted that Yeats's imagination was essentially dramatic — as Andrew Parkin has shown[36] — and that his many years of service to the Abbey Theatre were by no means a kind of amateur dabbling but a serious, if uneven, pursuit of his own art as well as being 'theatre business, management of men'.[37] We need to remind ourselves that when Yeats was awarded the Nobel prize for literature in 1923 he accepted on behalf of the Irish Dramatic Movement, as his address to the Royal Academy of Sweden testifies.[38] He knew that his achievements as poet could not be separated from the theatre, abrasive though his relationship to the Abbey could be. As he said in his note to *At the Hawk's Well*: 'I need a theatre; I believe myself to be a dramatist; I desire to show events and not merely tell of them . . . and I seem to myself most alive at the moment when a room full of people share the one lofty emotion.'[39] The proof of this self-description lies in Yeats's persistence. He kept returning to the theatre after intervals of disenchantment. In 1919, for example, he wrote his famous open letter to Lady Gregory (later reprinted in *Explorations*) in which he conceded defeat over his ambition to found a poetic drama at the Abbey. Yet, a few years later, when the Dublin Drama League staged *At the Hawk's Well*, *The Only Jealousy of Emer*, and *The Cat and the Moon*, Yeats took heart and started to write once again for the Abbey and the newly opened Peacock (1927). Significantly, however, he was leaving behind the notion of a drawing-room playing area and an aristocratic audience. He had to accept the vulgar conditions of the western theatre, as it were democratically formed by popular taste and (in the case of the Abbey) nationalist feeling. But the important point is that Yeats *did* accept, and did compromise his purest ideas on Noh and symbolism so as to find again an Irish audience. *Fighting the Waves* (1929) stands as an example of what this means, for it is a prose version, slightly simplified, of *The Only Jealousy of Emer*. It went down well at the Abbey, and must have encouraged Yeats to stage *The Words Upon the Window-pane* and *The Resurrection* soon afterwards. In the 1930s he also wrote for the Abbey several other plays influenced in varying degrees by the Noh tradition but, essentially, angled so as to admit the realistic conventions in some ironic relationship. The clearest example is *The Death of Cuchulain*, with its scornful prologue, use of blackouts, and inclusion of a final scene set in modern Ireland. Pragmatic is not a word usually applied to Yeats, but in his acceptance that Noh was not likely to take root in the modern, western theatre he was practical about the consequence. This shows that he was no mere closet playwright but one whose primary aim was to have (and please) an audience.

Moreover, T. S. Eliot, who was among the first audiences of *At the Hawk's Well* in 1916, was of the view that in the *Four Plays for Dancers* Yeats achieved his best dramatic work. In the early plays, Eliot argued, the characters were treated 'as creatures of a different world from ours. In the later plays they are universal men and women.'[40] The earlier plays represent 'a phase of confusion', whereas the *Four Plays for Dancers* represent clarification and starkness. Myth, says Eliot, was here 'not presented for its own sake, but as a vehicle for a situation of universal meaning'. If for 'myth' we substitute 'fable', Eliot's point may stand as a summary of the argument of this chapter.

Secondly, Yeats deliberately modelled *Four Plays for Dancers* on the Japanese Noh, as mediated by Ernest Fenollosa's translations and notes and Ezra Pound's enthusiasm. To quote Yeats himself: 'I have found my first model . . . in the "Noh" stage of aristocratic Japan.'[41] In his essay, 'Certain Noble Plays of Japan', in *Essays and Introductions*, he expands greatly on this indebtedness. It is clear, however, that there was nothing slavish about Yeats's imitation of Noh. Long before he discovered Noh, he was tentatively moving towards an idea of theatre startlingly similar in detail and emphasis. This is one of those extraordinary coincidences that occur from time to time in the history of literature. Yet it has to be understood that Yeats's use of the Noh was individualistic. Elsewhere in this volume Masaru Sekine shows just what the extent was of Yeats's departure from pure Noh. Indeed as Akhtar Qamber has remarked, Yeats's plays, although they 'came remarkably near capturing much of the artistic spirit and some of the spirit of the Japanesse classical theater', are 'not true Noh'.[42] Hiro Ishibashi went further, in concluding that Yeats's plays for dancers were 'born of a misunderstanding' of Noh.[43] This is surely as it should be where art is concerned. Little of lasting value comes from close imitation of originals; even translation becomes poetry only when it recreates the original anew. It is best, then, to take the view that Yeats's *Four Plays for Dancers* are worthy of attention as drama because they recreate anew the beautiful and spiritual ritualistic forms of the Noh. Such, indeed, is Richard Taylor's conclusion in *The Drama of W. B. Yeats: Irish Myth and the Japanese No*.

In the final analysis, Nō was not so much a direct influence on Yeats as the source of a new point of departure for continued experimentation with established themes and aesthetic concerns.   (p.161)

Recent commentators have tended to agree with this view. A. S. Knowland, while regarding the four dance plays and their successors as 'The Central Achievement' in Yeats's dramatic output, asserts that Yeats 'took from Noh drama what suited him' (*W. B. Yeats: Dramatist of Vision*, 1983, p. 109), and this, essentially, is also the view that informs Karen Dorn's chapter, 'An Intimate Theatre: The Japanese Noh Drama and Yeats's Dance Plays', in *Players and Painted Stage: The Theatre of W. B. Yeats* (1984).

To the last, in *Purgatory* and *The Death of Cuchulain*, Yeats clung to his life-long conviction that drama should be like a folk tale; indeed, he was still at this time saying that 'all must be like an old faery tale'.[44] The Noh form had enabled him to mould his chosen fables for maximum theatrical and emotional effects. Essentially, the Noh formed an episode in the history of Yeats's imagination and in the clarification of his aesthetics of theatre. By naturalizing it, Yeats so transformed its Japanese form into his own medium of intense and beautiful expression that it became his own unmistakable 'accomplishment'.

II.   WHAT IS NOH?

Noh is a Japanese traditional theatre, together with Kabuki and Bunraku. Noh is, however, the oldest, most sophisticated theatrical form in Japan. It has been an aristocratic theatre since it was first formalized by two actors, Kan-Ami and Ze-Ami, in the late fourteenth century. The young actor Ze-Ami won the patronage of the third *Shogun* Yoshimitsu in 1372 at a public performance organized to raise funds for a religious establishment, and he was fortunate enough to remain in this great man's favour throughout the latter's life.

The origin of Noh is obscure. Some scholars say it derived from an early dance form called ennen. Ze-Ami said the origin of Noh theatre was a dance by a goddess called Amano-uzumeno-mikoto in mythological times, while at the same time (with typical illogicality) stating that it had its origins in India. Thus the origins of the Noh are distinctly uncertain, most scholars preferring to think it originated, like most of Japanese culture, in China, and was a native adoption of a Chinese dance form known as *Sangaku*.

Sangaku, which was practised in China during the T'ang dynasty (618–907), reached Japan in the wave of Chinese culture which slowly swept Japan in the seventh and eighth centuries. It was, therefore, part and parcel of a cultural movement incorporating Buddhist ideas as well as a wealth of other art forms. *Sangaku* was a crude form of street entertainment, including juggling and mimes. It later became mixed up with *Wazaogi*, a Japanese form of entertainment. By the end of the Heian period (794–1192) *Sangaku* had been absorbed into Japanese life, and was rechristened *Sarugaku*. *Sarugaku* actors had no caste worth mentioning and, in an effort to attach themselves to the establishment and to gain standing, began work with the temples and shrines, providing religious entertainment.

It was during the Kamakura period (1192–1334) that the *Sarugaku* actors began to show a remarkable development in their ideas and skills. This was connected with the *samurai's* rise to power, which brought changes in Japan's social and financial structure. Until the establishment of the Kamakura shogunate, *samurai* were based in the countryside as guards for aristocratic estates, temples and shrines. When they invaded the political and financial centre, they brought with them religious entertainment widely performed in the countryside called *Dengaku*, which consisted of dancing and music. *Sarugaku* fused with this theatre and gained its strength by widening its scope of performance.

Samurai confiscated land not only owned by aristocrats but by temples and shrines. This put the latter in a financial straight jacket. The religious establishment therefore had to devise ways of raising money for keeping up their buildings and activities. They started sending their monks and priests around the country for this purpose. But this method of fund-raising depleted the monks' time and energy. In the middle of the Kamakura period, they invented an easier way of raising funds. They used actors and dancers to give public performances, charging their audiences, while at the same time encouraging them to give donations towards building new places of worship or rebuilding the old. These public performances awoke the actors' professionalism. The more popular their performing art was, obviously, the more people came to see them, and that meant more money for the religious establishment and, of course, for their protegées, the actors.

It was on such an occasion that the third *shogun* Yoshimitsu saw Ze-Ami and his father, Kan-Ami, on stage. The *shogun*, then eighteen, was personally charmed by the young actor, who was then only twelve, and gave him life-long favour and patronage. Till then, *sarugaku* was performed for the public, and the actors developed their skills to meet the taste of the common man. Ze-Ami then was called Oniyasha, which literally means devil and monster. He was soon given another stage name by an aristocratic poet, a cultural advisor to the third *shogun*, and was renamed Fujiwaka, literally meaning young wisteria. This symbolic change of name indicates a general trend, a movement from earthly to more refined tastes. The third *shogun* had aristocratic sensibilities, expressed poetically, especially in a short but intense art form, capturing the beauty of life's brevity and colour.

Ze-Ami invented the term *hana*, literally meaning flower. The concept of art, or theatre, as a flower or bloom provided an extensive metaphor describing the spiritual quality of a performance which could, therefore, be seen as sharing parallel aesthetic elements with flowers, such as colour, shape, seasonality, transience, and so on. Ze-Ami refined a tough and realistic theatre into a more sophisticated and recherché one. His obsessive desire to improve his troupe's methods and techniques lasted through his life and was inherited by his more conservative followers. Ze-Ami's troupe, called *Kanze-za*, was taken over by his nephew, Onnami. Successive *shoguns* favoured Onnami, throughout his lifetime. Noh was generally accepted as the theatre of the nobility and of *shoguns* and *samurais*.

Then Noh actors were scattered around the country during the civil war (1477–1573) seeking protection where they could find it. When the *shogun* Tokugawa Ieyasu (1524–1616) finally brought the country under control, he made Noh into an official ceremonial entertainment, guaranteeing employment and protection for four troupes: *Kanze, Kongo, Komparu* and *Hosho*. The shogunate, however, did not only want to impose social and political norms but cultural ones. Reflecting the static policy of the shogunate, the Noh theatre stopped experimenting with new developments. Noh drama was fossilized, depending on written stage directions secretly kept by each troupe leader. The *Kita* troupe was admitted among the other four troupes during the early Edo period (1600–1867). Since then Noh has been a purely traditional theatre.

The Tokugawa shogunate lasted over two and half centuries, and was replaced at the restoration in 1867. Noh troupes, having suddenly lost the all-powerful patronage of the shogunate and the prestige that went with it, were at a loss. Noh actors had to give performances to common people. They built Noh stages for public performances in Tokyo and Kyoto, and they started performing for paid audiences again after a four hundred years' gap. Noh troupes, however, never gained much popularity among these public audiences, but found new patrons amongst rich merchants and other industrialists from the new middle classes, the kind of people who, even now, like to employ Noh actors to teach them to become amateur singers and dancers.

Noh is a poetic theatre, which pursued the highest literary achievement with the inclusion of *waka* poems in its texts. When the great Noh actor, Ze-Ami, became one of the third *shogun's* favourites, he and his father started to polish the then realistic Noh theatre into a more sophisticated form of drama which would accord with the *shogun's* ultra-sophisticated tastes. Unlike the successive *shoguns* of the Kamakura period (1192–1334) who respected strong discipline and military strength, this ruler was intrigued by the aristocratic culture established earlier on by the nobles of the Heian period.

He had an aristocratic poet as his cultural adviser. He was Nijo

Yoshimoto, an aristocrat of the highest rank, whose chief interest
lay in improving existing *renga* poetry. *Renga* poems were widely
read, but they had never been regarded as a serious form of poetry
before. They were made and read, for example, at outings to view
cherry blossoms or autumn leaves, just as an entertainment and
amusement, contrary to *waka* poems which were written and read
much more seriously and were intended, in a pantheistic culture,
to show the participants' appreciation of natural beauty. Japanese
language is a syllabic language, and does not rhyme. When spoken,
it sounds flat and, unlike English, does not have metre, or intona-
tion, or accent. *Waka* has a definite pattern, comprising lines of
five, seven, five, seven and a final seven syllables. *Renga* starts like
waka but the fourth and fifth lines are seven, five and form a unit.
Renga was usually written by several people present at a poetry
making/reading session. Whoever wrote the fourth and fifth lines
could continue to extemporize with units of seven and five
syllables, finally concluding with two lines of seven syllables.
Renga, originally, dealt with comical situations and wit and
humour, and sometimes it became vulgar and rude. Nijo
Yoshimoto was convinced that while there was no room to develop
waka poetry (which had been continuously refined since the
seventh century), he could elevate *renga* to the height of the former
by choosing similar poetic subjects and aiming at a similar goal,
that of pure aesthetic achievement.

When Ze-Ami was favoured by the young *shogun*, he was
allowed access to his courtiers, highly educated aristocrats and
influential feudal lords. Ze-Ami was particularly influenced by the
poet Nijo Yoshimoto, who taught him the essence of Japanese
poetry. Ze-Ami tried to combine two forms of poetry by writing
the singing part of a play in *renga* style, and he also quoted old
well-known poems in his plays, usually relating to the main
character, or to the place where the play was enacted. Thus he
decorated the sentences in his plays; the words were used like
threads in a tapestry, waving complex decorative patterns. He
followed the same tradition of those of *waka* poetry.

One of the characteristics of *waka* poems is to describe some
human emotion symbolically in terms of natural phenomena. Thus
rain symbolized crying, or the changing of the leaves the ephemeral
nature of life and human affection. *Waka* also used a technique
called *makura-kotoba* (pillow words). These were used to create an
image or mood related as a subtle preparation for a specific feeling,
to make the statement more indirect, and thus, to the Japanese
mind, more poetic. Here is an example:

Kazefukeba Okitsushiranami Tatsutayama
Yowaniyakimiga Hitoriyukuran

The first and second groups of syllables in this *waka* poem (quoted
in the Noh play *Izutsu*) are pillow words and are used to bring
out 'Tatsutayama'. They describe the sea becoming disturbed by
high waves when the wind starts to blow. 'Tatsutayama' makes a
pun, meaning both the name of a local mountain and the winds rising. This image of a rough, windy sea evokes uncertainty and
possible dangers: This is associated with a poetess's anxiety about
her husband, who is crossing Tatsutayama mountain alone in the
darkness to meet his mistress. When he heard this he felt ashamed
of becoming involved with another woman whilst his own wife
loved him so devotedly, and consequently finished his affair.

Noh is a symbolic and stylized theatre. It started as a form of
public entertainment and was still crude in the thirteenth century.
Skills in dancing, singing, acting and miming were all basically
limited; they provided a realistic and sometimes vulgar display.
When Ze-Ami came into the limelight and gained the *shogun's*
favour, he started adapting the Noh to suit the *shogun's* courtly
standards. He refined not only the ideas and language of the Noh
plays, but the manners, in which these were expressed. He devised
stylized forms of acting to illustrate poetic concepts. Gestures and
movements were made symbolic and suggestive.

There are, for example, three ways of showing sorrow, according to the degree of the sorrow. One is just to look down. The
main actor (playing the role of a female, or of a ghost or a supernatural being) is masked. And while the smooth contours of the
mask were usually extremely impersonal, the slow tilting of the
curved surfaces, as an actor slowly let the angles of his mask dip
into ever-deepening shadow, expresses sadness in a symbolic manner. Deeply moving statements before or after such a silent show
of grief explains this restrained inner grief. The second method of
showing distress incorporates a hand movement. This synchronizes
with the face movements. The actor brings his hand up to his eyes,
but at a distance from his face, roughly of about fifteen centi-
metres. He holds his fingers together but keeps his hand open,
without stretching it out flat. The actor slowly repeats this gesture,
bringing his hand up to eye level. While the actor is performing this
gesture he may sing a sequence to express sorrow. Sometimes this
movement is performed in total silence. The third method is to
show deeper sorrow by using both hands. This action is usually

performed while the actor is sitting on the stage floor. He brings both his hands up to his eye level while he is looking down. He then repeats this movement with his right hand above the left without letting them touch. This may or may not be accompanied by sorrowful chanting. Thus a movement in the Noh theatre is reduced to a minimum, similarly with the stage props. The Noh is exposed to the eyes of the audience all the time. It has a square main stage, and a bridge to link it with the green room. Once an actor stands at the end of the bridge he is exposed to the audience. This arrangement of the stage and auditorium made any kind of realistic arrangement quite impossible. Unlike contemporary theatre audiences, people in those days were better trained for the spoken word. It was the same with Shakespeare's Elizabethan audience. Their imagination helped them to create invisible backdrops and sets for palace or castle, for inns or battlefields. Noh had the same stage conventions as the Elizabethan theatre. An actor would say that he was travelling from England to France, and the audience automatically accepted that the next scene took place in France. In Noh there is a sequence of singing, called *michiyuki*, in which the actor describes the changing scenery he passes while he is supposed to be travelling. At the end of his recital, he announces that he has arrived at his destination. The audience accepts this, and when he starts a new sequence they create a new setting in their minds.

The exposed stage makes any change of scenery and props difficult, as there is no curtain over the main stage. Ze-Ami and his contemporaries started using symbolic props. Their appearance was extremely stylized. They were usually simple structures of bamboo and cloth. The symbolic suggestion of a mountain, for example, was made of bamboo covered with cloth and small green branches. The whole structure, on a square base, would only be about six feet high and three feet wide, just sufficient for an actor to hide from the audience. Similarly, the shed or palace was simple and symbolic, and it was about seven feet high, three feet wide and six feet long. This simple symbol of a building was made of wood and bamboo; the whole thing was covered with decorative cloth to represent a palace, while when a few bamboo sticks were exposed, revealing the linear framework, it represented a cottage. The stage props and sets in the Noh, usually carried in before a play started, are reduced in size and turn concrete shapes into skeletons. They are nothing more than miniature symbols.

Acting in Noh theatre involves mimes. These are highly symbolic and sometimes it is quite difficult to guess what they meant. Ze-Ami explains his basic concept of acting as follows:

Acting consists of the movements of an actor's body. If an actor moves his body responding with his mind to the words and the lines of a play, . . . he will come to act naturally. For example, if he moves his head at the word 'looking' in the text, if he points or withdraws his hand at the word 'pointing' or 'withdrawing', and if he takes the posture of listening at the word of 'listening'. (*Fūshi-Kaden*)

As far as this quotation is concerned, the Noh acting may, in principle, sound the same as acting in any other type of the theatre. What is Noh, then? In the modern age, mime has become a purely silent art, in which the actor convey his ideas and emotions by gestures. The mime actor has to act in such a way that his audience is never at any time conscious of any lack of the spoken word. This form of theatre originated in Greece as a sketch of a dramatic and often crudely realistic sort. Mime theatre reached its height at the time of the *commedia dell'arte* in Italy, in which actors wore masks and used spoken words together with mime and gestures. Mime in Noh theatre is somewhat like that of the *commedia dell'arte*. There is, however, a great difference: one is comic and the other is serious. Kyogen, comic interludes between Noh plays, provide the kind of light relief based on improvised humour and everyday foolishness which may be equated with the European mime tradition of irresponsible gaiety. Although the Noh started realistically enough, it became increasingly sophisticated, and this sophistication was essentially philosophical. Noh actors in pursuit of aristocratic culture were influenced by Zen. Thus in Ze-Ami's later life he placed simple rustic beauty above rich and lavish beauty, and these aesthetic views led to increased minimalization throughout Noh productions. After his death, Noh had already become a traditional art, its acting style defined through a series of movements included in all the plays, called *kata*, designed to represent distinctive feelings and gestures.

Noh is a musical theatre. It has a chorus and musicians besides its cast. A Noh play has speaking and singing parts just like in western opera, but the total effect is completely different, since in the Japanese Noh threatre everything (except costume) was reduced down to a minimum to present action symbolically, while opera adopted every possible effect to add to its theatrical extravaganza.

A group of Noh musicians, or *hayashikata*, includes one Noh flute and three drums which provide sombre rhythms. They accompany the singing, but are silent during the speeches. In Noh music there is no absolute musical scale as in European music. This varies according to the mood of the tunes and players. If the singing part is by a happy young woman, the tone will hit the highest note of the scale, but if it is by a grieving old woman, even though her singing part is described as high-pitched, the tone considered suitable will be the middle tone of the happy young woman, or even lower. This is even more obvious in actual singing than in the accompanying music. Each measure in Noh music is divided into eight beats. The drummer who plays a drum called *okawa* or *ootsuzumi* leads the first four and the drummer who plays a smaller drum called *kotsuzumi* or simply *tsuzumi* leads the final four. The speed of their rhythm varies according to the scenes, characters and the plays; if it is a love scene, the tempo will be reduced and slowed down. Correspondingly the drummers' shouts between pauses will get gentler. If it is a battle scene, the beat becomes faster and the exclamations fiercer. As a Noh play is written as *renga* poetry, usually with twelve syllables in each measure, these syllables have to be distributed among eight beats. The vital role for Noh musicians is accompanying the dance which forms the play's climax.

The Noh is a dance theatre, in which dance was one of its original components before it became a courtly exercise; it was also one of its most distinctive characteristics once it had become an exercise and pastime of the nobility. Nobles, in the *shogun's* entourage, would practise Noh as a form of relaxation just as Louis XIV's courtiers would practise dances for royal performances. Precision and grace of movement, grandeur and elegance all had their impact on Noh dancing, its stately and refined form. Even dances of demons, or of *samurai* locked in battle, aimed at a heroic style, although the speed of a dance varied to suit the action depicted. Reunited ghostly lovers or a benign goddess blessing the company called for measured movements, but a demon trying to snatch a soul, or a wife jealously trying to murder a mistress, made for more dramatic movements. Often a slow chain of carefully executed steps culminating in a final dramatic and breathtakingly memorable moment of sudden action. The final part of the play is called *kyu*, literally meaning 'sudden or fast'. And the ending of a play focussing on demons or monsters or evil spirits presents a particularly spectacular and dramatic scene shaking the entire auditorium. Even the ending of a play dealing with the love of an aristocratic couple or the love of nature may be less violent, but will still speed up towards the climax. Thus the Noh play, in general, concludes with rhythmical singing and dancing.

The Noh is, in a way, a 'poor theatre', like that innovated by the Polish director, Grotowski. It is a theatre designed to show the actor's body, voice and movements with the minimum help from artificial sources such as lighting, costume, sound effects, and stage scenery.

The actors of the 'poor theatre' are exposed to the audience
without any way of camouflaging their shortcomings and lack of
ability. Noh theatre, however, is not altogether a 'poor theatre' in
this sense, since it uses highly decorative costumes for the main
character of each play. As the main character is frequently a young
court lady, or an aristocratic youth, they wear extremely elegant
and deliberately eye-catching costumes. Other characters such as
demons and evil spirits wear colourful yet terrifying costumes. The
waki, a secondary part such as a monk, wears rather more subdued
colours and designs. Players taking lesser parts such as members of
chorus and stage prompters/stage hands all wear black *kimonos*
and baggy trousers called *hakama*.

The Noh is 'poor' in lighting. This theatre was developed
hundreds of years before electricity was introduced. So Noh performances were given either by daylight or candle light. Specially
coloured lights have never been used in this traditional theatre.
The contemporary Noh stage is lit by ceiling light (a mixture of
ordinary bulbs and bar lights) which produce a flat light. There are
no spot lights, side lights or foot lights. This is quite close to the
lighting arrangement for the productions of W. B. Yeats's plays for
dancers.

Apart from the traditional accompaniment of drums and a Noh
flute, the Noh lacks artificial sound effects used to create credibility
and tension. The building up of an atmosphere is determined by the
very first short sequence of music and the first character to appear
to set the scene. During the middle or at the end of a performance
this role is taken by the musicians and the chorus, who sing and
exclaim dramatically.

Noh theatre, like the Elizabethan theatre, depends on verbal
images. A setting, a change of place, the description of a person,
all are suggested verbally, with relatively minute and minimal
props, such as a framework for a palace which can accommodate
a single actor, small items often being represented by the actor's
fan. The actor himself is visible to the audience throughout almost
all of every play and so, once he has passed through the small curtain at the end of the bridge leading to the main stage, it is up to
him to create whatever effects he can. The psychological insight
which this kind of concentrated acting can produce is similar to
Grotowski's 'poor theatre'.

Hana literarily means 'flower', and Ze-Ami says *hana* is the essence
of Noh; *hana* equates the degree of aesthetic quality; sophistication
surpassing ordinary material qualities.

When it comes to the definition of *hana*, however, it proves nearly impossible to render the meaning of the word, as the elements of this aesthetic concept are so versatile. Ze-Ami says in *Fūshi-Kaden*:

Seeing actual flowers, one must understand the reason why everything in the Noh has come to be compared to flowers.

All plants and trees flower at their appropriate seasons and people appreciate their flowers because they are fresh and novel.[3]

In Noh plays there are frequent references to natural beauty, and its transience, particularly in *waka* poems inserted into the texts. Poetic imagery in a Noh play is associated with the change of the seasons. There are about 240 Noh plays in the entire repertoire, and most of these are classified by the seasons and months; they are continually re-selected in varying groups to make up a complete programme which is produced once only, avoiding boredom through repeated programmes. The essence of Noh is a source of aesthetic refreshment, inner truths glimpsed through stylized form. It is an essential part of the understanding of *hana*, therefore, that the audience is capable of mental and emotional reactions of a distinguished and subtle nature.

The Noh, like western ballet and opera, is a highly professional theatre. Brief rehearsals are useless — Noh actors, who learn as children, are subjected to at least ten years' hard training before and after puberty (when their voices break), and are expected to continue with daily training to develop correct mental attitudes and physical fitness and strength. Singing is the most important part of the training. The actor has to learn to control both his voice and his breathing for correct voice production. A Noh actor has to be able to use strong and weak forms of voice and also has to be able to produce a range running from a young to an old woman. He has to raise the tone of his voice (without the kind of exaggeration found in the Kabuki theatre). The most challenging part probably is that of an old but refined lady, such as the poetess Komachi.

Dancing and acting training are also vital. As movement is highly controlled and limited, and as an actor has no liberty of physical expression, he has to learn to express variations in feeling by symbolic representations, as, for example, in the use of three different gestures to show sorrow. The actor's inner convictions are expressed physically.

Mind, however, is always stressed more than matter in this art where actor is in effect his own producer and should calculate the effect he creates by relying on his own powers and intuition, rather than on outside direction. The actor should gauge his audience and always keep them mentally on their toes. The Noh actor should never reveal his mental process, his creative intentions.[4]

Furthermore, the actor has to work at two levels of mind: he is partly identified with the role he is performing and at the same time he must be objective and critical. According to Ze-Ami, when an actor's conscious creative mind dissolves into his subconscious, then his acting flowers.

The Noh theatre, therefore, has to be professionally produced by actors trained rigorously over a long period of time. Indeed Ze-Ami says 'there is an end to our life, but there is no end to Noh'. He stresses that each actor should be always open to learning, however successful the world may consider him, and must train constantly, thus avoiding the pitfalls of conceit, and becoming wise enough to understand the art of true spiritual beauty.

The Noh theatre has survived for over six centuries and still attracts many audiences from inside and outside Japan. Its strength lies in the unique features of the performances and the fact that its actors are all highly skilled and experienced. Noh is the theatre of professionals, of the intelligentsia, of lovers of beauty. Although Yeats never saw a Noh play, he used his imagination, as a traditional member of a Noh audience would, to elaborate on the material available to him.

III. THEMES

As Richard Ellmann has shown in *Yeats: The Man and the Masks* (1961), Yeats only succeeded in coming to terms with his personal and poetic problems around 1916, coinciding with the writing of *At the Hawk's Well*. When he wrote it, says Ellmann, 'Yeats had at last found an adequate medium for his dramatic talents'.[1] His marriage in 1917 and his excitement at finding in his wife a collaborator for his philosophic writings, leading to the publication of the first edition of *A Vision* (1925), inspired and gave coherence to *The Only Jealousy of Emer*.

The political events of 1916, the rebellion and its aftermath, gave him images for *The Dreaming of the Bones*. His developing ideas on personality related to the phases of the moon, and the opposition of subjective (antithetical) nature and objective (primary) nature, gave him a basis for *Calvary*. Equally, these ideas, combined with the theory of masks, with which he had been working in the struggle to complete *The Player Queen* (1919), and which he had made philosophically coherent in the prose work *Per Amica Silentia Lunae* (1917), allowed him to see comedy as closely related to serious spiritual matters and facilitated the writing of *The Cat and the Moon* (1926).

At the same time, then, as his discovery of the Japanese Noh drama, Yeats was resolving a series of problems in his own life and poetics; the writing of the *Four Plays for Dancers* registered his breakthrough into a new stronger form and a more satisfactory mode of uniting conviction and communication.

Yeats's encounter with Noh drama was mainly through the translations of Noh plays by Ernest Fenollosa. Fenollosa was an American who went to Japan to teach economics at Tokyo University, but was soon enchanted by the traditional Japanese arts. He was puzzled to see the devaluation and the destruction of all these fine, sophisticated Japanese arts in the storm of westernization which followed two and a half centuries of isolation. All the old values were denied: some old Buddhist religious sculptures and

33

antique scrolls were destroyed; old Japanese paintings were sold for almost nothing. Fenollosa is now known as a defender of traditional arts in Japan, rather than a professor of economics. He thus saved thousands of works of art and they became the core of the Japanese section of the Boston Museum. Fenollosa was not only a collector, and champion of Japanese aesthetics, but also a practitioner of Japanese arts. For example, Fenollosa learned calligraphy, the tea ceremony, flower arranging, Noh singing and dancing. He was strongly attached to the Noh theatre, which had traditions dating back six hundred years, and started translating Noh plays with the intention of introducing this theatre to the west.

Fenollosa's translations of Noh plays were handed over by his wife to Ezra Pound, a poet who had shown a keen interest in Chinese poetry, and he thus came to edit the manuscripts for publication. Some of the translated plays appeared in the volume entitled, *'Noh' or Accomplishment, a Study of the Classical Stage of Japan.*[2] Editing was not easy, even for an expert on Chinese poetry, as a Noh play was a poetic drama with some spoken parts written in prose and most parts in syllabic poetry. Historically venerated *waka* poems were often quoted in the text. 'Pillow' words in Japanese poetry, for example, were a complete riddle for western minds, since they didn't literally fit into the context of a realistic speech, and yet gave a crucially reflective image. Quite often puns were used to evoke nature alongside descriptions of human feelings.

When Pound received Fenollosa's manuscripts in 1913, he showed them to W. B. Yeats, then searching for a new poetic form for the stage. Yeats was delighted with the discovery of these 'certain noble plays of Japan', in which he found an ideal example for his own drama. As he admits, Yeats wrote *Four Plays for Dancers* taking in general features from the Noh plays.

In fact with the help of these plays 'translated by Ernest Fenollosa and finished by Ezra Pound' I have invented a form of drama, and having no need of mob or press to pay its way — an aristocratic, distinguished, indirect and symbolic form.[3]

Yeats's first play for dancers, *At the Hawk's Well*, was based on the Noh play *Yoro* (and perhaps also *Kikujido* and *Makura Jido*), the second, *The Only Jealousy of Emer*, on *Aoino-ue*, the third, *The Dreaming of the Bones*, on *Nishikigi* and the fourth, *Calvary*, on no Japanese source at all. Formally, these plays marked a new venture into what Ian Kott calls 'the theater of essence', a non-literary manifestation of spiritual power and authority.[4] As Yeats himself put it, 'I seek, not the theatre but the theatre's anti-self'.[5] He had a sense of preparing a stage 'for the whole wealth of modern lyricism, for an art that is close to pure music, for those energies that would free the arts from imitation, that would ally acting to decoration and to the dance'.[6] So far as characterization was concerned, Yeats now moved away from the Shakespearean model, from the attempt (seen in *On Baile's Strand*, for example) to depict characters fully, with naturalistic details. Instead, he aimed for a more two-dimensional presentation. Anticipating the post-war expressionists, he used abstractions such as Young Man and Old Man to embody certain passions, states of mind or of being.

*

According to Richard Taylor, in his essay in *Yeats and the Theatre*, Yeats's dramatic themes include, 'the limitations of the human condition, the ideal of heroic action, and the transcendence of the spiritual world as projected through images of aesthetic creation, war or violence, and sexuality'.[7] In the *Four Plays for Dancers*, specifically, the themes are quite varied, and each play requires separate examination. The introductory songs (for the folding and unfolding of the cloth), while thematically relevant, do not always provide the keys to those themes most dramatically significant in the relevant plays: indeed, the songs may be misleading, and should be treated as 'mood music' rather than as supplying information as in a prologue.

Noh plays are divided into five groups according to their themes, and also the kind of representative figures which dominate them, although nearly all of them are religious to some extent. The theme of the first group is religious, with a Buddhist god or nature spirit as the leading character. The second group, concerned with the suffering of dead samurai, is dominated by a soul in purgatory. The third group, exploring love, is very often dominated by a tragic court lady. The fourth group, dealing with madness, is dominated by the mental suffering of a distraught character. The fifth group is varied, designed to give spectacular effects, and could be dominated by a colourful demon or theatrical supernatural creation. During the Edo period, the one-day programme was composed of one play from each group, plus some light relief provided by a couple of Kyogen or comic interludes. In a Noh play, apart from their function as commentators, the functions of the chorus are quite different from those in Yeats's plays. His use of chorus is much closer to that of Greek tragedies. His choruses comprise actual people who have been established on stage as a part of the play itself, though they do not get involved in the course of events within the play proper: the members of Yeats's choruses are commentators on and witnesses of his drama. The chorus in a Noh play, however, does not take any physical action; its members sit throughout a performance to the left (entering before the action starts, and remaining, statically, on the stage). They not only comment on the action supposed to be taking place on the stage, but also represent the main supporting role, or inner self of the lead.

The introduction of the play is done, in most plays, by the *waki*, or supporting role, who was often a travelling monk. In the period running from the tenth to the fifteenth centuries there were many travelling monks who sought enlightenment, or divine forgiveness for crimes that they had committed when they were still in the secular world. A travelling monk, or sometimes monks, will guide the audience at a Noh play in their imagination to a historic place, where the drama is going to take place, by standing and singing. The monk describes the changing scenery or makes a reference to fast-moving clouds, to indicate the process of travel. His singing is subdued, like the chanting by a bass singer, creating a serene, austere atmosphere on the stage. When the lead appears this character will become a sort of interviewer, provoking the lead into expanding on the historic site and people involved.

At the Hawk's Well/Yoro

Search: Both the Old Man and the Young Man are engaged in a search for the waters of immortality in *At The Hawk's Well*. A courtier is sent in search of the water of immortality by Emperor Yuryaku in *Yoro*.

The Supernatural: The Old Man refers to 'the unappeasable shadow', or power of the supernatural, by which the Guardian of the Well is possessed. Once she goes out, leading the young man in thrall, she raises up Aoife and the warrior women of the mountain to declare war on him. The 'pale windy people' whom Cuchulain complained of in *On Baile's Strand* have now become more particularized. The spirit who leads the Young Man away from the well of immortality is, in Yeats's term, a *daimon*; it creates Cuchulain's heroic destiny.

In *Yoro*, the supernatural power is represented by the god of mercy, Yoryu-kannonbosatsu, who turned a mountain stream into *sake*, or rice wine, which was regarded as a medicine for longevity. A loving, hard-working young man has been supporting his ageing parents. His love and loyalty to them has moved the god of mercy to reward him with sake to feed them, thus repairing their energy and strength.

Loss: *At the Hawk's Well* ends in failure for both the Old Man and the Young Man. The former bitterly berates 'the accursed shadows' of the spirit world for deluding him: 'You have deluded me my whole life through.' The Musicians indicate that the Young Man has 'lost what may not be found', and regret that he 'might have lived at his ease' if he had not risen to the challenge of the supernatural. Yet the sense of loss surrounding the Young Man's failure to drink from the well is counter-balanced by his initiation into his heroic life, tragic though its pattern will be.

In the original version of the play the sense of failure was stronger: it ended on an entirely pessimistic note: 'Accursed be the life of man . . . All his days are a preparation for what never comes'.[8]

Yoro is included among the first group of Noh plays which are almost religious rituals, just like medieval cycle plays. The power of Yoryu-kannonbosatsu is demonstrated by changing the mountain stream into a *sake* stream to reward the young man. In the second part, this god appears in front of the courtier sent by the Emperor, and passes his congratulations to the Emperor for his peaceful reign. The Emperor, at this time, was himself considered as a living Shinto god. The ending of this play can be interpreted as propaganda, linking religious belief and respect for the emperor's authority. The young villager secured the longevity of his parents by living in the kind of correct and faithful way advocated by the government.

The Only Jealousy of Emer/Aoino-ue

Death and the afterlife: Yeats introduces his theory that the dead inhabit a dream world: 'The dead move ever towards a dreamless youth / And when they dream no more return no more.' The Buddhist religion contains a lot of paradoxes. Death in this life is thought to be the beginning of the next life, quite often interpreted in terms of heaven and hell. In Buddhist teaching people believed (particularly from the eighth to the fifteenth centuries) that they had many lives, and that their present life had been determined by the results of their performances in their previous lives. They believed in many spirits. In *Aoino-ue*, however, it is not a vengeful ghost, but the thought power of a vengeful princess which causes the serious illness of Aoine-ue, one of her husband's favourite mistresses. It was commonly believed, when this play was created, that the evil soul of a person could cause actual physical and mental damage.

Buddhists also believed that after death they would wander about for forty-nine days in their bid to reach the other side. The other side is believed to be the Buddha's country, India, an entrance to the next life. Whilst they are wandering, spirits are in a state of transit, similar to purgatory. It is also believed that if a man dies with any negative or restrictive obsessions he will not be able to evolve spiritually, and his soul will remain earth-bound.

Remorse: as part of his theory of the afterlife, Yeats claims that a spirit can suffer guilt for sins, such as Cuchulain's infidelities to Emer: 'memory is beauty's bitterest enemy'. This guilt pulls him away from the spirit world and back to the material. Cuchulain is in an intermediary state, as it were imprisoned, with no possibility of escape except through Emer's bargain (sacrifice) with Bricriu. 'Intricacies of blind remorse' thus hold Cuchulain suspended between two worlds. This is more Buddhist than Christian in concept.

The Supernatural: the Sidhe, or fairy folk, especially Fand, wife of Manannan (the Irish version of Neptune), govern the action of the play. Bricriu, god of discord, complicates the supernatural intervention by his interposition between Fand (called the Woman of the Sidhe) and Emer. Bricriu takes over Cuchulain's body and (for motives of his own) instructs Emer in what she must do to save Cuchulain from Fand's power. Thus the supernatural world is divided in the play, and its discord is made to influence the human fate of Cuchulain.

In the original version of the play, the quarrel between Bricriu and Fand was given more prominence, so that her defeat might tend to distract the audience from Emer's situation. The irrelevant point was made that Fand, as a supernatural being, was unaware that humans are bound together by 'Intricacies of pain'.[9]

In *Aoino-ue*, the vengeful soul of Princess Rokujo appears at the call of the priestess Teruhinomae, who was ordered to find out if any evil spirits (dead or alive) have cast a spell over beautiful Aoino-ue, who is now critically ill. Princess Rokujo's vengeful soul appears and tells of her humiliation and anger towards her rival in love. The princess, obsessed with hateful feelings, renews her vow to get revenge on her husband's mistress.

In the second part, a powerful saint (who has gone through hard spiritual training process in isolation) exorcises these frightening, dangerous emotions. A piece of folded cloth is placed in front of the stage, signifying young Aoino-ue ill in bed. When the saint begins the exorcism, the vengeful soul of Princess Rokujo appears in the shape of a demon with the intention of killing Aoino-ue. There is a battle beween her evil soul and religious powers. After a while the evil soul loses its vengeful force when confronted with powerful prayer, and accepts the saint's guidance in the spiritual truths of Buddhism.

Loss: Emer loses Cuchulain's love forever, when she makes her heroic renunciation. Princess Rokujo loses her husband to his mistress, Lady Aoino-ue, twice; firstly she loses her husband's love to Lady Aoino-ue, and secondly after her confrontation with the powerful Buddhist saint, she gives up her revenge and stops causing her rival's destruction.

Love: The love of Emer and that of Eithne Inguba are contrasted: the domestic and the illicit. Ironically, it is because Emer is not Cuchulain's beloved that she can face Bricriu. Eithne is the ultimate winner solely because Bricriu strikes a bargain with Emer who 'renounce[s] Cuchulain's love for ever'.

The love of Fand for the Ghost of Cuchulain provides a secondary theme. This love is ethereal, a desire for a consummation that will provide her with unity of being, at the cost of Cuchulain's individual identity. Defeat for Fand, while pathetic, means release for Cuchulain; but as he rejoins Eithne and not Emer there is another kind of pathos established, in harmonic relation to that evoked for Fand, something the final and complex song attempts, with doubtful effect, to express.

Prince Genji is a great womanizer with exceptional advantages: the highest birth, handsome youth, sophistication. He does not find it difficult to make any woman fall in love with him. He is amorous. He loves women, but temporarily. He is always on the search for new lovers.

Princess Rokujo is his wife, but not his beloved. Prince Genji loves Lady Aoino-ue. Princess Rokujo's jealousy turns into vengeful rage when Lady Aoino-ue challenges her by colliding her carriage into hers and breaking it at a public festival. Intensive fury and jealousy drive Princess Rokujo into revenge. However, she gives up her envious outburst when she is confronted by the powerful saint. She accepts her fate (in Buddhism, suffering in the present world is explained as the result of an evil action in the previous world), and pacifies her rage. Princess Rokujo is doubly beaten in love and revenge, and creates a kind of pathos seen in Yeats's *The Only Jealousy of Emer*.

Beauty: This theme, introduced in the opening song, is related in the play to the theory of the phases of the moon. The ghost of Cuchulain recognizes the beauty of Fand by her being like the moon, close to completion at the fifteenth night. Yeats's complex theory, explained in a note,[10] is not allowed to obscure the action, and merely serves to motivate the mutual desire between the ghost of Cuchulain and the supernatural Fand. Essentially, Yeats is saying that beauty is a tragic gift.

Hana is the essence of Noh theatre. Beauty, elegance in subtlety and sophistication, should be created through the performance of any play, but a play such as *Aoino-ue* in which the lead is a noble person provides beauty and elegance naturally since she or he is sophisticated and poetical. Ze-Ami says the ultimate beauty, another typical Japanese paradox, is most present when it is marred by something. Ze-Ami gives two examples: the first is a flowering hedge; it looks most beautiful when seen through the lifting morning mist. The second is a legendary beauty, Komachi; Ze-Ami says her beauty would be heightened by a touch of sadness.

Princess Rokujo appears in deep sorrow, but her lamentation is soon overcome by rage and revenge. When her anger is spent, she falls back into despair. Princess Rokujo represents the utmost beauty in her tragic mood, since she then falls into Ze-Ami's category of ultimate beauty. Yeats's concept of beauty is, in a way, very close to Ze-Ami's.

Loneliness: The Ghost of Cuchulain refers to Fand as like the moon, 'lonely with extreme delight'. Her subjective nature, near perfection, is at odds with human objectivity or desire. Her longing for 'completion', being unsatisfied, expresses Yeats's tragic vision of life. Princess Rokujo, on the other hand, refers to a morning glory waiting for sunrise. Through this symbolical reference to the glory of a very short-lived flower, she is referring to the brief fulfilment of her desires; love, honour, social position and wealth. This achievement, however, once accomplished, was destroyed by the appearance of her rival, her husband's new mistress Aoino-ue. Her marital relationship was ruined, just as a perfectly beautiful morning glory will become withered by the light and heat of the sun. Nothing material lasts forever. The fall of a glorious princess represents the current Buddhist idea of cycles of experience, and thus present a tragic vision of life.

The Dreaming of the Bones/Nishikigi

Death and the afterlife: As in *The Only Jealousy of Emer*, the theory is introduced that the dead inhabit a dreamworld in which they live 'through their old lives again'. This reliving process is here given a Christian gloss, not used (because not appropriate) in *The Only Jealousy of Emer*. Now, because the action is set in modern Ireland, the dead are presented as doing penance in a dream-like state, an idea also underlying such later plays as *The Words Upon the Window-pane* and *Purgatory*.

The Dreaming of the Bones is believed to be based on a Noh play, *Nishikigi*, which has the form of a 'dream play'. A dream play has a convention that in the second half of a play the ghost of the hero appears in the dream of the supporting character, usually a travelling monk who has offered prayers to him in the first half of the play. This dream is regarded as an actual one, unlike Yeats's metaphorical dreamworld. The lovers' souls in *Nishikigi* have been earth-bound because they have been tied by their obsessive concern with pursuing and rejection. It is believed, in Japan, that the dead can temporarily transmigrate and take any shape to pass a message to a living person. The dead thus appear, in *Nishikigi*, in two different forms: first, as a local couple, and then as ghosts of the couple who died as a result of their tragic love affair. It is still believed today that even living people can contact the dead through a medium. In old Japan there seems to have been minimal separation between the dead and the living — particularly in the case of a soul of someone who died in anguish, obsession or revenge, who was believed to be going through hell, in a tortured realm between this world and the next. Pain and worry enabled them to transmigrate back into the present world, and it was believed that it happened frequently, as they tried to be released from their suffering. We must, however, bear in mind the time difference between these two plays: *The Dreaming of the Bones* was written in 1916, while *Nishikigi* was written by Ze-Ami at the end of the fourteenth century.

Remorse: As in *The Only Jealousy of Emer*, the dead suffer from remorse and seek release from it: the memory of a 'crime' keeps the lovers apart. Yeats, however, here gives remorse a partially Christian meaning, suggesting that the dead exist in a certain state of imprisonment (cf. purgatory) from which they can be delivered only by forgiveness. What is not fully Christian about this notion is the role given to the agent of forgiveness: if the Young Man will forgive Diarmuid and Dervorgilla they will be at peace forever, whereas in the Christian understanding of forgiveness, God is the source of forgiveness, 'And His will is our peace'.[11]

The dead couple suffer remorse and seek release from it. This is a Buddhist belief, and parallels the situation in *Nishikigi*. Here, the couple needed unification instead of forgiveness, since the causes of their deaths were an obsessive pursuit of love by a man and an obstinate refusal of it by the woman. They needed a 'match-maker' to free themselves from continuous torments. The travelling monk to whom they make an appeal prays for them, releasing them from their purgatory. They will be united in the next life. The differences between the plays, in the end, show contrasting ideas towards religion. Yeats did not believe in working within an optimistic, spiritual framework, nor in the release of suffering souls who had thrown Ireland into seven hundred years of subjection. So he placed the Young Man in the position of a judge, rather than of a servant to God.

The Supernatural: No gods appear in *The Dreaming of the Bones*, merely the 'accursed' spirits of historical figures. Yet their plea is interpreted by the Young Man as a 'temptation' and therefore demonic. The ultimate power of the Gods was represented in *Nishikigi* by the travelling monk who prays to the almighty to intervene and save the ghost couple from their sufferings.

Loss and Gain: In *The Dreaming of the Bones* when the Young Man refuses to forgive the spirits they drift away into eternal unhappiness. In *Nishikigi* the remorseful suffering spirits are saved by the monk. Through his intervention their souls are united and they will be married in the next life.

Love: This theme is very strong in *The Dreaming of the Bones*, since the action concerns the plea for release from guilt by two famous lovers in Irish history. Yet it is not their love, nor even their failure to love, that makes them guilty. Rather it is the political act of bringing the Normans to Ireland. Consciousness of this act destroys their union in the afterlife:

> Their manner of life were blessed could their lips
> A moment meet; but when he has bent his head
> Close to her head, or hand would slip in hand,
> The memory of their crime flows up between
> And drives them apart.   (*Variorum, pp. 771-2*)

This state is never remedied in the play. The theme is, accordingly, treated tragically. The ghost couple of *Nishikigi* also describe their tragic love. Unlike Yeats's *The Dreaming of the Bones*, there are no political aspects to the Noh drama. The tragedy takes place following the Woman's refusal of the Man's courtship after a thousand attempts to win her hand. In the northern region, there was a custom that a woman should accept a man's courtship after he carried a token of an ornate branch to her door for a thousand nights. The man was madly in love with the woman, though she stubbornly kept rejecting his courtship. He, however, had a hope that after a thousand nights' wooing he would be accepted. But, once again, he was rejected, and died in despair. The woman also died in remorse and lamentation. This obsessive courtship and her rebellion against the conventions brought tragedy to them both.

Beauty: Ireland itself is described as having a beauty ravaged by invaders and rebels. The city of Galway is singled out as typical of a lost culture, a symbol of hypothetical greatness overwhelmed by the historical consequences of Diarmuid's and Dervorgilla's 'crime'. But for that it would have been 'most beautiful', comparable to 'any old admired Italian town'. In this way, Yeats suggests the 'fall' of the whole country, comparable to the fall of mankind through the sin of Adam and Eve. Beauty in *Nishikigi* is likewise tinged with tragedy. The Michinoku region of the Northern Japan was then inhabited by the Ainu (a separate race who were near extinction after the Japanese invasion by the end of the Edo period (1867). Only some hundreds of Ainu survived this Japanese massacre, and they now live in Hokkaido). The Michinoku region at the time of this play (the twelfth century) was covered with thick woods, and the land was hardly cultivated, preserving its natural beauty. The small village of Kyo presents a remote scenic place with autumnal leaves. The Ghost couple carry a beautifully ornate tree branch called a *nishikigi*, and a piece of beautifully woven cloth, called a *hosonuno*. Those poetic symbols represent the situation of the play, since a *nishikigi* is a token of love, and a piece of *hosonuno* is beautifully woven, but not wide enough to make a *kimono*. A *kimono* made of a *hosonuno* is not wide enough to cross from both sides in the front. This is thus used as a metaphor to describe unhappy lovers whose breasts can never meet. Thus this tragic love story is revealed in poetic imagery and in a scenic surrounding, all of which contribute to build 'beauty', or 'hana', on stage.

Loneliness: An atmosphere of loneliness surrounds the setting of *The Dreaming of the Bones*: 'Even the sunlight can be lonely here.' The owl — for the play is actually set in the night time — is used to suggest loneliness. The Young Girl, in describing the state of the lovers suffering remorse, says they are 'more lonely' than those spirits who work out their penance on the mountain tops: 'These are alone, / Being accursed.' The play insists that their being together actually accentuates this sense of solitude. Loneliness and beauty in *Nishikigi* are inseparable. There is certainly a predominant atmosphere of nostalgia and forlornness, just as in *The Dreaming of the Bones*. But this sadness is the prevailing atmosphere in the Noh theatre, generally and not just this play. The Noh couple are not happy being with each other, being 'accursed', since they had never been lovers when alive, while Diarmuid and Dervorgilla rejoice in their love, blighted though it be.

Calvary/Sumidagawa/Miwa

Death and the afterlife: Here Yeats presents a unique attitude to a crucial Christian example of the miraculous. His Lazarus is not a spirit like the Ghost of Cuchulain, or the lovers in *The Dreaming of the Bones*, but he nevertheless has returned from the dead: 'I am the man that died and was raised up.' Yet he regards death as preferable to life, and resents his restoration. For him, death brought freedom: 'I was free four days, four days being dead.' The theme is thus inverted, since this figure, taken out of the element in which he was happy, curses the godhead that has miraculously overturned nature in his favour. Yeats's interest in death and afterlife is his own and no influence from the Noh is detectable at all in this theme. No single Noh playwright has ever tried to reverse their traditional cycle and bring the dead back to life in their plays, except as ghosts. According to Japanese beliefs, the peaceful — and contented — dead never come back since they are believed to be rejoicing in a happier existence.

The only exceptional play which deals with this subject is *Sumidagawa*, in which a child is called back from death by his mother. This child was kidnapped in Kyoto and brought to the East to be sold there; however, he dies from exhaustion and is buried by the roadside. When his mother arrives at the place where he died a funeral is being performed by a group of local people and travellers. His mother joins them there and soon realizes it is her own son who is being buried. She offers a sorrowful prayer to her dead son. Then he appears from the grave, and joins in with everyone in prayer. This situation is quite unlike that of Lazarus, since here the child appears as a ghost. It is now interpreted as an illusion of his mother; therefore the ghost is seen and heard only by her.

Remorse: The lack of remorse in Yeats's *Calvary* on the part of either Lazarus or Judas contrasts strongly with the other *Plays for Dancers*. It means we are being shown a world, as it were, upside down: shocking in its defiance of the expected moral response. In *Miwa* the disguised Shinto goddess of Miwa appears in front of a travelling monk, and invites him to her shrine. There she identifies herself, and asks him to save her from the results of a sin which she has committed. The Goddess had fallen in love with a man from Yamato and became his wife. But she managed to spend only night time with him. After a long time, he eventually became suspicious of her identity. Then the Goddess decided to sever their marital bond, and returned to her shrine. Since then, she has suffered from remorse. Here we can see an unusual mixture of religions; a Shinto

Goddess seeks relief from remorse through the intervention of a Buddhist monk.

The Supernatural: Christ is introduced in a dream state, reliving Calvary. His pain, in contrast to the pain of the 'dreamers' in the two preceding plays, is unrelated to any sin on his part, but to the frustration arising from contemplation of a world constituted free to reject his bounty. The attitude of the soldiers, in contrasting him with the 'God of dice', accentuates the ambiguity of Christ's position: he has to suffer the absence of intervention by the divine while knowing himself to be divinely empowered. Yeats's supernatural being is here a deliberate contradiction in terms. The Shinto Goddess of the Miwa shrine is the only supernatural existence in the Noh play, in the first half disguised as a village woman and in the latter half revealing herself as a Goddess. On a superficial level the supernatural being in this play seems to be a contradiction in terms, but Shinto gods are very close to human beings. They are thought to have human emotions, such as anger, love, and jealousy. This can be easily understood if the reader knows that the Emperor used to be considered the direct descendant of the Sun Goddess.

Loss: As in the other plays, failure is the dominant note of *Calvary*. Christ's last words are entirely despairing.

The despair of the mother in *Sumidagawa* creates an illusion of her son's presence from the tomb, and it gives her the temporarily reassuring joy of seeing and hearing him. But when the illusion disappears, she is doubly wretched.

Love: There is, of course, no romantic interest in *Calvary*, but there are present Martha and 'those three Marys, and the rest / that live but in His love'. Love in this play is a vacuum. It is a state against which most of the characters react.

Love in *Miwa* is not in a vacuum altogether, but it is seen in the way the Goddess escapes from a possessive kind of more materialistic human love: further amorous involvement with a male human being would have endangered her spiritual status and power.

Beauty: Appreciation of earthly graces is significantly dormant in *Calvary*. Both Lazarus and Judas cause terror in the crowd when they advance; their appearance is, in each case, ugly. Even Christ is described as having 'dirty / Blood-dabbled feet'. It is a play bereft of beauty. The appearance of a distraught woman in *Sumidagawa* should be ugly, but in Noh plays such a woman can provide a free and wide range of poetical expressions since she is meant to be ultra-sensitive towards natural beauty, changes of seasons, and any other happenings. Thus she reinforces the dramatic and poetic elements in the play.

Loneliness: From the opening song, Christ's loneliness is strongly suggested. Christ is not lonely for human company but because he is isolated by his perfection, unwanted by those represented by Lazarus, Judas, and the soldiers. Ironically, the latter say: 'To know that he has nothing that we need / Must be a comfort to him.' Their indifference drives him, finally, to despair. The closing song returns to the opening theme, 'Lonely the sea-bird lies at her nest', suggesting a correlation between bird life and God's non-appearance: their loneliness symbolizes Christ's agonized duality. On the other hand, loneliness is not the strongest strand in *Sumidagawa*, though the Mother is isolated after her son is kidnapped. Here, loneliness is replaced by the desperation of the Mother's pursuit of her kidnapped son, until the play comes to an end when she realizes that he has died and she is left alone.

In *Miwa* loneliness is deliberately created to build up austerity, piety and a divine atmosphere for the appearance of the Shinto Goddess. The season is deep autumn, the place is the Miwa shrine in a cedar forest. Originally loneliness had made the Goddess long for warm human contact. This provoked a dilemma for the Goddess since she could not be a human being and divine one at the same time. But finally her divinity triumphed, and led her consciously to seek solitude to become, again, a source and object of worship.

IV. CHARACTERIZATION

At the Hawk's Well/Yoro

As Richard Taylor has pointed out, Yeats divided the role of the *shite* and *tsure* between the Old Man and the Young Man, suggested by the Father and Son in *Yoro*; Yeats then set them in conflict. 'They share a common purpose, but differ dramatically in temper.'[1] It seems that in working on the play, Yeats depersonalized the characters and made them more allegorical.[2]

The Old Man is presented as unheroic. His nature is passive, for he has been waiting for fifty years for the waters of immortality to flow for him, and yet when they do he has hidden in terror. The Guardian, when possessed by the Sidhe, is what makes him turn away: 'I cannot bear her eyes . . . not of this world.' Although he sees the entrance of the Young Man as competition, and defends his prior right to the water, he is kind enough to warn his rival against the supernatural powers about to invade the place. He is, therefore, a reasonable, civilized man, *l'homme moyen sensuel*, while at the same time representing an attitude to life that values safety above risk. As Yeats said in 1904, 'the average man is average because he has not attained to freedom'.[3] The Old Man's plaintive expression of loss when he discovers that the water has come and gone further indicates his pathetic, enslaved character. Yeats allows him to complain of being cheated, whereas we see clearly that the loss is as a direct result of his own cowardice.

The Young Man, in contrast, is heroic. His whole attitude, from his first entrance, is brash and fearless. He speaks of a hawk he has seen that he would like to master and possess, even though it is suggested that this hawk is no ordinary or natural bird, but supernatural. His fearlessness is thus the Young Man's main characteristic. This, ironically, is his undoing; if, that is, one regards his loss of the water as more significant than his initiation into a tragic destiny. The play emphasizes, however, the moment of the Young Man's single-minded pursuit of the Guardian into battle, as he shoulders his spear and defines himself: 'He comes! Cuchulain, son of Sualtim, comes!' (p. 412) His heroic status is then presented as ominous: the consequences of his choice are not expressed, but from what the Old Man warned, we know it is inevitable that Cuchulain will ultimately kill his own son, and consequently lose all happiness.

The Guardian does not speak, as the Old Man complains. She, being possessed by the Sidhe, turns into a hawk-woman and as such has no 'character' but is the embodiment of supernatural energy, at once terrible and fascinating.

The characterization of Noh plays is very different from that of any European plays. Each whole play is centred around the lead, the central character, while other characters do not possess individual personalities. This convention is called *shite-ichinin-shugi*. Characters are usually divided into three groups; the first group is the *shite* and his spouse or relation or followers; the second is the *waki* and his followers; and the third is *ai-kyogen*, usually the part of a village man performed by a Kyogen actor who explains, more realistically, what happened in the first half of the play.

The *shite* in *Yoro* is an unusual case, as it takes two different characters: an old man in the first half, and the god of the mountain, Yoryu-Kannonbosatsu, in the second half. The old man is the proof of the mysterious water causing a miracle. He is not only given longevity but health and happiness. He, however, has no particular character. He is simply an old man who is most appreciative of his good fortune in tasting the miraculous stream. He appears in the play only to tell of the effects of this life-giving water.

The son of this old man is called a *tsure*, or follower: he is a hard-working young man, kind and thoughtful. He has been looking after his aged parents like a dutiful son. He is a simple-minded poor wood-cutter. His love and care of his aged parents move the mountain god, who then turns a spring into a source of longevity to revitalize the fatigued. The main part in the second half is the mountain god. Yoryu-Kannonbosatsu, whose hierarchical position amongst the gods is not very high, and consequently close to human beings. This god is known for his mercifulness. The mountain god stresses the importance of the Buddhist religion to maintain the monarchy and the welfare and peace of the country. The mountain god praises the reign of emperor Yuryaku, who is the direct descendant of the Sun Goddess, the highest ranked god in the Shinto religion.

The *waki's* supporting role is that of a courtier. He does not have any personality, except that of a faithful servant: he is fulfilling the emperor's commands in searching for the sacred spring. He shows his dogged loyalty to the emperor, and thus creates a foundation for the praise of the emperor, as a living God, by all other characters in the play. The *ai-kyogen* is a common man from the mountainous area in which the play is set. This role is taken by a kyogen actor. He acts as a commentator, telling the courtier the story of both the special water and the family who have benefited from it, in plain language so that the audience has a thorough grasp of the plot. (His long speech, incidentally, provides enough time for the main actor to change his costume and mask from those of the old man to those of the god of mercy, Yoryu-Kannonbosatsu.) Again, this ordinary man does not possess any remarkable personality traits.

This kind of a Noh play, which belongs to the first group of extremely religious pieces, does not need various characters, since it is more of a ritual than a drama.

The Only Jealousy of Emer/Aoino-ue

Eithne Inguba, Cuchulain's mistress, and Emer, his wife, are more naturalistically portrayed than are the characters in *At the Hawk's Well*. As Emer says, 'We're but two women struggling with the sea' (p. 541), so their feelings are strongly humanized. Eithne is timid, however, where Emer is courageous, as is shown by her reactions when Bricriu shows his distorted mask. Eithne is rather conventionally portrayed as the 'other woman' of traditional romance. She is the unheroic embodiment of passive beauty, contrasted with Emer, who is more masterful and shows a strong, active will. Emer's determination to save Cuchulain, to bring him back from the dead, is the mainspring of this play. In that regard, Eithne is no more than her unwitting beneficiary. Emer's courage is seen in the final decision: here her heroic nature is defined, as so often in Yeats's plays, by self-sacrifice.

Bricriu is the god of discord, presented as an abstract embodiment of whimsical motives. His role is to stand mid-way between Emer's human will and Fand's supernatural will to secure the soul of Cuchulain. Were it not for his explanation of what Fand intended, neither Emer, nor the audience, would be aware of the crisis in Cuchulain's spiritual history. His role, therefore, is both that of narrator and mediator. His motive for defeating Fand, however, seems weak: 'I am Fand's enemy come to thwart her will.' Yet one must bear in mind that he also wins against Emer, since she, too, loses the love of Cuchulain. Thus Bricriu represents malignant Fate, even if in his urging Emer to act he appears sympathetic.

The Woman of the Sidhe, or Fand, wife of Manannan, in love with Cuchulain, is depicted as Eithne's counterpart, an ethereal mistress-figure. There is a tendency among some commentators to see Fand as a Muse-figure, ambivalently seducing the psyche (represented by the Ghost of Cuchulain) away from the world of duty, and other quotidian concerns. Nevertheless, although she is described in aesthetic terms, she remains an actual Celtic spirit. Other commentators, bent on seeing the *The Only Jealousy of Emer* as autobiographical, like to see Fand as based upon Maud Gonne, haunting Yeats's imagination, following his marriage to Georgie Hyde Lees in 1917.[4] Such an interpretation emphasizes the essentially inner nature of the struggle between 'demon' lover and captive mind. Unfortunately for this view, the text indicates that Fand is identified by the Ghost as the hawk woman from *At the Hawk's Well* then 'Half woman and half bird of prey' but 'all woman now'. The text insists that (rather like the mermaid figure in folk tales who tries to adjust to loving a human) Fand needs Cuchulain's love and is unable to understand the nature of human remorse.

The Ghost of Cuchulain is depicted as mind itself, sunk into a dream state. He is the means whereby a private state (what Yeats called 'the deeps of the mind') is rendered visible to an audience. He has no energy, but is pulled this way and that by contrary feelings of remorse and fascination.

In *Aoine-ue* the central character is the vengeful spirit of Princess Rokujo, suffering from jealousy and humiliation. This princess is a proud lady of the highest rank, of the highest attainment. She enjoyed a scintillating existence as the wife of Prince Genji, but her misery began when her husband started having mistresses. Aoino-ue was one of her strongest rivals in love. When Prince Genji was still deeply in love with her, Aoino-ue crashed her carriage into his wife's as a deliberate challenge at a public event. The Princess's carriage was broken and she felt doubly insulted. Her mind became increasingly vindictive. Her vengeful curses caused a mysterious illness, weakening her husband's mistress to the point where her condition became critical.

In the first half of this play the vengeful spirit of Princess Rokujo appears and tells the priestess of her bitterness, and its distressing results.

The *tsure* in *Aoino-ue* is not exactly a follower of the Princess and appears only in the first half of the play. The *tsure* is Priestess Teruhinomae, who is asked to find the cause of Aoino-ue's illness by a courtier, after various cures have failed. Priestess

Teruhinomae represents the divine power of Shinto and, through her prayers, she manages to summon the vengeful spirit of Princess Rokujo. Then the priestess tries to pacify the spiteful spirit, but fails to subdue it.

The *waki* is a Buddhist saint, Yokawano-kohijiri, who appears only in the latter half of the play. Through his long, hard pursuit of truth and enlightenment, he has acquired certain powers represented by the Buddhist gods. Though he is a monk, he is different from any temple monks. He is called *yamabushi*. A *yamabushi* usually tries to strengthen his spiritual power, wandering about in wild places and sleeping rough. The name *yamabushi* derives from their habit of sleeping in the mountains. They spend days there, sometimes sitting under a waterfall while praying and meditating. Yokawano-kohijiri has gone through all these hardships and acquired spiritual power to overcome and pacify evil spirits and ghosts.

The *waki-tsure* is not a follower of this Buddhist saint, but a courtier serving the retired Emperor Shujakuin. This courtier introduced the opening of the play announcing that Aoino-ue, the daughter of the chief minister, is possessed by an unknown evil spirit and is seriously ill. The courtier does not possess any particular personality, but functions as a commentator and usher. He is sent for by Priestess Teruhinomae and Yokawano-kohijiri, and brings them to the stage, supposedly the Prime Minister's private residence, and introduces the audience to the scene of the action. He stays on the stage throughout the play and witnesses the drama happening.

The *ai-kyogen* is another servant in the private residence of the Minister. At the end of the first half of the play, he has a long dialogue with the courtier. As they talk in plain language, the author makes sure that the audience has understood what has happened already. (Thus the *ai-kyogen* gives enough time for the lead actor to change from Princess Rokujo to a devil at the back of the stage in full view of the audience: this change of costumes and masks on the stage is called *monogi*.)

Dreaming of the Bones/Nishikigi

Young Man: He is depicted naturalistically, as a modern man, recently engaged in Ireland's fight for freedom. He is early revealed as passionately anti-British, and this is his main characteristic, giving him his motive for refusing to pardon the crime of the ghostly lovers. He is a peasant type, with a knowledge of traditional beliefs about the afterlife. He knows what fear is, since he reacts nervously when his lantern is extinguished; but he nevertheless faces the possible dangers of the mountain at night, and its abbey grave-yard. He is thus resolute in character, ultimately too much so, when he demonstrates the primacy of head over heart.

Stranger and Young Girl: In contrast to the Young Man, they are stylized and presentational. The Stranger is more detached or neutral than the Young Girl. He offers to help the Young Man but asks nothing in return. He supplies information on the state of remorse of those who, after death, live on to haunt certain places. He is presented as a guide, both to the Young Man and to the audience. The Young Girl, on the other hand, is far more direct and persuasive. She speaks only when the Young Man asks about the fate of the spirits who haunt the mountain-top: as the Stranger falls silent, she takes over the narration and makes clear the state of the lovers, divided from each other by 'The memory of a crime'. Her role thereafter is to entice the Young Man to forgive the characters in her narration, Diarmuid and Dervorgilla. Although remaining involved with the Stranger, with whom she dances, she turns upon the Young Man a powerful, seductive appeal. She thus resembles the hawk-woman in *At the Hawk's Well* and Fand in *The Only Jealousy of Emer* in her attempt to lure the hero to enact her will, but she is made to appear more plaintive then erotic.

The lead, in *Nishikigi*, in the first half, is a villager from northern Japan. He accompanies a village woman, seemingly his wife. He does not show any particular personality, but seems quite content with his life, as they sell their own hand-made crafts to travellers. His are *nishikigi*, love-tokens in this area, and hers *hosonuno*, or narrow cloths. Being a local he naturally knows the sad tale of a man and woman who are symbolically brought into the story by mention of *nishikigi* and *hosonuno*. The lead, in the second part, is the ghost of the man mentioned in this love story. The ghost, in his lifetime, was madly in love with a village woman, who is the *tsure* in the latter half of the play. He was persistent and obsessive in his courtship. After his death, he suffered from remorse, his soul having been earth-bound. He has no heroic qualities, and his life and afterlife have been dominated by his emotion.

The *tsure*, in the first half, is a village woman. She sells *hosonuno* cloth, and seems to be happy accompanying her seeming husband. She is docile and obedient, like any good wife in the past. Consequently, she does not show her strong character here, in the first half. The *tsure* in the second half is the ghost of the woman the lead fell in love with. She, in her lifetime, showed her strength of will by rejecting this man's persistent courtship. This became obvious when she refused one thousand symbolic offerings of *nishikigi*, the love token, thus breaking the convention of the *ainu* people that after one thousand days had passed, and she had been offered a love token on each night, a woman should accept her suitor, because he had proved the truth of his love. This may not accord with western conventions and ideas, but by Japanese traditions she was to be condemned for her obstinacy and cruelty. Thus, in her afterlife, she also suffered from remorse for different reasons.

The *waki* in this play enacts the most typical functions assigned for this part in Noh drama. He is a travelling monk, who introduces the audience to the scene where the drama takes place, with his opening song, speech and travelling song. In a parallel with Elizabethan stage convention, he announces his trip to, and arrival at, the northern village of Kyo, and his audience automatically takes an imaginary leap into believing that they, too, are witnessing a drama there.

The monk then takes on the role of an interviewer, to get the love story out of a village couple, questioning them about the place, *nishikigi* and *hosonuno*.

Then he takes on a third role; after being guided to the tomb of the tragic couple, he prays for their release from earthly purgatory. Lastly, remaining sitting near the chorus, he becomes a witness to the play's conclusions.

The *ai-kyogen* is a villager. Questioned by the monk, he recounts the tragic love story which has become legendary in the region. He shows deep sympathy towards the deceased who appeared in the first half disguised as a village couple and also begs the monk to pray for them. This villager is not developed as a character, except for his strong empathy and his religious faith.

Calvary

All the characters here are either masked or made up to resemble masked figures; the characterization, accordingly, is non-naturalistic, non-representational, and actually quite close to the style of a medieval morality play.

Christ: He reacts to other characters, rather than acts himself. Okifumi Komesu argues, accordingly, that Christ is thus more like a *waki* than a *shite*,[5] although he also concedes that Christ is both.[6] Certainly, Christ is defensive towards both Lazarus and Judas, having fewer lines than either. He frequently uses words such as 'Yet' and 'But', which indicate this defensiveness. Also he asks several questions, as if at the mercy of events and/or of God. Although disputatious with both Lazarus and Judas, he is not forceful, and is clearly no intellectual. Finally, in his passive response to the soldiers, he is pathetic, for he is reduced to (emotional) despair at the accumulated opposition and indifference of all those around him with the exception of Martha and the three Marys (who in any case fly away at the approach of Judas).

Lazarus and Judas: In a note on *Calvary* in *Four Plays for Dancers* Yeats said he 'represented in Lazarus and Judas types of that intellectual despair that lay beyond His sympathy'. In the text of the play, however, intellectual despair can be attributed only to Judas, not to Lazarus.

Lazarus: He is resentful at having been raised from his 'comfortable' grave. He is insolent towards Christ, and here Yeats is unconventional in his characterization. Almost in the style of Shaw when presenting characters conventionally deserving of respect and deference, Yeats allows Lazarus to be impertinent; he makes him a representative of an intellectual position wanting to sweep aside expected reverence towards Christ. Lazarus is a surprise: raised from the dead, he wants only his death back again. But as A. S. Knowland points out, Lazarus 'cannot escape from the influence of Christ'.[7]

Judas: He is persecuted as a terrible figure, who frightens away those supporters who are left around Christ. Like Lazarus, he is arrogant and insolent towards the man he knows to be God. Explaining his motive in betraying Christ to his enemies, he displays a highly intellectual, indeed existential, nature. He values his own identity above participation in a divine plan, and so is a rebel against divine goodness. Cynical and embittered, he refuses to be dismissed by Christ. Commentators have often failed to notice that Judas does not exit (as Lazarus does), but is chosen by the soldiers to hold up the cross — an incident for which there is no biblical justification. But Karen Dorn is surely correct in saying that the stage image of heron and fish (in the opening song) is relevant here in reinforcing the conflict: 'Though Christ dismisses the man who had tried to free himself, they are joined together.'[8]

The Three Roman Soldiers: These are not distinguished one from the other. Instead of being individualized, they are presented as a group, in contrast to Christ's subjectivity.

One can refrain from comparing any characters in the plays mentioned earlier with those in *Calvary*, since this play was not modelled on any particular Noh plays. Noh plays as a whole are religious, but plays classified in the first group are more like medieval cycle plays and are almost religious rituals. Komesu could not accept Jesus as the equivalent of the lead of a Noh play when *Calvary* was compared with Noh drama. He is right there because the Son of God in despair will never make a ritualistic play. Ritualistic plays deliberately set out to create awe among an audience, to promote devotion and faith.

Thus, in *Miwa*, the representative of Shinto suffers from remorse from both committing and severing her relationship with a man. At the beginning of the play, the goddess is more like a human; she learns to reject her materialistic desires, and becomes, in the end, a true object of worship. This is a piece which concludes with praise of Shinto designed to strengthen the audience's faith in Shinto. Yeats had spiritual beliefs but did not have an ultimate faith in Christianity or any other religion. In writing *Plays for Dancers*, however, he ignored, or refused to take up, the harmonious blend of Shinto and Buddhism which permeated the Noh plays that he took as models: religious optimism was omitted.

V. PLOTS AND FUNCTIONS OF MUSICIANS

In general, Yeats was a neo-classical dramatist; he admired and sought to embody those qualities of plot which Aristotle describes in the *Poetics* as proper to effective tragedy. In dramatizing the Deirdre story, for example, Yeats began the plot close to the catastrophe, and placed great emphasis on suspense and accelerating tension. It is significant that, in his advice to Padraic Colum, who was attempting to write plays around the year 1902, Yeats advised him to 'Clear the decks for action':[1] plots should concentrate on clear progression, without a subplot, or other irrelevant materials. Likewise, in his 'Advice for Playwrights', which he formalized for all new Abbey dramatists, Yeats emphasized the need for unity of action:

... any knot of events, where there is passionate emotion and clash of will, can be made the subject matter of a play. . . . Young writers should remember that they must get all their effects from the logical expression of their subject, and not by the addition of extraneous incidents; and that a work of art can have but one subject . . . and it must possess a unity unlike the accidental profusion of nature . . . [T]he attainment of this unity by what is usually a long shaping and reshaping of the plot, is the principal labour of the dramatist, and not the writing of the dialogue.[2]

Yeats retained this dramatic concept — what he called the maintenance of a 'clean outline' — even after he encountered Noh drama. In 1928, for example, in his notorious letter castigating Sean O'Casey over the formlessness of *The Silver Tassie* (which Yeats rejected for production at the Abbey) his views were characteristically Aristotelian: he criticized O'Casey's play for lacking a 'dominating character' and a 'dominating action' which would have provided 'psychological unity' and 'unity of action'. Yeats insisted on one fundamental principle: 'there should be no room in a play for anything that does not belong to it'.[3]

Even when imitating the Noh form, Yeats put a high priority on action unified by the passions or motives of a play's characters. The

Musicians, however, who in a play like *Deirdre* clearly and effectively participate in the plot, become licensed in the *Four Plays for Dancers* to stand outside the plot and act as narrators and as evokers of mood and setting.[4] This represents a modification, then, of Yeats's own habitual dramaturgy, as a direct result of his discovery of the Noh form. In 'Certain Noble Plays of Japan' he admired the Japanese chorus, 'which describes the scene and interprets their thought and never becomes as in the Greek theatre a part of the action'.[5]

It must always be remembered, however that the sources of the *Four Plays for Dancers* were manifold: they included Irish folk tales, Irish sagas, and Irish traditional poetry, quite apart from possible interaction with the Japanese Noh plays which will be considered below. It is not here suggested, accordingly, that the Noh operated as exclusive influence on Yeats's dance plays: his imagination was such that he combined in active collaboration Celtic and oriental motifs, symbols, narrative patterns, and spiritual beliefs.

At the Hawk's Well/Yoro

Plots: The Old Man is challenged by the Young Man over the water expected from the well of immortality. The Guardian of the Well turns into a spirit of destruction and deprives both men of the water, in contrasting ways. But by his failure the Young Man discovers his destiny (the dance of the Guardian being the means whereby he confronts it). The plot thus concerns the moment of choice that makes a hero. Cuchulain's character is revealed *in action*: his being is tragically doomed, not from guilt as in Greek drama, but from the sheer energy that makes inevitable his diversion from a passive to an active challenge from the supernatural powers.

The plot of *Yoro* is not at all complicated. The *waki* sets the scene and introduces the action, which runs according to form, and, since there is no conflict to resolve, concludes in the traditionally optimistic manner of a ritualistic piece created to bolster the position of the establishment: the gods and their direct descendant, the Emperor.

The courtier easily finds the origin of the miraculous water being told this secret, since he is the representative of the living God. This discovery leads to another secret, revealed just as simply by the mountain god. He has turned the water into *kikusui* (*sake*) which betokens longevity, since he was impressed by the young man's behaviour. His benign attitude demonstrates the value of worship, whilst his praise of the Emperor's peace-giving rule reinforced the latter's authority.

Functions of musicians: In *At the Hawk's Well* there are only three musicians who play gong, zither and drum. They sing and also speak. The singing establishes the setting and emphasizes (symbolic) details of place; the speaking gives exposition and at the time of the dance tells the audience how the Young Man (who has no lines here) is reacting. This speaking is done by the first Musician. He also announces the splashing of the water (since the Old Man, too, is silent at this point) and describes the Young Man's response: 'Look, he has turned his head.' This sudden intervention by the Musician has been praised by Richard Taylor as 'particularly effective as it reintroduces their more freely and heightened speech with all its connotations of the supernatural world, and closely follows the practice of Nō where the chorus functions mainly as an extension of characterization or as an external commentator'.[6] The three Musicians then sing the consequence of the Young Man's failure to attend to the splashing water: 'He has lost what may not be found'; a little later they cry 'Aoife! Aoife!' to represent the off-stage battle-cry of the 'women of the hills', and they strike a gong to represent the sound of sword on shield. In the concluding song the Musicians lament what has happened.

The Musicians, then, narrate significant plot details, and alert the audience to the significance of what occurs; they establish setting and mood; and they also provide special effects to suggest off-stage events. William B. Worthen has argued that the Musicians do not interpose a fictive 'character' between each performer and the audience; they do not 'act' as such but 'perform a boundary function, articulating the difference between the play's acting and its observation'.[7] This assessment seems incontestable, if one bears in mind both the general choric function of Yeats's Musicians and his desire as dramatist to involve spectators in a performance. In addition; at times they accompany the movements of the players; for example, the Old Man moves to the tap of the drum and this establishes the acting style: the percussion emphasizes that his movements, *'like those of the other persons of the play, suggest a marionette'*. In his note on the play, referring to the first production in 1916, Yeats distinguished between these drum taps and the affect of zither (*or flute*, he says) which deepened the emotions arising from the story (*Variorum*, pp. 415–16).

The musicians in the Noh theatre are different from those in Yeats's plays. They are divided into two groups, one with musical instruments, and the other a chorus. The musicians with instruments do not sing at all. They call out, sometimes with high-pitched shouts, at some other times, low, subdued, groaning sorts of sounds, to measure the pauses between drum beats. They sit at the back of the stage, and they remain still throughout the performance. Similarly, the chorus sits, motionless, on the left of the stage.

The musicians for *Yoro* consist of four players, each playing: *okawa*, a big drum which produces an extremely sharp, high-pitched sound, *kotsuzumi*, a smaller drum which produces comparatively low-pitched sounds and *taiko*, a kind of drum used in religious festivals and when a divinity appears on stage. It produces a sound pitched between the other two drums. The sound of *taiko* produces a festive atmosphere. The final instrument, *fue* a, Japanese flute, is very high pitched, and its sounds are quite different from melodious European music. These four instruments are usually found accompanying all Noh plays.

The chorus in the Noh theatre undertakes several roles, such as interviewer, commentator, representative of various acting parts. But it does not, however, have any characters of its own, like the chorus in Greek tragedies. In *Yoro* the first chorus (divided into sections known as *ageuta, kuri* and *sageuta*) represents the lead, and expresses his gratefulness for having been given the life-giving water. The second sequence of the chorus (starting with another *ageuta* and ending with *rongi* and *agenta*) provides comments. This gives a Chinese example of a similar miracle provided by divine medicine for longevity, which produces seven hundred years of life. In the *rongi*, the chorus exchanges dialogues with the lead. Then it suggests that something mysterious is happening; the sky is lightening, there is the sound of water falling, music is in the air, and flowers have started to fall like rain. In the latter half, the chorus represents the lead, the mountain god, concluding with *kiri* singing in which the mountain god announces his departure.

The Only Jealousy of Emer/Aoino-ue

After the death of Cuchulain, his wife, Emer, and mistress, Eithne, both wish him back from the dead. His body, being inhabited by the spirit of discord, Bricriu, scares away Eithne but not Emer. She finds out from Bricriu that there is but one way to bring back her husband, namely, by renouncing her dearest wish of regaining his love. When Fand, the spirit of the underworld, dances before the Ghost of Cuchulain to win him for herself, it becomes clear that he must be lost to her unless Emer agrees to Bricriu's terms and gives up her one hope. At the price of her renunciation Cuchulain is brought back, to be united with Eithne. The plot is thus a struggle between two women, Emer and Eithne. It is also a struggle between a mortal woman, Emer, and supernatural powers. These conflicts result in an ironic restoration from the dead. If the plot culminates, after skilfully managed suspense, in the release of Cuchulain, it ends simultaneously in the defeat of Emer's private desire. The plot does not reconcile these two effects, although, as Emer's point of view dominates, Yeats stresses her tragic loss.

Aoino-ue is an unusually complicated Noh play. The *waki* starts by establishing that Aoino-ue, the prime minister's daughter, is seriously ill, that every known medicine has failed, and that he has sent for a priestess to determine, firstly, if she is possessed and, secondly, if so, by whom.

The priestess has sufficient power to summon Princess Rokyujo's spirit, and get it to explain its sufferings — jealousy and humiliation — but not enough to pacify it. The *waki* now sends for a saint who confronts the tormented and dangerous spirit. Good eventually triumphs over evil, after a dramatic fight between the demonic spirit and source of Buddhist faith.

The plot of *Aoino-ue*, described at length, is relatively complex. There are four musicians in *Aoino-ue* plus a chorus of eight singers. They create different atmospheres according to the Princess's changes of mood; sometimes gentle and sad, at other times fierce and angry. During a fight, the musicians give a fast, vibrantly dynamic performance to add to the drama. They change tone altogether after she gives in, and produce comforting music to indicate that the evil spirit has reached the nirvanic state of mind.

The Musicians, employing string, drum and flute, set the mood of *The Only Jealousy of Emer* by singing the opening and closing choruses. The First Musician also plays an expository role at first by speaking fifteen lines introducing setting and situation. He does not intervene to explain what happens, however, when Emer pulls the curtains to allow the actor to change his mask: instead, the three Musicians play to accompany her movements. Therefore, the audience is kept in the dark regarding the stage 'trick' which allows Bricriu to enter. Again, in contrast to the commentary offered on the dance in *At the Hawk's Well* the First Musician does *not* speak either when Emer is shown the Ghost of Cuchulain or when Fand enters and dances. Instead, Bricriu supplies whatever commentary is needed. Thus the Musicians have no role in the plot itself; their role is theatrical and, apart from supplying atmosphere and introduction, they accompany and are subservient to the central episode of the dance.

In *Aoino-ue*, however, the chorus in its first sequence represents the lead in *sageuta* and *ageuta* and explains the Princess's suffering and her determination to get revenge. In the second singing sequence, the chorus, again, representing the swaying mind of the Princess describes her past glory and present misery, and finally her determination to go and kill Aoino-ue.

The chorus in the latter half of the play has two major singing parts. It first represents the *waki*, singing vigorously, symbolizing attempts to pacify the evil spirit, and then the resignation and pacification of the Princess, singing peacefully, as she reaches a state of grace.

The Dreaming of the Bones/Nishikigi

The plot of *The Dreaming of the Bones* concerns an encounter between a couple and a Young Man fleeing through the night from the aftermath of the Irish 1916 rebellion. This man and a woman narrate the historical love-story of Diarmuid and Dervorgilla who were responsible for the Anglo-Normans' invasion of Ireland in 1169. They then beg forgiveness for the lovers. The Young Man, anxious to get away safely to the Aran Islands, agrees to be guided by these two strangers up the mountainside of Corcomroe on the borders of Clare and Galway. He refuses, however, to pardon the historical lovers in the narrative, in spite of the pleas of the Young Girl. The strangers dance, during which the Young Man discovers their identity but persists in his refusal to forgive their crime. Accordingly, the play ends tragically.

In an early volume of stories, *The Secret Rose* (1897), Yeats had imagined an encounter similar to that recorded in the play: the story was entitled 'Hanrahan's Vision'. But there the emphasis was on the supernatural, not on the conflict between the individual and historical consciousness. A few years before he wrote *The Dreaming of the Bones*, at the time when Pound revealed to him the riches of the Noh drama, Yeats referred to *Nishikigi* in some detail in the essay, 'Swedenborg, Mediums and the Desolate Places' (1914), but it was not until the rebellion broke out in 1916 that Yeats had a plot which suited his interest in heroic action and its dilemmas.[8]

The plot of *Nishikigi* is typical of a dream play. A travelling monk, who introduces the story, prays for unhappy souls, and consequently communicates with the spirits of those he has liberated in a dream sequence. The travelling monk, in this case, sets the scene in the northern village of Kyo, and encounters a village couple who recount the pathetic story of a local man who, after wooing a woman for three years, and being constantly rejected, died heartbroken. Their tale is interwoven with repeated references to both *nishikigi* and *hosonuno*. These local handicrafts add realism to the village couple, provide colour on stage, link the text and, most significantly, provide poetic images for their ill-fated love: the love tokens the man repeatedly leaves at his beloved's door, *nishikigi*, or decorated branches. The cloth she constantly wears is *hosonuno*, or narrow cloth, too narrow in practical terms, to make the two overlapping, front sections of a *kimono*, and therefore an apt symbolic description for an ill-matched couple. The supposed villagers lead the monk to the lovers' tomb, asking him to pray for the deceased.

The monk prays and spends a night by their tomb. The now freed ghosts, delighted, wish to thank the man whose goodwill released them from remorse. No longer earth-bound, they appear in front of the monk, expressing their gratitude by demonstrating the customary courtship rituals of their region. The man, in conclusion, performs a vigorous *otoko-mai* dance, celebrating the fact that he and his beloved will marry in the next life, until dawn breaks, and they disappear. Thus, although the theme of this play is tragic, the conclusion, like that of a medieval miracle play, shows God's power, symbolized by the priest's intervention to prevent human suffering.

In *The Dreaming of the Bones* the Three Musicians have roles similar to these in *At the Hawk's Well* and *The Only Jealousy of Emer*: they supply lyrical mood and set the atmosphere as with the opening song. Here details of place lend solidity to the subsequent action. Yeats's emphasis on night and the dead establishes an atmosphere of unease. The First Musician speaks introductory lines, as in the other two plays cited, but he is more detached and offers less exposition. Instead, he stresses the loneliness of the place, as Yeats consciously prepares his audience for a ghostly drama set at night on a bleak mountainside. The Musician knows nothing about the Young Man: 'He *seems* an Aran fisher'.[9] It is left to the Young Man himself to inform the audience where he is coming from and where he is going. Likewise, in the play itself the Musicians do not intervene with explanatory comments on the action, other than to provide descriptions of the journey being undertaken by all three characters. As the characters go around the stage, on their way to the mountain top, the First Musician first speaks and then sings: his speech narrates the details of their journey while his song expresses fear, loneliness and defiance. When the characters journey for the third and final time, however, the First Musician neither speaks nor sings. Instead, the three Musicians play, after which the Young Man himself takes over the role of commentator on the topography. Technically, his speech is an expansion of the expected Musician's description. Dramatically, it is effective, partly because of the breach with the earlier patterns, and partly because Yeats characteristically uses this setting to express his political views. Thus the ritualistic function of the First Musician, as narrator, yields to the dramatic function of the Young Man who, similarly, becomes an authoritative spokesman.

In *Nishikigi* the musicians provide subdued tonal music which creates a tragic atmosphere. The tempo remains slow throughout until the climax when the hero demonstrates his delight. An *otokomai* dance provides the opportunity for a vigorous, active dance accompanied by similarly invigorating music, to celebrate a joyous conclusion.

The chorus starts by representing the *waki*, and expresses his concern on hearing the lovers' tale. This is expressed, concisely, as a *waka* poem. It is built around the length of sounds, rather than European rhyme. ('Nishikigiwa Tatenagarakoso Kuchinikere Kyoonohosonuno Muneawajitoya'.) Then, at the end of the first act, the chorus comments on the development of the play: it describes the journey to the lovers' tombs, and describes the sudden disappearance of the supposed village couple.

In the second act the chorus (in an *ageuta*) expresses the hero's pain. While the Woman weaves cloth inside the house, the chorus tells of his repeated rejection and his sorrows. Then follows a *kuri* sequence, in which the chorus, now representing the monk, expresses his comments on the odd courtship being enacted before him. Becoming an extension of the hero, once again, the chorus now explains to the audience that the couple have appeared to show their courtship in the monk's dream. This is, in fact, an illogical contradiction, since they have already appeared in the monk's dream. Indeed, apart from the monk's prayer at the beginning, all of this concluding part takes place within the monk's dream. In the subsequent lengthy sequence, starting with *kuse*, the chorus has a far more flexible part, since it blends the roles of commentator and representation of the Man. In the ultimate *kiri* sequence, the chorus represents the hero, before providing a final comment.

Calvary

The plot concerns the visit to Christ (being crucified) of Lazarus and Judas, each claiming independence of his act to save mankind. The plot establishes the loneliness of the heroic Christ, whose passivity as he fulfils God's will contrasts with the activity of the embittered renegades. Three soldiers, whose job it is to crucify Christ, dance 'The dance of the dice-throwers' around him, to show their indifference. Christ ends in despair. The plot, as always in Yeats's plays, consists of the spiritual conflict of the main character with the opposing representatives of some other philosophy or attitude to life. As usual, also, the plot of *Calvary* culminates in failure, rather than fulfilment. As Okifumi Komesu puts it, Yeats's dance plays end in 'a failure to resolve the conflict to which the characters have been subjected, while Japanese Noh plays usually end in a Nirvanic vision or a redemption of the spirit'.[10]

Musicians: Use drum, flute and zither. The song for folding and unfolding the cloth is more relevant to character and theme than is the case with the preceding plays. Moreover, lines are distributed among the three Musicians. Otherwise, the role of the Musicians is the same: one Musician acts as narrator, providing exposition at the start and (after Lazarus exits) later in the play; this Musician also sings solo after his speech narrative, both before and after the appearance of Lazarus. A variation occurs since Judas does not exit but stays to hold up the cross; there is no narrative from the Musicians at this point, where a stage direction is called for instead: 'During what follows, Judas holds up the cross while Christ stands with His arms stretched out upon it' (p. 786). This arrangement does not appear in any other of the dance plays.

Thus the role of the Musicians is quite limited in *Calvary*: it is to introduce the situation and to establish the theme of loneliness. In his note on *Calvary* Yeats said:

I have written the little songs of the chorus to please myself, confident that singer and composer, when the time came for performance, would certainly make it impossible for the audience to know what the words were. I used to think that singers should sing a recipe for a good dish, or a list of local trains, or something else they want to get by heart, but I have changed my mind and now I prefer to give him [*sic*] some mystery or secret.(p. 789)

When a piece belongs to the first group of Japanese religious plays, there is virtually no conflict to solve. *Miwa* is a rare exception. If there are conflicts in religious plays, they are intended to show up the divine power of either Buddhism or Shinto. The plots conclude with a reassuring religious ritual. The dances for such plays are usually *kami-mai*, vigorous, vivid, divine, concluding the ritual. Yeats, however, was uninterested in ritual for any particular religious establishment, using biblical characters and events as starting points for more private interpretations of overlapping kinds of reality.

The traditional choice of three drummers and a flute player contributes to the smooth running of a ritualistic piece, until a god or goddess dances. If it is a male god (usually dancing a *kami-mai*) they create dynamic sounds. But if it is a goddess (usually dancing a *Kagura*) their tunes are more gentle and harmoniously rhythmical.

Correspondingly, the chorus, in the first half of a Japanese Noh play helps the action along, singing austerely. But in the second half it helps to build up the tension by contributing more dramatically — even if still slowly, with more consciously impressive, and often more cheerful, chanting to accompany a god's dance, and a similarly evocative, although more highly pitched singing, to accompany a celestial dance by a female deity.

VI. CONCEPTS OF MASKS

Noh and Masks

Masks are essential in the Noh theatre. They were felt necessary as actors had to perform roles which are sometimes supernatural beings such as gods, spirits of mountain, trees, *tengu* (imaginary monsters), besides ghosts and women.

The difference between the Greek masks and Noh masks is in size, Greek masks are large and cover the head of an actor altogether, while a Noh mask is small and scarcely covers his face. Greek masks have a device for amplifying the voice, while a Noh mask tends to act the other way round. There was a long tradition of using masks in Japan's early, primitive theatre: they were used in Bugaku and Gigaku performances. The masks for these theatres were much bigger than Noh masks, and they were used for religious festival performances or religious processions. These masks were not designed to look human, but represented some supernatural powers; their features were crudely exaggerated. The influence of these masks on those of the Noh is seen in the Noh masks representing supernatural beings.

The importance of Noh masks increased when the Noh theatre became more realistic, more dramatic. More subtle masks of various kinds were made towards the end of the Kamakura, and the beginning of the Muromachi periods. Since the Noh theatre never had actresses until the last war, they needed masks for all kinds of women — young and old, rich and poor. The masks became very stylized, and the same masks came to be used for similar roles in different plays. Although the number of the Noh masks exceeds two hundred, over two hundred and forty plays can be performed with around eighty masks today. These Noh masks can be grouped as follows:

1. *Jomen*: masks for old men ranging from *kojo* which are to be used for a god in disguise, for an old man in a play such as *Takasago* to *asakurajo* for a common old man in the first half of *Yashima*.

2. *Akujomen*: masks for wicked and bad old men, seen in such plays as *Koino-omoni* and *Domyoji*.

3. *Iso-men*: masks for supernatural beings such as Obeshimi for a frightening tengu in *Daie*, *sarutobide* for a monkey-faced creature in *Nue* and *kurohige* for a dragon god in *Kasugaryujin*.

4. *Shinbutsumen*: masks for various gods such as those in *Takasago* and *Yoro*.

5. Masks for young men such as *doji* for *Tamura* and *shakkyo* and *imawaka* for noble young men in *Kiyotsune* and *Tadanori*.

6. Masks for middle-aged men such as *heida* for the leads, in the latter halves of *Tamura* and *Yashima*.

7. Young women's masks such as *koomote* for a young lady in *Toboku* and *Izutsu*, and *Oomionna* for slightly more mature women in *Dojoji* and *Ama*.

8. Middle-aged women's masks such as *fukai*, in *Miidera*, and *shakumi*, in *Sumidagawa*.

9. Old women's masks such as *uba* for an old woman in *Obasute* and *rojo* for old Komachi, a noble poetess in *Sotoba-Komachi*.

10. Masks for characters in a state of temporary madness. These include *masugami* for *Ukifune*, *deigan* for *Kinuta*, *hashihime* for a jealous old woman in *Kanawa*, and *hannya* for the vengeful woman in the second part of *Dojoji*.

The use of these masks requires preliminary meditation. Some Noh masks are very expressive but others more impersonal. It is often more difficult to use a subtle mask, as it requires harder work on the part of an actor, identifying himself with the role he is to play. These masks do not carry any obvious expressions. It is the actor's internal creative force, accrued during his intense, Zen-like, contemplative studies of his mask, prior to wearing it, which creates his intensity of expression. During a performance, the masks themselves, often highly revered objects of art, are designed, when tilted downwards, to show shadows, and thus sadness, and greater degrees of serenity and joy as the angles of the face are tilted upwards, into the light.

Yeats and Masks

From 1908 Edward Gordon Craig had been advocating a style of acting which was 'symbolic gesture'.[1] Use of the mask was integral to Craig's ideas, and Yeats, of course, was deeply influenced by Craig. Craig designed a mask for the Fool in a new production of *The Hour Glass* in 1911. He also designed a mask for *On Baile's Strand* (the Blind Man). Liam Miller has claimed that these two designs 'remained always in his [Yeats's] thoughts as central to his concept of the mask'.[2]

Yeats's decision to revise several of his early plays at this time was closely bound up with his interest in Craig's ideas on scene design and staging, and, as Karen Dorn has pointed out,[3] the revisions using Craig's concept of stage space anticipated Yeats's adaptations of the Noh drama.

Craig's interest in physical masks coincided with Yeats's growing interest in the subject of mask as a philosophical concept related to personality. In January 1909 he uses the word 'mask' in his Journal to signify the opposite of conventionality: 'Active virtue, as distinguished from the passive acceptance of a code, is therefore theatrical, consciously dramatic, the wearing of a mask.'[4] A few weeks later he expanded further on the idea: 'The tragic mask expresses a passion or mood, a state of the soul; that only. (The mask of a musician or of the dying slave.) The mask of comedy an individual. (Any modern picture.) The mask of farce an energy: in this the joyous life by its own excess has become superficial, it has driven out thought. (Any grotesque head.)'[5] As A. N. Jeffares has pointed out, the theory of the mask can be associated with Yeats's theory of the anti-self, which he gradually evolved.[6] The mask is associated with the pursuit of the heroic ideal. Yeats said in his Journal, March 1909: 'I think all happiness depends on the energy to assume the mask of some other life, on a re-birth as something not one's self, something created in a moment and perpetually renewed.'[7] The mask is thus not an escape from life, or an evasion of reality, but a constraint or discipline imposed on the self in order to achieve victory over circumstances. Yeats explains: 'What I have called "the Mask" is an emotional antithesis to all that comes out of their [subjective men] internal nature. We begin to live when we have conceived life as tragedy.'[8]

While he was elaborating this theory of the mask as a means of expressing the anti-self, Yeats was also writing *The Player Queen*. Significantly, he abandoned it in frustration and was unable to complete it until after he had encountered and adopted the Noh form. (*The Player Queen* was first staged in 1919.) He did, however, publish 'A Lyric from an Unpublished Play' in *The Green Helmet* (1910), under the title, 'The Mask'.[9] Once he had studied Fenollosa's translations of the Noh plays, however, Yeats was able to clarify and develop his theory of the mask. This may be seen in 'Anima Hominis' (1917),[10] especially sections VI, VII and IX. Yeats then refined the theory of the mask to include his idea of tragedy: 'The poet finds and makes his mask in disappointment, the hero in defeat'.[11] This is the germ of his *Plays for Dancers*, where every protagonist makes a decision in which heroism and defeat are equated.

At The Hawk's Well/Yoro

The Old Man and the Young Man are masked; the Guardian of the Well and the Three Musicians have their faces made up 'to resemble masks'.

In the opening stage direction Yeats comments: 'These masked players seem stranger when there is no mechanical means [of lighting] of separating them from us' (p. 399). This point is clearer if one refers to a passage in the essay 'Certain Noble Plays of Japan':

A mask will enable me to substitute for the face of some commonplace player, or for that face repainted to suit his own vulgar fancy, the fine invention of a sculptor, and to bring the audience close enough to the play to hear every inflection of the voice. A mask never seems but a dirty face, and no matter how close you go is yet a work of art . . .[12]

In his original note on *At The Hawk's Well*, however, Yeats implied that the use of masks was something that the staging conditions imposed, rather than something deliberately chosen: 'the masks forced upon us by the absence of any special lighting, or by the nearness of the audience who surround the players upon three sides, do not seem to us eccentric'.[13] This cannot be accurate: surely, one feels, masks were essential to a form modelled on the Noh? This remark reveals, however, the conservatism which inhibited western theatre at this time. It may also explain why the other actors do not wear masks. Liam Miller has made the point that the musicians were probably made up to inhibit naturalism, to 'speak and sing their lines without emotive facial expressions or body movements'.[14] But in this case why wasn't the Guardian masked? The head-dress, designed by Dulac, covered the sides of Ito's face in the first production, giving an Egyptian effect.[15] Ito, apparently, approved and preferred a painted face to a mask.

In the Noh theatre, supernatural beings are represented by masks. Since it is hardly suitable for a mere human to enact a divinity in mortal guise, Noh actors always wear masks. In the Kabuki theatre, however, make-up takes the place of masks. Perhaps Yeats (or Ito) in deciding not to mask the Guardian of the Well, was influenced by the Kabuki theatre.

In *Yoro* only the lead wears masks (*kojo* for the first part, and *kantan* for the second). The rest appear unmasked, the Woodcutter (*tsure*), the Courtier (*waki*) and his servants (*wakitsure*) and a Village man (*ai-kyogen*) do not wear make up, but remain con-

sciously expressionless throughout the performance. Thus there is
no discrepancy between the masked and the unmasked.

The Only Jealousy of Emer/Aoino-ue

Here masks are worn by the Ghost of Cuchulain, the Figure of
Cuchulain, and the Woman of the Sidhe, while the three Musicians
have their faces made up to resemble masks. Eithne Inguba and
Emer may either be masked or have their faces made up to resemble
masks, a hesitation which reveals Yeats's continuing uncertainty.
The Figure of Cuchulain has two masks, one heroic and one grotesque (which the actor changes behind the curtain of Cuchulain's
bed, before he appears as Bricriu). In the Preface to *Four Plays for
Dancers* (p. vi), Yeats said *The Only Jealousy of Emer* was written
'to find what dramatic effect one could get out of a mask, changed
while the player remains upon the stage to suggest a change of personality'.[16] As A. S. Knowland has pointed out, this use of a
grotesque mask is not in accordance with Noh practice.[17] But
Yeats may be thinking of *Aoino-ue*, in which, he said, the evil spirit
is represented by a dancer wearing a 'terrible mask with golden
eyes'.[18] In a letter of 27 May 1921, Yeats remarks: 'I knew that a
grotesque mask was enormously effective.'[19] The mask for the
Woman of the Sidhe (Fand) is described in a stage direction in connection with her costume: both 'must suggest gold or bronze or
brass or silver, so that she seems more an idol than a human being'.
This description echoes what Yeats wrote as a note to the early edition of *At the Hawk's Well* already quoted from above:

> We are accustomed to faces of bronze and of marble, and what could be
> more suitable than that Cuchulain, let us say, a half-supernatural legen-
> dary person, should show to us a face, not made before the looking-glass
> by some leading player . . . but moulded by some distinguished artist?
> . . . It would be a stirring adventure for a poet and an artist working
> together to create once more [like the Romans and Japanese] heroic or
> grotesque types that . . . would seem images of those profound emotions
> that exist only in solitude and in silence.[20]

In *Aoine-ue* the vengeful spirit of Princess Rokujo wears two
masks, *deigan* in the first part, and *hannya* in the latter. *Deigan*
represents a woman obsessed, and *hannya* a woman turned into a
devil for revenge. Priestess Teruhinome wears a *tsure-men*, a
young woman's mask, but the saint, courtier and servants do not
use masks: they remain expressionless, creating a parallel effect.

The last part of the sentence quoted above emphasizes how Yeats saw masks as expressive of emotion, rather than disguises of any kind. Karen Dorn suggests that Yeats's interpretation of *Aoino-ue* 'as a Japanese version of the Irish tales he and Lady Gregory recorded in *Visions and Beliefs*, in which supernatural spirits seek power through possession of living bodies', influenced Pound's account of the play. Pound said that Princess Rokujo's jealousy made her subject to possession by a demon who comes first in a disguised and beautiful form, which 'is a sort of personal or living mask, having a ghost life of its own'.[21] Dorn is surely correct then in concluding that, 'The notion that intense emotion could produce a "living mask" or image of itself is the *modus operandi* of *The Only Jealousy of Emer*'.[22] In this regard, the Woman of the Sidhe (Fand) is the 'mask' of Emer's own jealousy.

The Dreaming of the Bones/Nishikigi

The Stranger and the Young Girl are masked. (In a note to *Four Plays for Dancers* Yeats says she could wear Cuchulain's mask from *At the Hawk's Well*. He also pays tribute to Edmund Dulac as designer of the masks.) The three Musicians present faces made up to resemble masks; but the Young Man wears no mask, and is thus emphasized as being outside the realm of experience of the others. His (naturalistic) modernity withstands the aristocratic power of the others. Because he sees the place itself, for example, Galway, as vestigially aristocratic and noble the Young Man is depicted as not immune to the 'temptation' identifiable with the world of Diarmuid and Dervorgilla. He has, after all, a 'mask', which is his love of ancient Irish culture; otherwise there would be no conflict in the play, and Yeats's drama subsists on irreconcilable conflict.

In *Nishikigi* the Woman wears a *tsure* mask throughout. As there are no actresses, all female Noh parts are masked. The Man, on the other hand, starts unmasked. The reason for this is that, although he is, in fact, a ghost, he starts by acting a role in which he appears to be a living person. He appears, realistically enough, to the monk, who takes him for an ordinary villager. In the monk's dream, however, the same character appears in an *awaotoko* mask, thus adding to the drama, and also, according to Ze-Ami's theories, making it easier for the actor to perform this more challenging sequence. For Ze-Ami says that only the most experienced actors can perform well, without a mask (*hitamen*). *Hitamen* implies that one is acting without a clue to one's role; one has no substantial guide, and may end up simply being oneself on stage, rather than producing creative acting. In *Nishikigi*, the monk, his followers, and the villagers are all unmasked, but their parts pose no specific problems since they are all just representing orthodox, contemporary characters.

Calvary

Christ, Lazarus and Judas are masked, but Yeats did not decide about the Three Roman Soldiers: they may be masked, or painted as though masked. The uncertainty, as over *The Only Jealousy of Emer* above, may indicate Yeats's continuing lack of practical experience, since *At the Hawk's Well* remained the only one of the *Four Plays for Dancers* to be staged before the 1920s.

It is not quite clear what kind of masks Yeats wanted in *Calvary*. In the text there is the unusual formulation: 'A player with the mask of Christ and carrying a cross has entered', where even the tense is untheatrical. What kind of mask is intended? A conventional image, recognizable as the suffering Christ? This would indicate a different concept from the heroic mask used in the other three plays. A similar formulation is used to describe Lazarus: '*A player with the mask of Lazarus has entered.*' What could this mask be? It might have been grotesque, like Bricriu's in *The Only Jealousy of Emer*, but Yeats does not describe it thus. Can it, perhaps, have been representational, suggesting Lazarus's return from burial? Judas, to make matters worse, is described only as having '*entered*': no mask is mentioned in the stage direction, and he introduces himself with the line, 'I am Judas / That sold you for the thirty pieces of silver'. Again, this is the conventional description, although its crude use resembles folk drama more than Japanese Noh. It is quite clear that Yeats had not worked out a style for the use of masks in this play. (In a note to *Four Plays for Dancers* he plaintively appealed for a sculptor to do the masks.)

In Noh, the masks used for gods are: *fudo, shintai* and *tenjin*: a god disguised as a man wears a *kojo* or *koujijo* mask, a goddess wears a normal young woman's mask, such as *koomote* or *zoona*. Except for some terrifying gods, such as the Buddhist god, Fudo, the distance between human and divine seems to be much closer in the Noh plays. This is particularly true in the case of goddesses, since there are no masks specially designed for goddesses. In Noh plays, almighty gods such as Buddha and The Sun Goddess are often mentioned but they are never shown on stage: the celestial beings who appear in the Noh are relatively low-ranked gods in the Buddhist and Shinto hierarchy. If Almighty God was represented on stage a theatre would really become a place of worship, and it would seem inappropriate to make a play so directly representative of the divine.

VII. STAGE PROPS AND COSTUMES

Yeats rejoiced in the use of a bare, simple stage. Gordon Craig's style of decoration, with its symbolic, abstract scenery, encouraged him to think of a break with nineteenth-century illusionism. In his essay in the 1904 issue of *Samhain*, 'The Play, The Player, and the Scene', he commented:

> We must have a new kind of scenic art. I have been the advocate of the poetry as against the actor, but I am the advocate of the actor as against the scenery.[1]

Illusion, he continued, is impossible 'and should not be attempted', a tenet that goes far to explain and justify his use of props and symbolic scenery in the dance plays. He elaborated his views:

> Having chosen the distance from naturalism which will keep one's composition from competing with the illusion created by the actor, who belongs to a world with depth as well as height and breadth, one must keep this distance without flinching. . . . But, whatever the distance be, one's treatment will always be more or less decorative. We can only find out the right decoration for the different types of play by experiment. . . . This decoration will not only give us a scenic art that will be a true art because peculiar to the stage, but it will give the imagination liberty, and without returning to the bareness of the Elizabethan stage.[2]

The scene, the setting, in short, should mean nothing 'until the actor is in front of it'.[3] Nevertheless, Yeats remained — *faute de mieux* — faithful in his fashion to the proscenium-arch stage and its attendant conventions until 1916, when *At the Hawk's Well* was first staged in a drawing room. (This is not to deny his experiments with lighting and curtains for *On Baile's Strand* and thereafter.)

The stage was now 'any bare space before a wall against which stands a patterned screen'.[4] Yeats now saw that he had discovered, or recreated, a single form of theatre, such that 'its few properties can be packed up in a box or hung upon the walls where they will be fine ornaments'.[5] Props would be either practical or symbolic.

A Noh stage, which is square, has a unique feature, a long bridge leading in from the right (from the left when viewed from the

auditorium). Although there is a curtain of five coloured stripes at
the entrance of the bridge, there is nothing to hide the actors or
stage hands while they change their costumes and masks (in
monogi), or rearrange the set. Technically, it is impossible to set up
a large-scale scene change for any part of a performance without
damaging the overall effect of the production. Another technical
problem is that the main stage is quite small, compared with a
European proscenium stage.

Apart from these technical difficulties, the Noh theatre, under the
influence of Zen, tended towards symbolism and minimalism. Props
have to be small, even a mountain is reduced to a miniature, con-
structed with bamboo and covered with a cloth. A mountain prop is
only six feet high, three feet wide and three or four feet at its base.
There is, therefore, hardly any space for an actor to hide inside this
structure, since the bamboo sticks from the four corners are joined up
at the peak. Bamboos are often used because of their flexibility, as,
for example, in making the suggestion of a royal carriage by a skeletal
outline of the essential framework. This kind of a prop is typical
throughout the Noh, a theatre whose costumes, often including
many layered brocade kimonos, can be breathtakingly lavish, but
many of whose props remain minimal.

At the Hawk's Well/Yoro

The following props are specified: 1. A folded black cloth is
brought on by the First Musician; on it there is 'a gold pattern suggesting a hawk'. 2. A square of blue cloth 'to represent a well'.
3. A spear for the Young Man. He drops it on his first exit but
shoulders it before his final exit, 'no longer as if in a dream'.

Yoro requires no set or props, except a walking stick for the Old
Man. This (together with the mask of Kojo and his costume) symbolizes his old age. The play, consequently, takes place on a bare
stage (as in the Elizabethan theatre). The audience is requested,
imaginatively, to conjure up a wild mountainous environment.

Fans are considered essential in the Noh theatre. Almost all the
characters, even the chorus and musicians, carry them. The chorus,
when they sing, hold their fans pointing with the wide end towards the
floor, in front of them, in the traditional way, or put the fan, with the
handle near them, vertically, on the floor, through the performance.

The most significant use of the fans is by the main characters.
They use them symbolically, replacing swords or other props, or
simply to make their dancing more graceful. In *Yoro*, the Mountain

God in the latter half of the play uses a dancing fan specially designed for a divine god, called a *kami oogi*.

The Only Jealousy of Emer/Aoino-ue

The text calls for: 1. the same black cloth as used in At the Hawk's Well. 2. A 'curtained bed or litter' on which the Ghost of Cuchulain lies. The curtains are practicable and close off the bed like a pavilion.

Aoino-ue does not require any complicated sets either. The performance takes place on a stage, bare except for a piece of folded cloth at the front of the stage. This symbolizes Lady Aoino-ue, ill in bed. The title role Aoino-ue, is thus, symbolically present on the stage, throughout. As far as this play is concerned, its audience is expected to witness the events of the play through the symbolical existence of Aoino-ue, rather than through the medium of the *waki*.

Major props are a red stick held by the vengeful demon of Princess Rokujo, and rosaries held by the priestess and the saints. Rokujo tries to kill Aoino-ue by beating her with this stick. The priestess and the saint pray using their rosaries to stop her murderous attack. This saint carried a small sword, since he is a *yamabushi*, not an ordinary monk. There is a particularly spectacular scene, as the monk fights the stick-swinging princess, as he tries to overcome her demonic ravings.

The Dreaming of the Bones/Nishikigi

The text calls for: 1. A screen, 'with a pattern of mountain and sky, can stand against the wall, or a curtain with a like pattern hung upon it, but the pattern must only symbolise or suggest'. 2. A lantern for the Young Man. It is, presumably, practicable, with a candle lit inside it when he enters. Presumably, also, he keeps it with him even after it is blown out by the Young Girl.

Nishikigi requires five stage props: 1. A mountain. This is, however, more of a mound than a mountain in this context. It is made of bamboo, and covered with a cloth, with leafy branches on top. In the latter part the cloth covering is taken off, and the same structure then symbolizes the house in which the woman once lived. 2. *Hosonuno*. A piece of narrow cloth. This symbolizes unattainable love. 3. *Nishikigi*. An ornate branch. This is a love symbol to be placed in front of the door of a house where a woman who is being courted lives. 4. Fans. The lead carries *otoko oogi* in the first part, where he is performing as a villager. He then uses *Shura-oogi* in the second part, acting the ghost of the obsessive lover. 5. Rosaries. They are carried by the travelling monk and his followers: they use them while praying for the spirits of the tragic couple.

Calvary/Religious Noh plays

The text requires: 1. A cross for Jesus. Presumably a solid piece of wood, since he leans on it, but probably not naturalistic. 2. Possibly dice for the dance of the dice-throwers, although there is no stage direction for dice. They would probably be presentational, larger than life. As Richard Taylor says of the props in the *Four Plays for Dancers* generally, they 'express complex relationships as concrete symbols.'[6]

In the Noh, god plays do not usually need any particular props or sets. In *Hagoromo*, however, a pine branch is erected to symbolize a pine forest along the beach. The divine characters use fans, as any other leading character mentioned earlier. The gods are omnipresent, the audience's imagination moves from place to place, following clues given in dialogues and songs.

COSTUME

There seems little point in making a detailed comparison between Yeats's use of costume and that which distinguishes the Noh: it is well known that the latter has traditional riches unknown and unavailable to western theatre. To suggest grounds for comparison merely serves to expose Yeats, perhaps, to obloquy. Yet the subject is too important to omit entirely, and what follows is a brief attempt to indicate how much of a gap exists between *Four Plays for Dancers* and the Japanese Noh.

Noh and costume

Costumes in the Noh theatre are versatile, mostly colourful and decorative, sophisticated and stylised. The designs and materials of these costumes are similar to those worn by ladies and courtiers, *samurai* and monks in the Heian, Kamakura and Muromachi periods — with some exceptions for imaginary creatures and supernatural beings. Even the costumes for the ordinary people are stylised and beautiful, such as those for a wood-cutter, a salt-maker and a fisherman. Noh costumes are set outside the over-riding principle of simplicity dominating the zen aesthetic, since the ultimate purpose of the Noh theatre is to create *yugen*, elegant beauty. Dirty rags would not have appealed to an audience who sought highly sophisticated art forms, particularly in the Noh.

A Noh actor usually wears a proper *kimono*, and then wears an outer *kimono* costume of various colours and shapes. Though colours and designs are different they can be grouped into twelve types:

Atsuita: Costume often used for a male character with thick material similar to *karaori*. It can be worn as either an outer or under-*kimono*.

Choken: Costume usually worn by a female character whose acting involves a long dance. It is an extremely beautiful, light, unlined, broad-sleeved *kimono*, also occasionally worn by male characters.

Happi: Costume for a *samurai* warrior. It is similar to *kariginu*, a hunting costume, but has broader sleeves. An unlined *happi* is used for a *samurai* of the defeated Heike clan, and the lined ones for the triumphant Genji clan.

Hitatare: Costume for *samurai*. The designs are simlar to another garment for *samurai*, the *suo*. Originally worn by commoners, when the *samurai* rose to power they almost monopolised it. This is worn with baggy trousers called *okuchi*.

Karaori: Costume for a female character. This is decorative and gorgeous. A colourful *karaori* with red in the design is used for a young woman, and one without red for an older woman.

Kariginu: 'Hunting' costume for male courtiers. It is sometimes used for gods and supernatural characters, when gold brocade is applied.

Maiginu: 'Dancing' costume usually for female characters, similar to a *choken*.

Mizugoromo: Costume for both male and female characters. This is a plain *kimono* often used for a travelling character.

Noshi: Costume for an emperor or a courier. Its style is similar to a *kariginu*.

Nuihaku: Costume for both male and female characters. This is decorative, with gold and silver foil embroidered over the essential material. This is often worn in the style of *koshimaki*, the top half draping from the waist.

Sobotsugi: Costume for a samurai. This is similar to a *happi*, but does not have sleeves and is usually worn by a lesser *samurai*, or to indicate a Chinaman.

Suo: Costume for an ordinary person. This is often worn by a *waki* actor, in the role of an ordinary *samurai*, and is worn together with the baggy trousers known as *okuchi*.

Significance of the ways in which a kimono is worn

There are a few distinguishable ways of wearing a *kimono* for Noh performances and some represent the psychological state of the character.

Kinagashi: This is the standard way of wearing a *kimono*, where the outer garment hangs from the shoulders almost to the floor, is tied in the middle, but the cord is not visible. This style is particularly common for a female role.

Nugisage: This irregular way of dressing, in a society obsessed with personal neatness, traditionally indicates mental imbalance as a stage convention. The right shoulder of the outer garment is slipped off the shoulder and left hanging over the back. Sometimes madness is also symbolised by a character carrying a branch of bamboo.

Mogido: An unusual way of wearing a *kimono*, this style symbolises a character who is half-naked. The *nuihaku kimono* is stripped off the shoulders, and left hanging from the waist.

Tsuboori-koshimaki: This symbolises that the character is hiding his or her fury or vengeance, and is seen in such plays as *Dojoji* and *Aoine-ue*. The top half of the under-*nuihaku kimono* is slipped off the shoulders. The outer garment is then tucked up and draped over the hanging under-*kimono*. This gives an extra bulky central section to the costume, and, because of the extra tucks, usually reveals the lower section of the under-*kimono*.

Tsuboori-okuchi: This way of dressing is used for a court lady. The under-*kimono* is tucked into baggy trousers called *okuchi*, the outer-garment hanging from the shoulders down to the floor, and tied in the middle, with the hem spread over the baggy trousers.

Yeats and costume

Yeats, of course, never experienced any of the richness of Japanese costume indicated above. He would, in all probability, have had a problem in integrating such wealth into the concept of a bare, symbolic stage he longed to bring (back) into use. He thought always of costume in association with scenery. Consequently, rich and colourful costumes were as suspect in his eyes as the whole paraphernalia of nineteenth-century illusionism. Writing in May 1899, when the Irish Literary Theatre was launched in Dublin, Yeats attacked the theatre of commerce, to which he was opposing a theatre of art, and he linked scenery and costume as partners in the conspiracy against art:

As audiences and actors changed, managers learned to substitute meretricious landscapes, painted upon wood and canvas, for the descriptions of poetry, until the painted scenery, which had in Greece been a charming explanation of what was least important in the story, became as important as the story. It needed some imagination, some gift for daydreams, to see the horses and the fields and flowers of Colonus as one listened to the elders gathered about Oedipus, or to see 'the pendent bed and procreant cradle' of the 'martlet' as one listened to Banquo before the castle of Macbeth; but it needs no imagination to admire a painting of one of the more obvious effects of nature painted by somebody who understands how to show everything to the most hurried glance. At the same time the managers made the costumes of the actors more and more magnificent, that the mind might sleep in peace, while the eye took pleasure in the magnificence of velvet and silk and in the physical beauty of women. These changes gradually perfected the theatre of commerce, the masterpiece of that movement towards externality in life and thought and art against which the criticism of our day is learning to protest.[7]

A few years later, in 1903, when he wrote on the necessity for reforms in the theatre Yeats commented: 'Just as it is necessary to simplify gesture . . . it is necessary to simplify both the form and colour of scenery and costume.'[8] Here was the dilemma: to simplify and at the same time to provide artistic impact. Yeats could only proceed on his pre-supposition that 'All art that is not mere story-telling, or mere portraiture, is symbolic,'[9] and attempt to transform — by infusion of romantic imagination — the ordinary into the beautiful and significant: hence his interest in the ideas of Edward Gordon Craig. Hence also his concentration of the role of *colour* rather than design of costume. For example, when he first staged *The Hour-Glass* in 1903, with costumes designed by Robert Gregory, it was the colour scheme that attracted his attention.

Writing in 1922 Yeats commented:

Up to the present year we always played in front of an olive-green curtain, and dressed the Wise Man and his Pupils in various shades of purple (with a little green here and there); and because in all these decorative schemes, which are based on colour, one needs, I think, a third colour subordinate to the other two, we dressed the Fool in red-brown, and put touches of red-brown in the Wife's dress and painted the chair and desk the same colour.[10]

James W. Flannery tells us that Yeats took an active role in the production of *The Hour Glass*, 'from approving the material, colour, and patterns of the costumes to personally designing the Botticellian costume of the Angel'.[11] When the production proved successful Yeats was emboldened to insist upon his colour sense in the staging of subsequent plays, such as *The Shadowy Waters*, *On Baile's Strand* and *The Green Helmet*.

It would appear he was his father's son — not to mention his brother's brother — and shared the family interest in fine composition. It would appear also that he had the right approach for developing a theatre of all the arts. Indeed, Liam Miller believed that from the beginning Yeats shared with his Japanese counterparts a sense of unified design. Just as in the Noh the design of the costumes 'assists rather than hinders the stage movements and often a change in character or personality . . . . is indicated by a costume change devised as part of the movement so that the whole concept of costume contributes to the dramatic effect of the performance', so too, according to Miller, Yeats visualized his plays since the 1890s, 'particularly after he had made contact with Craig and Ricketts in the first decade of this century'.[12] Charles Ricketts eventually designed the costumes for a revival of *The King's Threshold* in 1914 which Yeats, in a letter, describes as 'the best stage costumes I have ever seen. They are full of dramatic invention, and yet nothing starts out, or seems eccentric . . . . such is the effect of costume that whole scenes got a new intensity.'[13] Ricketts also designed costumes for London productions of *Deirdre* and *On Baile's Strand* but had no part in *Four Plays for Dancers*. Somehow, Yeats got side-tracked and did not follow the trail his artistic instincts were pointing towards in costume design, for Edmund Dulac was not the right man for *At the Hawk's Well*.

It has also to be borne in mind, when considering Yeats's attempts to write in the Japanese manner, that the theatre he had founded and knew best was essentially a 'theatre of poverty': sumptuousness was never a feature of Abbey productions.

Standards were really rather low, as James Flannery makes clear:

Naturalistic peasant plays and the more poetic peasant plays of Synge and Lady Gregory again were dressed with relative ease and charm simply by utilizing authentic peasant shawls, colourful petticoats, ancient frieze coats, and even "pampooties" — the cowskin wrap-around sandals still worn by the fisherman in the Aran Islands. The plays of Yeats, however, demanded special treatment, not only in the design and colour of costumes but in their material, cut, and fit. A glance at photographs of the first productions of *The King's Threshold*, *The Shadowy Waters*, and *Deirdre* . . . tells an unrelieved tale of tasteless shoddiness. One would think it far more likely to find these ill-fitting, crudely decorated costumes made of dyed hessian, with street shoes peering out from beneath the stiffened cloth, in a school pageant than on the stage of the famous Abbey Theatre.[14]

The fact was that the 'famous Abbey Theatre' was small, underfinanced, and more interested in developing writers and actors than in mounting high-quality productions. Yeats, intent upon restoring *words* to their ancient sovereignty, can have had little time (or money) to expend on costume design. Thus conditioned, he envisaged a style of theatre wherein meagreness was to be taken for granted.

It seems clear, then, that Yeats's concept of the Noh was impoverished. His *Four Plays for Dancers* make very few demands indeed on a scene designer. His stage directions mention costume only when it is functional.

At the Hawk's Well

Only the Guardian's costume is described. She is 'entirely covered by a black cloak' at the beginning, solely to allow for its sudden removal for the dance, when 'Her dress under the cloak suggests a hawk'. Of course, we know fairly well what this hawk costume was like because there are photographs extant of Michio Ito in the first production of 1916. What is not, perhaps, appreciated is that Yeats left the design to Dulac and Ito between them. Dulac's design, according to Ito, [15] was Egyptian in style, which he liked, though he disliked the Egyptian style also given to the masks of Young Man and Old Man. It was a colourful costume : red tights for the legs, cream and black for the front, brown with gold feathers for the back, and a blonde head-dress to complete the picture.[16]

Yeats does not seem to have asked why the costume design should be Egyptian when the characters were Celtic and the play was supposed to be in imitation of the Japanese. He was quite happy, it would appear, to leave this matter in the hands of the supposed experts.

Yoro

Costumes in *Yoro* do not delight the eyes of the audience, since all the characters are men, and they wear similar costumes. The Old man, the lead, in the first half, wears an *atsuita kimono* with a discreet checked pattern to show his age, and white baggy trousers, *okuchi*. He carries a fan appropriate for an old man, and a walking stick. His outer garment is a *mizugoromo*, tied in the middle.

His son, the *tsure*, appears in a similar costume, but with a bolder and more dramatic checked pattern, suggesting the stronger vitality of youth. He carries a fan for a man and does not carry a walking stick.

The courtier, the *waki*, wears an *atsuita kimono* for his under-*kimono*, and baggy trousers, white *okuchi*, over which is a *kariginu*. He also wears headgear called *daijin-eboshi*, to symbolise his status as a courtier.

The mountain god, the lead in the latter half, wears a white and red *atsuita* as his under-*kimono*. He has baggy trousers, white *okuchi*, and a *kariginu* as an over-garment. He also wears *sui-kamuri* headgear, to symbolise his divine status.

The Only Jealousy of Emer

Two costumes are described. One is for the Figure of Cuchulain, 'a man in his grave-clothes', which is also the costume worn by the Ghost of Cuchulain ('Another man with exactly similar clothes'). The Woman of the Sidhe, who performs the central dance just as the Guardian does in *At the Hawk's Well*, is also described:

> Her mask and clothes must suggest gold or bronze or brass or silver, so that she seems more an idol than a human being . . . . Her hair, too, must keep the metallic suggestion.   (p. 551)

Thus there are two actors in grave clothes, of indeterminate quality or design, and one in a metallic costume : all three being other-wordly. But what are the 'wordly' to wear in contrast? Is there a *style* for saga? Is Emer, as wife, distinguishable through her costume from Eithne Inguba, Cuchulain's young mistress? Is the costume Celtic in some ways or quite plain? And what of the Musicians? Alas, Yeats provides no answers.

Aoino-ue

Princess Rokujo wears a *rimpaku* under-*kimono* which has

triangular patterns on a silver background, representing scales, and also a black-based *koshimaki* with a bold design of a symmetrical crest. She wears a *karaori*, an outer garment in the *tsuboori* style. She carries a fan suitable for a devil. At the *monogi*, or interval, the lead changes his mask from a *deigan* to a *hannya* mask, and then takes a beating stick.

Priestess Teruhinomae, the *tsure*, wears a *surihaku* under-*kimono* or *karaori*, and a white *mizugoromo* for an outer garment in the *kinagsahi* style.

Yokawano-kohijiri, the *waki*, wears a plain *asuita kimono* covered by *suzukake* (a symbol of *yamabushi*). He wears baggy white *okuchi* trousers, and carries both a fan suitable for a *yamabushi* and a *irataka* rosary.

The courtier, the *waki-tsure*, wears a colourful *atsuita* under-*kimono* and baggy white *okuchi* trousers. He also wears a *awase-kariginu* on top and carries a man's fan.

The Dreaming of the Bones

The stage directions here give no attention to costume. The First Musician, however, describes the Young Man on his entrance:

> He seems as Aran fisher, for he wears
> The flannel bawneen and the cow-hide shoe.   (p. 763)

Such attire could come straight out of the Abbey Theatre stock : Bartley's costume in *Riders to the Sea* would do nicely. The play, after all, is set in the year 1916. But what of the other two characters, both masked, the Stranger and the Young Girl? As they are revealed to be Diarmuid and Dervorgilla from the twelfth century one would imagine that their costumes would contrast with that of the Young Man. Yet the Young Man never comments on their attire as he might be expected to were they roaming the hills at midnight in what must strike him as fancy dress. What is called for is clearly a noncommital design for the ghostly characters : all-purpose cloaks which might play a part in the climactic dance. Once again, however, Yeats seems not to have given thought to this matter of design.

Nishikigi

The man, the lead in the first half, wears either a *suo* or a *mizugoromo* for an under-*kimono*, to show his common origin. He wears white *okuchi*, baggy trousers, and usually a *suo* as an outer garment, tied in the middle. He carries a man's fan, and a *nishikigi* branch. The man's ghost (the lead in the latter half) wears an *atsuita kimono*, *okuchi* baggy trousers, and a *happi* coat as a covering garment on top of them. He carries a *shura oogi*, a fan used by a spirit suffering in purgatory.

The woman, the *tsure*, wears a *surihaku kimono* as an underkimono covered by a *karaori* in the *kinagashi* style. The *surihaku kimono* has small sleeves and is enriched with gold appliqué, suggesting the decorative aspects of youth.

She carries a *hosonuno* cloth and a *mizugoromo* in the *kinagashi* style. He carries a fan with a *sumi-e* ink drawing and a rosary.

Calvary

There are no indications, either in stage directions or in textual descriptions, of the costumes. Presumably, the Three Roman Soldiers must look like three Roman soldiers : here, at least, Yeats encounters a specific tradition. But as the play is essentially a dream play the costuming of Christ, Judas and Lazarus may well be indeterminate. Certainly, as the play itself confronts tradition in an abstract, non-representational form the costuming could well be ahistorical. All that is clear, finally, is that by this stage Yeats had abandoned even his earlier interest in colour when conceiving the staging of his plays, for *Calvary* is stark and devoid of colour. His failure to comment on the costume design indicates his distance from the treasure-house of the Japanese tradition.

VIII.   DANCING AND ACTING

Dancing in Noh comes towards the end of a play and contributes to the climax. Dancing was added to Noh plays during the Kamakura period, when various arts became fused and developed into a much more complex theatrical form. Consequently, even though almost all Noh plays have a dance at their conclusion, these dances have not been developed individually. The same dances may be adapted for many different plays. There are about forty dances, against about two hundred and forty plays. For example, a fast, vigorous and austere *Kamimai* dance suits such plays as *Awaji, Ema, Shiga, Takasago, Yumiyawata* and *Yoro* (all these are from the first group of God plays). There are, however, some exceptions: for example, the dance of *kaneiri* in *Dojoji*. Here, the lead (a jealous woman equated with a serpent) moves slowly but intensely, drawing patterns of scales with foot movements on the floor before she jumps into a temple bell. In some other plays, dancing is replaced by a fight, as in *Aoino-ue*. As Princess Rokujo, in demon form, tries to pass the saintly monk trying to stop her taking her revenge, a fierce battle ensues.

Noh is a traditional theatre art and as a result it has not accepted any new choreography to any dancing parts. So the same dances have been danced for hundreds of years; each detail of their movements has been recorded in scrolls, kept by troupes as vital, aesthetic secrets. Even today, no new choreography is permitted in the Noh.

Some dance pieces last for a few minutes, others for as long as half an hour. During the dances, there are no speeches or singing. These independent patterns of movement are usually accompanied by the music of a flute and two or three drums. These dances consist of many decorative movements and rely heavily on their harmonization with music in order to convey the dancer's inner feelings.

Such independent dances as *kamimai, chuno-mai, jono-mai, otoko-mai* lead us on to the dance finale which is combined with chanting from the chorus, called *kiri*. Both the dancing and chanting in *kiri* are much faster than any other part of a play. There are

85

many symbolic, yet highly comprehensible movements in this part, since the dance accompanies, and often illustrates, the chanting of dramatic poetry.

On the other hand, dance was never an organic part of any of the western forms of drama available to Yeats, apart from ballet. Indeed dance was never a major feature of English drama. Even in Shakespeare's plays, such as *Love's Labour's Lost, Romeo and Juliet, Much Ado about Nothing* and *The Tempest,* dance appeared only occasionally, a subordinate part of a masked encounter, with dramatic implications for the plot. Once realism was established on stage, in the nineteenth century, dance was banished from modern 'legitimate' drama. Yeats's discovery of the Noh form opened his eyes to a nonverbal mode of expression which consorted very well with his own concept of dynamic imagery, and in imitating this form he was excited by the symbolist possibilities of the dance. He saw the dance in Japanese Noh as 'a series of positions and movements which may represent a battle, or a marriage, or the pain of a ghost in the Buddhist Purgatory'.[1] He observed that the *rhythm* discovered in the dance suited the ideal of 'reverie' which he held as an aim in all tragedy:

I have lately studied certain of these dances, with Japanese players, and I notice that their ideal of beauty, unlike that of Greece and like that of pictures from Japan and China, makes them pause at moments of muscular tension. The interest is not in the human form but in the rhythm to which it moves, and the triumph of their art is to express the rhythm in its intensity. There are few swaying movements of arms or body such as make the beauty of our dancing. They move from the hip, keeping constantly the upper part of their body still, and seem to associate with every gesture or pose some definite thought. They cross the stage with a gliding movement, and one gets the impression not of undulation but of continuous straight lines.[2]

As is well known, Yeats used Michio Ito as the dancer for *At the Hawk's Well* but Ito soon left for New York. Yeats greatly admired what he called Ito's 'genius of movement', which is more significant than the fact that Ito was not actually a trained Noh performer and, apparently, held no very high opinion of the Noh arts.[3] What Yeats admired in Ito was his 'minute intensity of movement',[4] and his ability by his gestures to create images of an inner, spiritual world of experience; his ability to 'recede from us into some more powerful life . . . to inhabit as it were the depths of the mind'.[5]

Once Ito had left, in Autumn 1916, Yeats seemed to lose any clear idea of what he wanted in his dances. In his note to *Four Plays for Dancers* he says, as if depressed by his failure to stage any other of the dance plays:

Should I make a serious attempt, which I may not, being rather tired of the theatre, to arrange and supervise performances, the dancing will give me most trouble, for I know but vaguely what I want. I do not want any existing form of stage dancing, but something with a smaller gamut of expression, something more reserved, more self-controlled, as befits performers within arm's reach of their audience.[6]

Later, he recovered his sense of purpose. Ninette de Valois danced in the second revival of *At the Hawk's Well* at the Abbey Theatre on 22 July 1933. She clearly had Yeats's approval, since he had been so impressed by her dancing when he first saw her in 1927 that he had invited her to Dublin to perform in his *Four Plays for Dancers* and set up a school of ballet at the Abbey.[7] Dame Ninette described to Richard Taylor how she performed the dance in *At the Hawk's Well*:

She danced barefoot in the modern style then known as abstract expressionism, and the choreography was created to express the emotional content of the mask through stylized forms. Both movement and maintained emotion were determined by the fact of the Hawk's hood, and the dance progressed from an evocation of brooding power, through suggestive seduction, to the violent ecstasy of a wild bird. From the snatches of description that have been preserved, photographs of Ito in costume, and what is known of his later dance style, it is quite certain that his concept of the Hawk's dance was much closer to that of Dame Ninette than to the classical choreography of Nō.[8]

But towards the end of the 1930s Yeats again despaired of finding the right dancer for his plays, as appears from the prologue to *The Death of Cuchulain*.

At the Hawk's Well/Yoro

The crucial stage direction in *At the Hawk's Well* is brief and uninformative: 'He [the Young Man] has sat down; the Guardian of the well has begun to dance, moving like a hawk. The Old Man sleeps. The dance goes on for some time.' (Perhaps the most repeated story connected with Ito's hawk dance relates to his visit to the London Zoo with Dulac, in order to study the movements of a hawk. This hawk, having been fed, remained inert in the corner of his cage, even when poked by an umbrella; and so Ito's research came to nothing.)

Yeats's stage directions continue to be sketchy: following three lines of song from the First Musician, another reads: 'The dance goes on for some time. The Young Man rises slowly.' After two lines of speech by the First Musician, 'The dance goes on'. Three more lines of verse by the Young Man are followed by the stage direction, 'The dance goes on'. Typically, it is not clear exactly when this particular dance finished. After the First Musician speaks three lines starting, 'I have heard water splash', a stage direction says that the Guardian 'has gone out', presumably as the Musician speaks. In the first edition (1917) the dance is described as continuing for 'some two minutes' at a time, instead of the above vague description. This Beckett-like precision, however, may be misleading as a total of six minutes seems excessive. In a note on the music, Dulac says the dance should be only three and a half minutes in duration (*Four Plays*, p. 95).

In *Yoro, kami-mai* (the god-dance) is danced towards the end of the play. The Old Man and his son show the courtier the miraculous spring. As he leaves, he hears heavenly music, and the mountain god appears, speaks and dances. This dance is to be danced by a young male god and, consequently, it is quite fast, dynamic and majestic. By dancing *kami-mai*, the lead in the role of the mountain god, demonstrates divine power and celebrates ever-lasting divine presence keeping the world of Shinto and Buddhism in peace and harmony.

The Only Jealousy of Emer/Aoino-ue

The dance is executed by the Woman of the Sidhe (Fand), described in a stage direction as follows:

The Woman of the Sidhe moves round the crouching Ghost of Cuchulain at front of stage in a dance that grows gradually quicker, as he slowly awakes. At moments she may drop her hair upon his head, but she does not kiss him. She is accompanied by string and flute and drum . . .

In the later, prose version, *Fighting the Waves*, in which Ninette de Valois danced in 1929, the above stage direction is followed a few lines later by an explanatory addition:

The object of the dance is that having awakened Cuchulain he will follow Fand out; probably he will seek a kiss and the kiss will be withheld.[9]

Even here, however, 'probably' is an irritating example of Yeats's general imprecision over directions for the dances in his plays. Does the Woman of the Sidhe dance first and then speak the dialogue which follows the above stage direction? Or does the dance continue while she speaks? The latter seems the preferable choice, but it raises the question of how the dancer is to punctuate

the dance with speech. It is certainly true in general, as Yeats confessed in a note to *Fighting the Waves* in 1934, that he 'left
imaginative suggestion to dancers, singers, musicians'.[10]

In *Aoino-ue* dance is replaced by conflict, as the saint and the
chorus vigorously chant Buddhist prayers, and he uses his rosary
to counteract the demon's attack, in a dramatic evocation of
spiritual triumph.

The Dreaming of the Bones/Nishikigi

In this play there are no stage directions for the dance. It begins
while the attention of the Young Man is focused on the distant pro-
spect of Galway city, and in the course of his political commentary
on its 'fall' he notices the dancers. One must infer from the text
when exactly the dance begins. He asks:

> Why do you dance?
> Why do you gaze, and with so passionate eyes,
> One on the other; and then turn away,
> Covering your eyes, and weave it in a dance?   (p. 774)

'Weave it in a dance': what can Yeats mean? A graceful, eighteenth-
century cotillion? A piece of Dalcroze eurhythmics? Any modern
director must take pause here, for this is certainly the crucial area
of the play, the dramatic climax, and yet Yeats offers no help as
to its expression. The Young Girl has two lines to speak while dancing, and these are probably directed (in appeal) to the Young Man.
Yet when he speaks, it is to comment on them and their dance
rather than to reply. Indeed, part of his comment is to say, 'They
cannot hear, / Being folded up and hidden in their dance', which
sounds like very close dancing indeed! He continues, with lines that
make clear, at least, that the dance goes through at least two
distinct phases:

> The dance is changing now. They have dropped their eyes,
> They have covered up their eyes as though their hearts
> Had suddenly been broken . . .   (p. 775)

For performers who are masked, these lines suggest a good deal of
gesture and inclination of head and neck, always maintaining a
rhythm. As the Young Man issues his final refusal to forgive Diarmuid and Dervorgilla he comments on their sudden fading away,
suggesting another phase in the dance:

> They have drifted in the dance from rock to rock.
> They have raised their hands as though to snatch the sleep

That lingers always in the abyss of the sky
Though they can never reach it. A cloud floats up
And covers all the mountain-head in a moment;
And now it lifts and they are swept away.   (p. 775)

At this point, the Stranger and Young Girl *'go out'*. They do not,
it seems, dance out. But when, then, does the dance end? This is
one of the most infuriating examples of Yeats's carelessness as to
detail in the dance plays. In a note on the play, in *Four Plays for
Dancers*, Yeats says that Dervorgilla's lines in the play 'can be
given, if need be, to Dermot [*sic*], and Dervorgilla's part taken by
a dancer who has the training of a dancer alone; nor need that
masked dancer be a woman'. This would mean, of course, that the
dance was a solo performance. What is the Stranger to do while
Dervorgilla does her dance? He may consult the moon for an
answer, for he will not get any from Yeats.

In *Nishikigi*, after the earth-bound spirits of the tragic couple are
released, they appear in front of their saviour the monk to show
their gratitude. The Man, delighted, dances *oshikihayamai*. The
dance is extremely swift and intense. In the after world, they are
finally united, and he demonstrates his climactic joy. The accompanying music is provided by a Japanese flute and two drums:
Okawa and *Kotsuzumi*.

Calvary/Religious Noh plays

In *Calvary*, as in *The Dreaming of the Bones*, there is minimal
detail on how the dance (of the Three Roman Soldiers) is to be performed. There is merely a brief stage direction in *Four Plays for
Dancers*: 'They dance round the cross, moving as if throwing dice',
a direction which in *Collected Plays* becomes, simply, 'they dance'.

Karen Dorn suggests that Yeats had in mind the 'Sacred Dance
of Jesus', as described by G. R. S. Mead. According to this source,
taken originally from the letters of St. Augustine, Jesus made his
disciples form a ring around him at the time just before his
betrayal: 'Then follows the mystery-dance of his Passion, the
earliest Passion play of Christendom.'[12]

Katharine Worth's comments on the dance are telling, since she
relates the dance to the final song and to the overall meaning of the
play:

They move into a dance which is one of the most arresting and complex
in all the plays. The dance of the dice-throwers represents gamblers falling
out, settling the quarrel by throwing dice, and then, reconciled by chance,
taking hands and wheeling about the cross. The configuration of the stage

forms a silent language: on one hand, the rigidity of the cross, on the other, the choral revolutions, a spectacular dancing out of the image of change and chance with which the play began. Two truths are there: Christ and Judas can never change, but there must be change; the full moon must give way to crescent, everything must become new.[13]

In the Noh, several dances can be adapted for specifically religious plays. Thus in *Yoro*, *kami-mai* is performed by a young male god, in *Takasago* by the spirit of an old pine tree. Other dances are as follows:

Mai-bataraki: a demonstrative fierce dance by a dragon god, sometimes by a demon.
Shinno-jono-mai: a sublime slow dance by a goddess or aged god.
Jono-mai: a majestic dance by a celestial being, or by a spirit of flowers and trees, basically a female dance.
Kagura: an enchanting ecstatic dance by a goddess, or sometimes by a priestess.

Acting

Yeats was always interested in an acting style that would strike a balance between natural feeling and artificiality. He seems to have shared Bernard Shaw's dislike of the popular London style in the 1890s: 'I hated the existing conventions of the theatre',[14] and no doubt had his fill of the English tradition by the time Frank Benson and his company were done with *Diarmuid and Grania* at the Gaiety Theatre, Dublin, in 1901. It was after this débâcle that Yeats decided to throw in his lot with the Fay brothers, and their carefully cultivated compromise between modern naturalism and traditional French-style formalism. In writing of the first productions in 1902 by Fay's company of his own *Cathleen Ni Houlihan* and of AE's *Deidre*, he said:

> . . . it [*Deirdre*] was the first performance I had seen since I understood these things in which the actors kept still enough to give poetical writing its full effect upon the stage. I had imagined such acting, though I had not seen it, and had once asked a dramatic company to let me rehearse them in barrels that they might forget gesture and have their minds free to think of speech for a while. The barrels, I thought, might be on castors, so that I could shove them about with a pole when the action required it.[15]

This interest in, indeed obsession with, stillness on stage remained a life-long preoccupation. Yeats disliked naturalism intensely, thinking it common, graceless and unimpassioned. In 'The Play, the Player, and the Scene', in *Samhain* 1904, he stressed the need to maintain poetry on stage, in acting style as well as in drama. What he wanted, he said, was an art 'essentially conventional, artifical, ceremonious'.[16] There had also to be music in the actors' delivery: 'An actor must so understand how to discriminate cadence from cadence, and so cherish the musical lineaments of verse or prose, that he delights the ear with a continually varied music.'[17] Without being monotonous, actors should keep to a musical note in their delivery. (Ironically, Yeats was tone deaf.) In short, all acting should be rhythmical and ceremonious. Yeats's ideal Irish actor was Frank Fay,[18] whom he praises in a late essay (in 1937) as 'openly, dogmatically, of that school of Talma which permits an actor, as Gordon Craig has said, to throw up an arm calling down the thunderbolts of Heaven, instead of seeming to pick up pins from the floors'.[19] It is no accident, then, that in the Prologue to his last play, *The Death of Cuchulain*, the Old Man, a most Yeatsian figure, declares he is the son of Talma. François-Joseph Talma (1763–1826) had reformed the Comédie Française in several ways, including the suppression of 'exaggerations of the declamatory style', thus 'allowing the sense rather than the metre to dictate the pauses'.[20]

As time passed, Yeats formed the view that the Abbey players lacked sufficient passion to do justice to the highest dramatic form, tragedy. When Synge's *Deirdre of the Sorrows* had its posthumous premiere in 1910 Yeats saw that not even Synge's beloved Molly was up to the mark:

Then as I watched the acting I saw that O'Donovan and Molly (Maire O'Neill) were as passionless as the rest. Molly has personal charm, pathos, distinction even, fancy, beauty, but never passion — never intensity; nothing out of a brooding mind. All was but observation, curiosity, desire to please . . . [H]er talent showed like that of the others, social, modern, a faculty of comedy.[21]

This remained his general view of the Abbey company, publicized in his open letter to Lady Gregory in 1919. He had become disillusioned with what he saw as its growing objectivity, realism, and proficiency in comedy; the Abbey had become a theatre of the 'head', rather than of the 'heart'.[22]

In the Japanese Noh Yeats rediscovered a theatre of the heart. In his essay, 'Certain Noble Plays of Japan', he recounts the story, 'traditional among Japanese players', according to which an old woman rebuked an actor who followed her in the streets in order to imitate her movements: 'If he would become famous as a Noh player, she said, he must not observe life, nor put on an old face and stint the music of his voice. He must know how to suggest an old woman and yet find it all in the heart.'[23] Yeats saw Noh drama as essentially tragic, full of the deep feeling he wanted from the theatre. The acting style he imagined for it, since he never actually witnessed a Noh play in performance, was simple, intense, and ceremonious. These were, accordingly, the qualities he wanted in the performance of his *Four Plays for Dancers*.

Acting in the Noh theatre is completely different from the conventional contemporary theatre. Yeats was right to recognize it as the theatre of the heart. The Noh theatre rejected realistic movements and gestures (losing physical freedom of expression, and verbal freedom of speech). Noh acting provides a stylized, poetic form of the contemporary Zen beliefs and symbolic concerns. Gestures are no more than clues for understanding the emotional developments. So a gesture does not tell everything; it tells the minimum. Changes of emotion created inside a character have to be made known through artificially devised movements called *kata*. The retained emotion, not spent in impromptu exuberance, lends restrained strength to the actors' superbly controlled performance.

The Noh theatre, for example, created its own unique way of walking on the stage, called *suriashi*. All Noh actors adopt this way of walking right through the performance, including the musicians and chorus. They walk, sliding their feet alternately against the floor, so that their walk does not look rough. Sometimes in a Noh theatre the audience will hear a board of the connecting bridge under the feet of a passing actor, because the actor is pressing his feet hard against the floor while he slides his feet along. Thus even when portraying running, an actor has to keep one foot on the floor.

While an actor is on stage, he retains an artificial posture: standing as if he is an amateur skier, knees bent, hips sticking out, making his back hollow and keeping his head upright. This artificial posture, together with the way he walks, means that he gains more control over his body than in any other position for Noh acting. His body and all his movements are like those by a person in stiff, overstarched clothes or in armour.

The Noh theatre has a limited number of fixed gestures for some particular expressions, called *kata*. For example, to show grief there are three patterns of movements according to the depth of the sorrow portrayed. Firstly, slight sadness is suggested by an actor looking downwards a fraction, thus creating shadows under his own eyes and mouth, on those of his mask. Secondly, *kata-shiori* suggests the character in deep sorrow. An actor, while looking downwards, brings his closed right hand towards his eyes and moves his hand away from his face without actually touching his face: weeping in stylized form. He repeats this same gesture twice. While he is performing this gesture, he may say a simple sentence to indicate his grief, but it is always minimal. Thirdly, *moroshiori* suggests that the character is in despair. An actor will use both hands to show the character is in deep tragedy.

There are a few symbolic gestures such as crying, indicating praying, sleeping, drinking, looking and so on. But there are also abstract gestures as well, such as *sayu* and *hiraki*. Such abstract movements are mixed with other movements, symbolic and realistic.

Realistic movements are themselves relatively stylized. For example, in a fighting scene, using either swords or *naginata* (designed for warrior monks or lady fighters), their movements are controlled and measured, and they never actually strike each other's sword or body. In *Matsukaze*, the lead performs a realistic gesture, for example putting sea water into a pail she carries. Here the actor uses his fan to take water from the sea. This is a long way from twentieth-century realism.

These symbolic gestures provide clues for the audience's creative imagination. The subtler the actor's gesture is, the more elegant the images they will stimulate in his audience. To produce a truly moving effect, as Yeats realised instinctively, a Noh actor has to act with his heart. Ze-Ami is relevant here:

Mind, however, is always stressed more than matter in this art where the actor is, in effect, his own producer and should calculate the effect he creates by relying on his own powers and intuition, rather than on outside direction. The actor should gauge his audience and always keep them mentally on their toes. The *Noh* actor should never reveal his mental processes, his creative intentions. So, even though every actor is trained in formal patterns, and every play has its own material, he should not let anyone know how he will interpret his part. Keeping his intentions a mystery, he gains power over his audience, gives his impersonations life, brings inner vitality to an artificial process. In *Kakyo*, Ze-Ami chooses the telling image of a puppeteer to explain this, saying that the dead or lifeless puppet symbolizes a body whose soul is leaving it, and that just as a skilled puppeteer can put life into this puppet so a skilled actor can put life into his work (See *Kakyo*, pp. 100–101). The actor, in effect, is doing this physically, for just as the puppeteer moves strings to give the illusion of physical life, so the Noh specialist manipulates his powers to give an illusion of psychological reality.[24]

Above left: *Zo* or *Zo-onna,* a mask used for a mature woman; above right: *Hannya,* a mask used for a devil, or vengeful spirit, such as in the latter part of *Aoino-ue* and *Dojoji.* Below left: *Shiwajo,* a mask used for an old man; below right: mask designed by Edmund Dulac for the Old Man in the 1916 production of *At the Hawk's Well,* reproduced from *Four Plays for Dancers.*

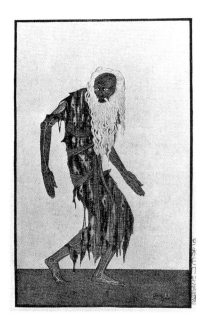

Edmund Dulac's designs for the 1916 production of *At the Hawk's Well.* Above left: the Old Man; right: Young Man (Cuchulain); left: a Musician.

Above: Edmund Dulac's design for the Black Cloth for the 1916 production of *At the Hawk's Well*. Below left: the Old Man in *Yoro;* right: the god Yoryo-kannonbosatsu, photographs by Ken Yoshikoshi.

Michio Ito wearing the hawk head-dress for the 1916 production of *At the Hawk's Well* (photograph by Alvin Langdon Coburn).

Michio Ito dancing in Scriabin's 'Prelude' No. 10, performed in London and Hollywood (photograph by Soichi Sunami).

The 1984 production of *At the Hawk's Well* at the Peacock Theatre, Dublin.
Above: Martina Stanley, Maire O'Neill and Linda McDonnell as the Three
Musicians. Below: Brid Ni Neachtain as the Guardian of the Well, Maeliosa
Stafford as the Young Man and Martina Stanley and Linda McDonnell as
Musicians.

Takahime (The Lady Hawk) by M. Yokomichi, a Noh adaptation of *At the Hawk's Well,* photographs by Tatsuo Yoshikoshi from the collection of Shotaro Oshima. Above: The Guardian of the Well and the Old Man. The hazel wood and the well are hidden by a black screen, and the rocks are symbolised by the six seated, masked figures. Below: *Old Man:* 'Why do you not speak to me? Why do you not say anything?' *Young Man:* 'I am called Cuchulain.'

Aoino-ue. Above: Princess Rokujo, performed by Koichi Sekine, confronts the Priestess Teruhinomae.

Below left: Princess Rokujo beats her rival in love, who is symbolised by the folded cloth. Below right: the vengeful spirit of Princess Rokujo (performed by Koichi Sekine), confronts Yamabushi.

Nishikigi by Ze-Ami. Above: a village woman and man. Below: their ghosts re-enact their courtship. Photographs by Ken Yoshikoshi.

Above: *The Dreaming of the Bones* in rehearsal, directed by Masaru Sekine at University College Dublin in 1986, with Christopher Murray as the Stranger, Colleen Hanrahan as the Young Girl, and Glynn Kelly as the Young Man, with Miriam Kenny (flautist) and Miriam Purtill (prompter). Below: the 1984 Peacock Theatre production of *The Cat and the Moon*, directed by Raymond Yeates, with Martina Stanley, Maire O'Neill and Linda McDonnell as the Three Musicians, Vincent O'Neill as the Blind Beggar, and Barry McGovern as the Lame Beggar. Photograph by Fergus Bourke.

Above and facing page: the 1986 Peacock Threatre production of *Calvary,* with Maire Ni Ghrainne, Aine Ni Mhuiri and Eileen Colgan as the Three Musicians and the Three Soldiers, Jonathan White as Lazarus, Brendan Conroy as Judas, and Sean Campion as Christ. Photographs by Fergus Bourke.

Facing page above: the 1989 Peacock Theatre Production of *At the Hawk's Well,* with Ciaran Hinds as the Young Man, Olwen Fouere as Aoife, and the Chorus — Fidelma O'Dowda, Kevin Reynolds, Brian McGrath, Eithne Dempsey, and Maire ni Ghrainne. Facing page below, and this page: the 1989 Peacock Theatre production of *The Only Jealousy of Emer,* with Ciaran Hinds as the Ghost of Cuchulain, Fedelma Cullen as Emer, Orla Charlton as Eithne Inguba, with Siobhan Miley as Figure of Cuchulain (Bricriu). Reproduced by courtesy of the photographer, Tom Lawlor.

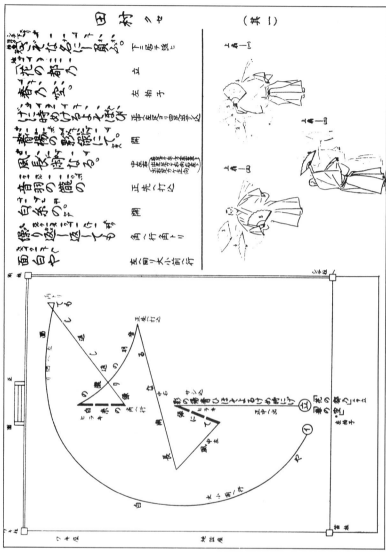

This illustration shows the extreme care that is taken to exactly instruct a Noh actor in every movement he makes during a play, in this case, *Tamura*. He is not permitted to make any change to these rules, which have remained the same for over 500 years. The only difference between a 15th-century and 20th-century production of a Noh play would be in the speed. Productions are now very much slower, and take perhaps three to four times as long to perform.

At the Hawk's Well/Yoro

As the only one of the four plays to be staged as Yeats desired, *At the Hawk's Well* deserves special attention. It is regrettable, for the historian, that Yeats enjoyed the high-handed attitude towards the press which he gleefully records in his note on the play, when he ejected a photographer willing to give a whole page to his premiere: 'What a relief after directing a theatre for so many years . . . to think no more of pictures . . . nor of all those paragraphs written by young men, perhaps themselves intelligent, who must applaud the common taste or starved!'.[25] Had there been reviews, it would be possible in some measure to recreate that first production. As it is, there is little to go on.

The acting style was formal and retrained. The word 'slowly' is used in relation to the unfolding of the cloth. The text also tells us that the Old Man moves in a non-naturalistic manner: 'His movements, like those of the other persons in the play, suggest a marionette'. This latter stage direction, however, is a later addition (1921): the original editions of *At the Hawk's Well* in 1917 limit the suggestion to his keeping time to the drum taps. Yeats, in adding the detail of the marionette, may have meant to allude to Gordon Craig's well-known, if frequently misunderstood, notion of the *über-marionette*. Reg Skene, at any rate, believes that Yeats's familiarity with Craig's ideas 'certainly prepared him for the enthusiastic acceptance of Japanese acting technique when he came to study the Noh tradition'.[26] In his preface to *Four Plays for Dancers* Yeats says, in general: 'the players must move a little stiffly and gravely like marionettes'.[27]

We learn from Yeats's letters that the actor cast as the Young Man was Henry Ainley (1879–1945). Although a professional of considerable reputation (having played Leontes in Granville-Barker's production of *The Winter's Tale* in 1912), he was obviously of the modern school Yeats disliked, because the latter described him (in a letter to Lady Gregory) as unsatisfactory in rehearsal: 'The play goes on well except for Ainley, who waves his arms like a drowning kitten'.[28] Yeats determined to get rid of Ainley at the first opportunity, because he told Lady Gregory after the premiere of 2 April, 1916: 'We shall not do it again until June in order to get rid of Ainley and the musicians'.[29] There seems to be no further record of a performance in June, with or without Ainley, who seems to have appeared in the second performance, given a few days after the first, according to Yeats's note on the play.[30] It would appear that experience showed Yeats that it was one thing to despise contemporary standards and styles of acting, and quite another to get his plays performed in a style of which he would approve:

A man who loves verse and the visible arts has, in a work such as I imagined, the advantage of the professional player. The professional player becomes the amateur, the other has been preparing all his life.[31]

Acting in *Yoro* does not require any complicated acting techniques, since this is a typical play of the first group, god plays. This play focuses on the revelation of the miraculous water. The *waki*, a courtier, opens the play with his *shidai* song; creating a peaceful and calm atmosphere, which represents the peace enjoyed during the reign of Emperor Yuryaku. While singing his travelling song, the *waki* does not move, but the words of his song suggest his implied movements and what he sees on his journey. When the *waki* meets the *shite* and the *tsure*, an old man and his son, they will take over the key role of reinforcing the peaceful atmosphere on the stage, whilst explaining that the secret of the old men's longevity is the miraculous water. They have to establish the credibility of the miraculous water, but this is not difficult, since most Noh plays are based on well known stories, and their audience would have known about the miraculous springs of Chinese legends.

In the second half of the play, the lead is the mountain god, Yoryu-kannonbosatsu. Acting a god requires strength, and Ze-ami explains in his theories of Noh drama how an actor should portray divine roles:

A God: (To be acted in in elaborate costumes to suit a God's magnificence). One should act this character in the same way as one acts a devil. This part should have an element of rury about it, so it is quite acceptable to act like a demon but with a divine appearance. Nonetheless, there is a basic difference between the two. Acting a god naturally leads to dancing, but the character of the devil never includes dancing.

The Only Jealousy of Emer/Aoino-ue

Stage directions are of little help to an attempt to rediscover the acting style Yeats required here. There is, however, a clear indication of the importance of mime. When Emer tends the fire which is to keep Mananaan's power at bay, she:

goes to one side of the platform and moves her hand as though putting logs on a fire and stirring it into a blaze. While she makes these movements the Musicians play, marking the movements with drum and flute perhaps. Having finished she stands beside the imaginary fire . . .   (p. 539)

This stage direction can be taken, perhaps, as an indication of the ceremonious, ritualistic style to be used throughout performance. The folding and unfolding of the cloth at the beginning and end of the play, likewise, reinforces the ritualistic quality of performance. Acting in the role of Princess Rokujo in *Aoino-ue* is the most difficult of all roles referred to in this comparative study. Princess Rokujo was one of the highest-ranking fictional characters ever portrayed in Noh drama, making it extremely difficult for an ordinary Noh actor to create a suitably sophisticated, aristocratic rendition of this part. And to make the acting of this particular role yet more difficult, the Princess is distraught because of her husband's love affair with Aoino-ue. When the actor representing her vengeful soul is called on stage by the Priestess Teruhinomae, Princess Rokujo makes an emotional confession — a touching mixture of nostalgic regret and present anger. The difficulty in the first half is to retain the Princess's nobility, while showing her violent reactions. If an actor exaggerates the emotional elements of this part, his interpretation may lose its intrinsic refinement. The second half of the play requires more straightforward acting based on physical strength, where the actors portray spiritual conflict. The difficult, complex acting techniques required in the first half of the play have been explained by Ze-Ami in his *Fushi-Kaden*.

A Monogurui [a mad person]. Acting a mad person is most dramatic and intriguing. There are various characters in this genre, so that if one excels in acting a role such as this one can act a whole range of similar characters. Many devices are required for this kind of impersonation. For example, if a character is distraught because they are possessed by a ghost, or the spirit of a dead or a living person, one can easily get suggestions for one's performance by imitating the being possessing them. It is not easy to impersonate a mad person who is distraught, suffering from a quite different kind of misfortune, such as being separated from parents, being deserted by a husband or lover, being left by a wife, or searching for a lost child. Even if an actor is skilled, his acting will not appeal to an audience if he performs without taking into consideration the different causes of madness. If the cause of the madness is the result of being overcome with emotion, one should act so that one looks pensive, and appears to be deep in thought, and then one should try to present *hana* at the scene where the character goes mad. If one presents the scene of madness, identifying oneself emotionally with the character, one's performance will become impressive and moving. One can be called a real expert if, by one's skill, one makes the audience cry because of sympathy for the character portrayed . . .

In general, one should choose a suitable costume for one's part. One can, however, occasionally dress in a more exhibitionist costume than usual to indicate the distraught mind of a character. One should also put a seasonal flower on one's hair ornament. There is something one should bear in mind. On the whole, one should portray a mad person as obsessed. But there are unsuitable cases in which a demon, or the fighting spirit of a warrior, possesses a woman and makes her mad. If one acts this kind of role, like a demon or the fighting spirit of a warrior, it will result in the presentation of a furious woman, which will not please the audience. And if one tries simply to look like a female, then one will fail to suggest that this character is possessed by a strong and violent spirit. Acting a man possessed by a female spirit will come to the same; after all it is best not to perform such characters. This is because some *Noh* playwrights do not understand the basic rule. [That is, that these roles of human and spirit do not go together.] An experienced writer would not write such a contradictory play. It is vital to keep this theory in mind.

As for a mad person who should be acted without a mask, only an experienced actor can perform this well enough. One has to change one's facial expression to look like a mad person, otherwise everything will become unconvincing; and yet the changes of facial expression can quite often ruin the performance. It is twice as difficult because it is *hitamen* [without a mask] and because the character has a distraught mind. So it is extremely difficult to present *hana* through the impersonation of this kind of character . . .[32]

The Dreaming of the Bones/Nishikigi

The only clue to acting style lies in the stage directions for the journey undertaken by the Young Man and his ghostly guides. There are four such stage directions, punctuating the action, each taking the same form: '*They go round the stage once*'.

In contrast to the conventions of naturalism, this stage direction implies a use of space and time which is medieval and presentational. Shakespeare had inherited this medieval convention, as may be seen from the journey undertaken by Gloucester to Dover in *King Lear*; but even at this point Shakespeare was defying the neo-classical rules on the so-called unities. With the establishment of changeable scenery on the Restoration stage in 1660 the older flexible conventions of time and space disappeared. Yeats, feeling constrained by the modern, basically realistic conventions, felt liberated when he discovered that in traditional Japanese drama the pre-Shakespearean usage of time and space still operated, and although he was basically neo-classical in his dramaturgy Yeats adopted this romantic, symbolic usage in *The Dreaming of the Bones*. The adoption suggests the overall style of acting as contra-naturalistic, and (for its time) daringly ceremonious. What is not apparent from these stage directions is something that is fundamental to the play's meaning, namely, that the Young Man does not inhabit the same heroic world as the ghosts, just as he does not inhabit the same world of time. In production, since he is not masked and is dressed realistically, a style would have to be found whereby this essential conflict became palpable: the 'signs' would have to be created for audiences to read.

In *Nishikigi*, the lead (unlike his female companion) appears without a mask. This implies that, at this stage, his role should be performed realistically because, although he is a ghost, he is desperately trying to convince the monk that he is a real, an ordinary villager, in order to get the monk's support. Ze-Ami says *hitamen* (performance without a mask) is very difficult.

A *Hitamen* (a man without a mask): This is also a taxing and valuable role. An actor is by nature secular and worldly, thus it seems easy to perform a role like this, but it is actually difficult, if one's ability is limited. As for this type of impersonation, there is no other way to do it than to imitate actual characters in existence around oneself . . . One should only imitate their behaviour. As for their facial expressions one should not try to imitate them, but keep one's face as it is and look natural.[33]

The actor's main concern, in the first part, is to attract the monk's sympathy for the ill-fated lovers. Although the audience no doubt guesses his real ghostly identity, he pretends to be an ordinary person.

The actor's chief concern, in the second part, is to show his gratitude to the monk. The ghost appears wearing the mask of a man obsessed — *ayakashi* or *awaotoko*. He re-enacts his unhappy courtship — (the cloth is removed from the bamboo 'mountain' structure, so that it can now represent the woman's house) — and then demonstrates his joy, on being released from purgatory, and about to be united in love.

Calvary/Religious plays

The opening stage direction, having described the business of the unfolding of the cloth, indicates that the three Musicians are 'singing and moving rhythmically'. This emphasis on rhythm is doubtless a key to the style of movement Yeats wanted in the play itself. Earlier (in 1904) he had said of poetic drama: 'The actors must move, for the most part, slowly and quietly, and not very much, and there should be something in their movements decorative and rhythmical as if they were paintings on a frieze.'[34]

In the opening stage direction, also, Yeats says that the Musicians repeat their actions at the end of the play, 'which enables the players to leave the stage unseen'. This emphasis reminds us of the instruction towards the end of *At the Hawk's Well*: 'During the singing, and while hidden by the cloth, the Old Man goes out'. Yeats, perhaps conditioned by the convention of the stage curtains on the proscenium stage, wished to mask these exits, no doubt so as to leave his stage bare at the end. Whereas this usage does, indeed, suggest the dream-like atmosphere in which the dance plays exist, it seems unnecessarily fussy, even amateurish.

The stage direction for Christ's entry suggests an element of the statuesque in this play: 'A player with the mask of Christ and carrying a cross has entered and now stands leaning upon the cross.' The pose, 'leaning upon the cross', defines an attitude which the play goes on to sustain: the languid passivity of Christ, who exists in a remote, timeless agony, surrounded by those he cannot save. As A. S. Knowland has emphasized, 'Imaginatively the structure of the play can be seen as circular',[35] and so Christ is the still centre around whom the others revolve, as it were, endlessly, in a dream.

Acting in most Japanese plays does not require complicated effort so much as a smooth flow of energy, and some strength, as already discussed for *Yoro*, but if the lead is a female divinity, the dancing, in particular, will be different.

Jogakushin: dancing grandly to the music accompaniment. This is a most important dance. The dance of a Heavenly Being is to present yugen in itself, like a bird flying about in a gentle spring wind. One should dance in full, sometimes dancing with control and sometimes dancing spontaneously, marking the difference between slow and fast movements clearly . . . One must practise hard to learn this role.

The Dance of a Heavenly Being: This should be placed outside the three basic characters, as her dancing is not seen in the human world. However, this is like the female dancing. This is a grand dance in scale and if one takes in the main characteristics of this dance, one should be allowed to interpret the role in the same way that one interprets that of a human being. This is the basis of learning this art, as to dance the Heavenly dance one is required to use one's whole spiritual energy all through one's body. The Heavenly dance consists of five pieces: one *jo* piece, three *ha* pieces and one *kyu* piece. The order is sometimes changed to *ha, jo, kyu* and en [extension]. This order can be adopted for the convenience of the occasion and this is called *jungyaku*, upside down.[36]

A Noh play featuring a male god is designed to create strong religious belief, but a piece featuring a feminine deity is primarily concerned with creating exquisite aesthetics, of *hana*.

IX. POETRY AND IMAGERY

Japanese poetry is purely syllabic. It does not have rhymes like western poetry. Two types of poetry were popular at the time of Ze-Ami, *waka* and *renga*. A *waka* poem consists of five groups of syllables; five, seven, five, seven and seven. A *renga* poem has much more flexibility. The middle part of a *renga* poem, a set of five and seven, or seven and five syllables could be repeated as many times as a poet or poets liked.

Ze-Ami wanted to cater to the aristocratic tastes of his powerful patron, the third *shogun*, Yoshimitsu. Therefore, this poet playwright eagerly adopted the courtly, literary traditions established over the past centuries. He became particularly keen on the minimalist aesthetics of *waka* poetry. He embellished his Noh plays with famous poems relating to dramatic characters or historical sites. Ze-Ami was also influenced by an aristocratic *renga* poet, called Nijo Yoshimoto and tried to blend his sophisticated elegance with rich simplicity. Thus the text of a Noh play is often compared to a tapestry: various elements are interwoven. Japanese poetry has subtle allusions provoked by various nuances in descriptions of nature and in expressions of human feelings. Direct expression was considered crude and vulgar. Indirect expression was thought ultimately to create a beauty.

Let us look at a *waka* poem mentioned earlier: *Seohayami Iwanisekaruru takigawano waretemosueni awantozoomoo*. The first three groups of five, seven, five syllables provide a description of fast-running mountain water: *seohayami* means fast-running water, *iwanisekaruru* means a rock in the river dividing a stream, *takigawano* means a river running as fast as a waterfall or a stream with many waterfalls.

Natural imagery suggests the course of a sad love affair: the turmoil in a lover's heart being compared with the tumbling of a mountain stream: the first three groups of syllables indirectly expressing passion as the lovers are divided, as by some unavoidable political mission forcing them to part, like a huge rock in the centre of a stream. The concluding groups of seven syllables express their determination to reunite, after the mission is completed, as the divided current will meet again once it has passed the rock.

Ze-Ami believed that it is most vital to choose a suitable figure for the lead of a play. Since dances and poems are crucial in creating *hana* on stage, the leading characters should be as naturally well acquainted with these arts, as an author with poetry.

For a male lead character Narihira, Kuronushi and Genji are ideal figures since they are cultured men, and for a female lead character Ise, Komachi, Gio, Gijo, Shizuka and Hyakuma are ideal since they are known for their talents as poetesses and dancers. If one chooses one of them, one can create a great dramatic effect in elegance quite naturally.[1]

Ze-Ami also says that if the lead is a commoner, he should be a woodcutter, or salt maker. Thus, in *Yoro*, the son is a woodcutter by profession and so he and his aged parents naturally live in the woods, in a wild mountainous setting, which allows for poetic illusions and reflections.

There are two ways of looking at Yeats's poetry and imagery in the plays. One is purely literary: the extrapolation of Yeats's rhetorical devices in the name of textual exegesis: '. . . without fine words there is no literature'.[2] This is the approach which tended to give Yeats the reputation of a non-playwright, since it tended to establish him as a lyric poet out of his element. The other, more fruitful way of regarding this question is to subordinate language and imagery to the theatrical and dramatic effects of a particular play taken as a whole. This method, long in use in relation to Shakespeare's plays since it was introduced by G. Wilson Knight and Caroline Spurgeon, has the merit of taking Yeats seriously as a playwright. What follows, accordingly, is an examination of Yeats's poetic imagery, not for its own sake but as one of several means of communicating and enriching meaning on stage. It is a method peculiarly apt for Yeats's drama because he was quite conscious of the role of imagery as an organizing and thematic force in poetry and drama. In 'Certain Noble Plays of Japan', for example, he asks tentatively:

I wonder am I fanciful in discovering in the plays themselves . . . a playing upon a single metaphor, as deliberate as the echoing rhythm of line in Chinese and Japanese painting [?] . . . In European poetry I remember Shelley's continually repeated fountain and cave, his broad stream and solitary star. In neglecting character . . . they [Japanese dramatists] have made possible a hundred lovely intricacies.[3]

In his own plays for dancers, Yeats elaborated key images for two basic purposes: to establish a sense of place, rendered sacred by

mystic or supernatural associations; to articulate currents of feeling
hidden beneath various calm surfaces.

At the Hawk's Well/Yoro

Images of wind, hazel tree, leaves, stones and the well in *At the
Hawk's Well* establish at the outset a setting of a sacred place in
wild and desolate surroundings: this 'barbarous spot'. The condition of tree, leaves and well is quite significant: stripped, withered
and empty, respectively, indicating the sterility which the Young
Man is about to oppose by his heroic attitude to experience. Thus
the topography is metaphoric. The water and the hazel trees, in
particular, are symbols of life and wisdom.

The Old Man is associated with the dry leaves. This is done
indirectly through his gradual alignment with the Guardian, who
is 'Worn out from raking its [the well's] dry bed, / Worn out from
gathering up the leaves'. This listlessness is commented on by the
Old Man: 'You seem as dried up as the leaves and sticks.' At the
end of the play, however, the Musicians sing on behalf of the
withered tree: 'Who but an idiot would praise/A withered tree?'
The Old Man's feelings, his attitude to life, are thus defined in relation to the barren tree and dead leaves. He think she is more alive
than these (and than the Guardian), but his prudence nevertheless
drives him to hide away from the water that flows, from genera-
tion, and from the Guardian transformed into demonic energy.

The Young Man, on the other hand, is associated with the hawk.
This is both an actual hawk in nature and a symbol. The Young
Man describes it:

> As I came hither
> A great grey hawk swept down out of the sky,
> And though I have good hawks, the best in the world
> I had fancied, I have not seen its like. It flew
> As though it would have torn me with its beak,
> Or blinded me, smiting me with its great wing.
> I had to draw my sword to drive it off . . .
> Could I but find a means to bring it down
> I'd hood it. (pp. 406–7)

The hawk is a powerful image of energy, which the Young Man
by his nature wishes to harness. When the Guardian is possessed,
she becomes a hawk-woman and the image takes on a sexual meaning. It is hard to agree with Richard Ellmann that the hawk 'symbolizes logic and abstract thought'.[4] The hawk is clearly
associated with supernatural power, as is the hawk in Ibsen's *Brand*

which eventually leads Brand to the ice-palace where, in the avalanche which destroys him, he hears the answer to his appeal for divine illumination: 'He is the God of love.'[4a] The hawk is also a symbol of freedom, like the eagle in romantic imagery such as Sheridan Knowles used in his version of *William Tell* (1825):

> Scaling yonder peak,
> I saw an eagle wheeling near its brow:
> O'er the abyss his broad expanded wings
> Lay calm and motionless upon the air,
> As if he floated there without their aid,
> By the sole act of his unlorded will . . .
>   . . . Instinctively
> I bent my bow; yet kept he rounding still
> His airy circle, as in the delight
> Of measuring the ample range beneath . . .
>   . . . I could not shoot! —
> 'Twas liberty.[5]

In Yeats, however, in contrast to Knowles, the bird does not remain a mere icon, an external image of liberty, but becomes integrated in the action as an expression of the fatal attractiveness of supernatural energy.

Whereas the desolate imagery at the beginning of *At the Hawk's Well* creates a certain emptiness, the naturalistic imagery of *Yoro* produces a quite different effect; one of peace. The *waki* establishes this tranquillity (in nature and also, by implication, in Japanese society) by telling his audience that there is no wind blowing through the oak branches; it is calm — there is not even the whisper of leaves.

Similarly, the old man's first sequence of songs establishes his ethereal state:

> An old man wakes up early,
> His mind talks to the moon above the thatched roof
> His body floats on the frost of a wooden bridge
> The snow on his head accumulates

His metaphors, suggesting his frailty prior to taking the miraculous water, are poetic images conveying a wistful loosening of his bonds with the earth. His mind, described as discoursing with the moon, drifts away romantically from everyday concerns. His body loses substance; it floats, whilst the wintry images of frost and snow indicate his extreme old age, his white hair.

The water images in *Yoro*, similarly, combine naturalism plus poetry. The miraculous water itself forms a fountain (an archetypal fountain of life) in a pool under a rocky waterfall, and then joins the mainstream. The text refers to the sound of the mountain stream, and also to the water of a mountain well, to waves; it likens a man's life to the foam on a stream, it refers to water as beautiful water, implying that it is also valuable, to be equated with gold, silver and precious stones. The chorus, which was given some of these descriptions, is also given one of the most beguiling suggestions, making a more cosmic, if fanciful link — 'let's scoop some water together with the reflection of the moon on it'.

The old man says the water is medicine, and also refers to a Chinese legend about *kikusui*, which proved a medicine for longevity (and also inspired another Noh play entitled *Kikujido*). This kind of reference to Chinese culture assumed the kind of knowledge European writers assumed their readers would have through their own classical heritage.

Ze-Ami uses water as it moves through different stages — spring, stream, river, torrent — as a metaphorical way of representing the then obviously hierarchical Japanese. Thus the limpid spring represents divinity, and, by association, the Emperor, descendant of the gods. The wider river, filled by many streams, and so less pristine, still has its value as it assures the cultivation of the fields, and is thus associated with the (food-producing) peasantry. When the upper reaches of the stream are clean, cleaner water fills its lower reaches. Consequently, as the noble Emperor Yuryaku acts impeccably, his noble actions permeate all Japanese society.

The eternal aspects of water are suggested in various ways. Right at the beginning of this piece the old man tells us about the colour of the mountain stream, saying 'clean water is green'. The implication is that this clear water reflects the surrounding green of the pine trees growing behind it, themselves symbols of the unchanging.

The succouring aspects of water, as an essential source of life, are evoked by a reference to rain and dew being the parents of every tree, plant and flower. Different forms of water, whether inland or oceanic, are linked: they are the same element. And, finally, there is a spiritual understanding of water as *nori-no-mizu*, a Buddhist symbol for attaining inner cleanliness, whereby obsessive desires are washed away, the soul purified. This play, unlike *At the Hawk's Well*, is definitely a religious, ritualistic, piece. The presence of the benign god, Yoryu-kannonbosatsu, representing Buddhism in the area, illustrates this. His dancing to divine music, as flowers fall from the heavens, proves the power and grace of the spiritual in life.

The Only Jealousy of Emer/Aoino-Ue

A fisherman's house close to the seashore is the basic setting for a play in which 'the Sidhe / Are dexterous fishers and they fish for men / With dreams upon the hook'. The most active and dangerous element in the play comes from below the sea, namely Fand, wife of Mananaan Mac Lir. Thus the opening song, establishing the setting, uses images that the audience soon find repeated in a metaphoric guise, signifying the spiritual plight of the dead Cuchulain. The image of the sea is also used by Emer to express her common interest with Eithne Inguba: 'We're but two women struggling with the sea.' But it is only Emer who so struggles, since Fand is her major rival now. Thus the last moments of the play suggest that the Ghost of Cuchulain has left the confines of the fisherman's hut and is being led by Fand along the seashore: 'Hear how the horses trample on the shore.' That shore is the limit between two worlds, of nature and the supernatural. The final irony, after Emer has released Cuchulain from the danger of that limit or boundary is seen in Eithne's claim: 'And it is I that won him from the sea.' Only the audience knows how literally she means this and how totally false the claim is.

The imagery of seabird and shell, in the opening song, relates to the tragic trial which Emer has to undergo; it is paralleled in the play by the imagery of the moon, associated with beauty. Fand, the Woman of the Sidhe, possesses almost perfect beauty, but she suffers a lack of human love which might give her completion. Sea and moon are naturally related; the tides being governed by the moon. But the beauty of seashells are in turn created by tidal motions. All is connected, just as are dead and living in a mighty cosmic pattern. Yeats's imagery powerfully evokes Emer's dilemma in the face of this natural conspiracy.

To a lesser extent, images of hearth and flames, of kisses and of arms and hands, serve to integrate characters and themes in the action. Emer tries to keep a fire going in order to keep at bay the power of Mananaan, but, ominously, she fails. Here one recalls, perhaps, the fire in *On Baile's Strand* which was part of the oath ceremony binding Cuchulain to the values of the hearth and to Conchubar's will. That fire has now been extinguished by the power of the sea, by Mananaan, and in order to redress that power Emer must release Cuchulain from the hearth and its values, from fidelity. Cuchulain's inability to kiss Fand recalls both Emer's and Eithne Inguba's fear of kissing the Figure, and lends significance to Fand's pressure for unity of being. As to arms, there is Bricriu's withered arm, which Eithne finds unbearable; contrasted with Cuchulain's cry upon returning from the dead: 'Your arms! Your arms!' The warmth of embrace which Fand desired is denied her; the arms of Emer will never embrace Cuchulain in love either; never again will come the moment he dreams of in his remorse:

> O, Emer, Emer, there we stand;
> Side by side and *hand in hand*
> Tread the threshold of the house
> As when our parents married us.[6]

Instead, Emer in her isolation will resemble a statue, though her heart will beat just as warmly for Cuchulain: so the final song says.

Aoino-ue's most striking use of symbolism is the folded cloth, which represents the sick woman, Aoine-ue. (It is a folded *kosode*, a *kimono* which a court lady of the Heian period wore under a ceremonial one.) This gains symbolic life when a courtier announces that the Prime Minister's daughter is seriously ill, and that neither medical treatment nor exorcism has helped her.

The lady who has caused Aoi's pain is Rokujo, herself suffering intensely from hatred and jealousy. Rokujo's own anguish is summed up by several images — such as a combination of broken wheels and transitory flowers.

When the vengeful spirit of Princess Rokujo, recalling how her rival, Aoi, had insolently crashed into her carriage at a religious festival, sings 'I am sorry for *yugawo* and the carriage with broken wheels', she is elaborating on her own misery. This public humiliation, symbolized by her broken carriage wheels, and linked with a reference to *yugawo*, a short-lived flower opening briefly on summer evenings, shows that she feels her happiness with her husband to have been as temporary as the evening-flowering *yugawo* (now pronounced *yugao*, and misinterpreted by Ezra Pound as a reference to another mistress in *The Tales of Genji*). Similarly, another flower image, suiting this very sophisticated, courtly play, is that of a morning glory. In comparing herself with this dazzling, but equally short-lived bloom (which withers as the day develops) Princess Rokujo indicates the brevity of her triumphs at court. Images such as these reinforce basic Buddhist beliefs in the transience of all things. Whilst the strong contrast between her recollection of past pleasure and the heat of her present anger, symbolized by images of fire, adds to the piquancy of her position, a reference

to a mirror, finally introduces a note of realism as the play's
emotional temperature begins to cool.

The Dreaming of the Bones/Nishikigi

Yeats sets the scene economically and at the same time suggests
that it is an image of occlusion or shadow. He wants to suggest the
twilight world between the living and the dead:

> The hour before dawn and the moon covered up;
> The little village of Abbey is covered up;
> The little narrow trodden way that runs
> From the white road to the Abbey of Corcomroe
> Is covered up;[7]

The repetition of 'covered up' supplies the image of a veil that shuts
off the unseen world.

There is fairly conventional use made of imagery of owl and
cock, representing night and dawn, but these could also be
registered as symbols of the occult, the owl of Minerva and the
cock of Hades.

The most interesting use of imagery lies in the topography itself,
first the ruined abbey and then the view of Galway 'in the breaking
light'. Whereas there is a certain amount of realistic detail here,
especially in the description of the abbey and its tomb of Donough
O'Brien, the point made is that these places are despoiled:

> In the old days we should have heard a bell
> Calling the monks before day broke to pray;
> And when the day had broken on the ridge,
> The crowing of its cocks.   (pp. 768–9)

'In the old days', but not now. The place is no longer sacred; prayer
is no longer heard here; the cocks are no longer associated with
matins. To the Young Man, it is 'the enemy', the English, who are
responsible for this profanation. Likewise 'the enemy' is responsible for the desecration of Galway: here the language is violent in
its mimesis of the attack on the abbey buildings:

> The enemy has toppled roof and gable,
> And torn the panelling from ancient rooms;   (pp.773–4)

The detail of the 'roof' echoes the earlier line: 'Is there no house
. . . the enemy has not unroofed?' Thus the despoliation of Galway
is made to seem a profanation too. The non-existence of a possible
rival to Bayeux or Caen (in the first edition) or 'little Italian town'

opens up to the imagination (like the non-existent bell earlier) a vacuum. This vacuum is filled by two different kinds of dreaming: the Young Man's political kind and the lover's penitential kind. Thus the subject of the play arises with beautiful appropriateness out of the imagery of place.

The feelings of the Young Man, also, are early on established as fearful, superstitious and militantly republican. Buildings lend — as it were — concreteness to these feelings: between the General Post Office, the wall against which he would be shot if caught, and the crumbling walls of both the abbey and of Galway the Young Man runs his course.

The feelings of the lovers are expressed by the image of 'shadows, / Hovering between a thorn-tree and a stone'. They can have no definition, no constancy, until that gap is stopped, and that 'hovering' terminated. The insubstantial character of their relationship, after death, is finally expressed by the Young Man in imagery that combine several of the preceding images: the architectural ruins, art-work, and clouds covering light (recalling the First Musicians' opening speech):

> All the ruin,
> All, all their handiwork is blown away
> As though the mountain air had blown it away . . .
> A cloud floats up
> And covers all the mountain-head in a moment;[8]

Then comes the resolving line: 'And now it [the cloud] lifts and they are swept away.' The dispersal of the cloud exposes the abbey, the road, the facts of historical reality; and with that exposure comes the dismissal of the lovers' presence: they become absent like the bell, like the glory that once attached to Galway, like the sanctity that attached to the abbey. The plangency of the moment is reinforced by this imagery of natural dispersal attuned to supernatural inter-dependence. It is if the Young Man, in controlling history, also controls nature: an awesome responsibility, which he is finally relieved to relinquish.

Nishikigi is particularly rich in the kind of literary overlay, punning and linguistic suggestion found in all Noh plays. It relies heavily on background information — anecdotal, and geographical, for example, as well as literary. Where one word carries double, or treble, images it is hardly surprising that non-native Japanese speakers can rarely gather the fullest implications of a poetic clue or telling the guide line.

Thus in *Nishikigi* the travelling monk draws the audience's attention to the scene of the action, mentioning 'There was never anybody heard of Mount Shinobu but had a kindly feeling for it'.[9] Shinobu, the name of a mountain north of Tokyo, is also synonymous with having an affectionate feeling for someone, or something, and so is deliberately used to evoke the underlying nostalgia of the opening tale. As well as puns such as this, accepted Japanese metaphors are also employed to heighten the poetic imagery. The monk's discovery of the haunted site evoked in the plot is supposed to be by chance. His journey is compared with that of clouds blown hither and thither by the wind: 'I go about with my heart set upon no particular place what so ever, and with no other man's flag in my hand, no more than a cloud has.'[10] This, according to Ezra Pound, in *The Classic Noh Theatre of Japan*, is a reference to the monk's not following any man's banner (being free, by inference, from any aristocratic or military authority). In fact this flag image is a classical Japanese metaphor for clouds billowing in the breeze.

The lead's frustrated love is summed up, concisely, by two telling quotations (altered very slightly at the ends to run into the text), which would have been as immediately recognizable to native audiences as, say, key quotations from Shakespeare to a later English-speaking public. Thus, brief lines from the poets Tooru Minamoto and Narihira Ariwara establish the lead's anguish, and in no uncertain terms.

Narihira's *waka* poem refers to an unhappy man passing a sleepless night thinking of his love. References to insects singing incessantly indicate his tragic predicament since *naku*, in Japanese, means both to sing and to cry. Similarly, another telling pun is employed in the phrase:

> *mininasukotowa namidagawa*
> *nagarete hayaki toshitsukikana*

In this, the first line suggests that the man has abandoned himself to grief and that his tears have formed a river. While the second line indicates the speed with which this has happened. The word *nagarete* plays on the poet's links between a swift-flowing river and passing time, since it refers to both the flowing of a river and the fleeting of time.

Calvary

The opening and closing songs are dominated by bird imagery. The white heron, solitary and motionless, 'Shivers in dumbfounded dream'. He symbolizes something which lies outside the divine plan, insofar as the human imagination can conceive that. In another context, the poet John Montague speaks of the heron as a 'radiant initial, illuminating the gospel of the absurd'.[11] Yeats, however, while seeing the heron as radiant, and as within nature's framework, does not see him as illuminating a gospel of the absurd but as standing (rigidly) outside the Christian gospel: 'God has not died for the white heron.' Thus place is far less important in *Calvary* than philosophical theme. The imagery conspires to elucidate the nature of Christ's agony, viewed as a timeless reflection on love united with freedom.

In his note on *Calvary*, Yeats said:

I have used my bird-symbolism in these songs to increase the objective loneliness of Christ by contrasting it with a loneliness, opposite in kind, that unlike His as can be, whether joyous or sorrowful, sufficient to itself. I have surrounded Him with the images of those He cannot save . . .[12]

In the final song, as Karen Dorn points out, the imagery of lonely seabird and ger-eagle recall Lazarus and Judas earlier on.[13] In the play itself, however, Lazarus uses an image of a rabbit in a hole to describe his perception of Christ's deliverance:

> You dragged me to the light as boys drag out
> A rabbit when they have dug its hole away;   (p.783)

This image indicates how for Lazarus, as rabbit, Christ's love was a violation of natural rights: the violence of his language registers the resistance to Christ's attention. Judas also uses animal rather than bird-imagery: 'I could not bear to think you had but to whistle / And I must do.' He did not want to be God's working dog. The moment of betrayal, however, is linked with the heron's experience: 'There was no live thing near me but a heron.' The heron, as Judas saw it, was 'So full of itself that it seemed terrified'. Ironically, he does not see that the identification of himself and the heron implies his own enslaving self-love.

The image of the dice, made from animal (sheep's) bone, serves to characterize the Three Roman Soldiers in their indifference to Christ's love. They gamble with the dice for Christ's cloak, indifferent to who wins:

> What does it matter?
> One day one loses and the next day wins.   (p. 786)

Related to material goods such indifference is liberal; but linked to the owner in this situation the indifference reveals a horrific surrender of choice. The soldiers represent a godless society, exposed to chance and disguising this exposure as the essence of freedom. Yeats imagines their saviour as knowing all this and suffering the effect: despair.

The poetic images employed in religious Noh plays are limited. Their primary function is to build up an impression of peace and prosperity. There are clichés: the continuous sound of a waterfall, the evergreen quality of pine trees suggest eternity: turtles and cranes are seen as symbols of longevity, of happiness. Such symbols tend to outweigh negative imagery, such as *shurado*, or Buddhist references to souls of *samurai* encapsulated in their own obsessions.

Just as the tolling of church bells marked time in medieval European society, so the tolling of the slower, indeed often lugubrious, Buddhist temple bells punctuated the lives of the early Japanese. The prevailing resonance of Buddhist temple bells is evoked in *Takasago*, as a symbol of the spread of Buddhist principles, of the orderliness of a society run according to Buddhist teaching.

Similarly, in *Miwa*, the idea of regularly giving offerings to the dead, a crucial aspect of the whole pattern of Buddhist rituals, is stressed by the monk's tale of a woman who regularly shows her respect for other realities by bringing water and a *shikimi* branch to a tomb. When we later learn that this woman is none other than a goddess in disguise, the value of her actions is enhanced still further: they provide an obvious example to be echoed in everyday existence.

X. RITUALS

As early as 'Samhain: 1904' Yeats saw a link between ritual and the folk. He wanted, he said, audience involvement such as greeted the performance of Douglas Hyde's play in Gaelic, *An Posadh*, and he continued:

> It was not merely because of its position in the play that the Greek chorus represented the people, and the old ballad-singers waited at the end of every verse till their audience had taken up the chorus; while Ritual, *the most powerful form of drama*, differs from the ordinary form, because everyone who hears it is also a player.[1]

Some twenty-five years later he wrote to the artist T. Sturge Moore. 'I always feel my work is not drama but the ritual of a lost faith.'[2] This claim implies that Yeats consciously wrote plays which sought to put on stage spiritual realities now ignored or forgotten. His prime interest was, of course, in symbolism; he said: 'All symbolic art should arise out of a real belief.'[3] Belief in the supernatural, and its powers of intervention in human affairs, was what he had here in mind.

In the *Four Plays for Dancers*, the ritual of the folding and unfolding of the cloth, while on one level a mere invented device to replace the unwanted stage curtain, was also an image of order, giving formal design to the action. It was, however, purely theatrical, purely gestural, without either Celtic or Christian significance. It served to set the tone of each play as ceremonious; no more. Contrast, instead, the final lines of a poem by Thomas Kinsella, in which he has confronted his own image in a mirror while shaving, and discovered the end of youth:

> I fold my towel with what grace I can,
> Not young and not renewable, but man.[4]

In these lines, the folding of a real towel is combined with the word 'grace', and suddenly releases Christian and aesthetic meaning: the folding becomes a moral act, of acceptance and courage. In Yeats's plays such meaning is never inherent in the ritual of the folding and unfolding of the cloth.

Those dramatic rituals that do exist in *Four Plays for Dancers* apparently contain ironies. In *At the Hawk's Well* the Old Man goes through the motions of lighting a fire, which serves as a sacred flame at this shrine where the well of immortality is situated. But the Old Man lacks the courage suggested by the fire: his ritual is an empty one, or it is simply irrelevant in the context of the terrible powers surrounding the well. Instead, the fire within the Young Man, who grasps his spear to join in battle with fate, appears of greater moment. In all of the *Four Plays for Dancers* it is as if existing rituals are ineffectual. Emer's attempt to keep alight a fire which will keep at bay the feared arrival of Mananaan or his forces to claim the spirit of Cuchulain is likewise in vain. She has hardly finished tending the ceremonial fire when the Woman of the Sidhe arrives from the Country-under-Wave; Emer must put out the fire in her own heart in order to defeat this rival and release Cuchulain's spirit from thrall. In *The Dreaming of the Bones* the night on the mountain-side is a vigil, an experience for the Young Man which would have had his 'Grandam' on her knees praying for the souls in purgatory. This modern Young Man, while still conversant with the traditions of penance exacted from dead sinners, refuses to participate in the ritual or scenario the ghosts lay before him. His faith is in the new republic, not in the 'lost kingdom' of the dead. In *Calvary*, too, Christ's crucifixion, the supreme ritual of Christian worship, is given a form which shuts off the flow of love which might (as in Dante's final image of the rose in *Paradiso*, for example) set up a current unifying man and the supernatural. Yeats's vision is tragic. He uses ritual so as to express the breakdown in modern times of the human-divine relationship. The rituals he fabricates are all ironic, all eloquent of human failure.

*

Yeats's plays are not religious in the oriental sense. Although this poet dealt with supernatural realities in his plays, he tried not to make them religious, since he believed in the supernatural but did not believe in any existing form of religious establishment. Noh developed along with Buddhism as Noh troupes developed their art form. These troupes depended on powerful religious establishments, such as temples and shrines, and provided an extension of their teaching. There is a piece called *Okina* which is usually performed first of all to start a full day's programme on festive occasions. This piece is not a dramatic play. It is, itself, a ritual within the tradition of the Noh theatre; its lines do not carry conventional meanings. Some historians claim that it is an imitation of an early Buddhist service. Like miracle or mystery players in the medieval European period, Noh actors (then called *sangakushi*) were commissioned to interpret services for the ignorant. Though Noh later developed into a highly sophisticated form of performing art, it never severed its original links with the Japanese religious establishment. Buddhist influence is strongly felt in all these plays with characters constantly praying to appropriate deities for spiritual relief. Yeats's plays are 'rituals of lost faith', while Noh plays demonstrate a strong spiritual faith in both Buddhism and Shinto (which co-exist happily).

Secondly, in a ritual the place of performance turns into a place of worship. But Yeats used Lady Cunard's drawing-room for the first performance of *At the Hawk's Well*. He chose a more sympathetic, sophisticated, invited audience for his first daring attempt, probably from the fear of ridicule. His *Four Plays for Dancers* were rarely performed in a theatre before a public audience. Since Yeats's plays are not religious, they are incapable of turning a theatre into a place of worship. They merely provide glimpses into this poet's visions, of an unreal, supernatural world. Noh plays, on the other hand, expound religious doctrines and encourage the worship of both Shinto and Buddhist gods.

Thirdly, a ritual will change the persons involved in it, as Richard Taylor says in his *A Reader's Guide to the Plays of W. B. Yeats*. But Yeats's characters do not change throughout his plays. Taylor argues (p. 59) that in *At the Hawk's Well* young Cuchulain changes when he hears the challenging war cries of 'Aoife and all her troop'. He then realizes his own destiny as a warrior. In this sense, Taylor claims this play can be regarded as a ritualistic play. The realization of Cuchulain's fate is a by-product, however, since Cuchulain was at the well to gain water to get immortality. In *The Only Jealousy of Emer* Cuchulain's wife makes a bargain with Bricriu (who tried to stop the Sidhe winning Cuchulain) but realizes that, despite her love, she herself will never have her husband back. Yeats is negative in *The Dreaming of the Bones*. He does not free the ghostly couple from the curse laid on them, from which they have already suffered for seven hundred years. In *Calvary* no characters change: Jesus Christ dies not so much as a divine being, but as an ordinary man lost in his own doubts. None of Yeats's *Four Plays for Dancers* inspires worship of any kind, except of the beautiful. This merely reflects Yeats's loss of faith in all established religions.

Noh plays, on the other hand, show dramatic psychological changes in their main characters, when spiritual power is evoked, often by prayer. In *Aoine-ue*, for example, Princess Rokujo gives up her demonic revenge on her rival, Lady Aoino-ue, when she is powerfully moved by the telling prayers of the monk, *yamabushi*. Again, in *Nishikigi*, a travelling monk's devout prayers save the earth-bound souls of a man and woman who died in a state of emotional obsession. The growth and attainment of personal harmony, which are obvious in the evolution of the main characters in *Aoino-ue* and *Nishikigi*, are reflected by all the other characters. In *Yoro*, and other god plays, the human characters receive blessings from the divine characters. (If, occasionally, as in a play called *Shunkan*, the conclusion is not resolved happily, the main character is punished for his atheism.) Specific blessings, as souls are released from their private purgatories, are shared with the audience who, by their emotionally sharing in the drama, have experienced a re-enactment of a ritualistic duel between good and evil (often represented by a demon), in which good triumphs. The underlying faith of authors, actors and audience forms a common ground of understanding in which a trance-like intensity can be evoked to re-enact the necessary miracles inspiring an optimistic community. In Yeats's plays, the poet's own mistrust of self, of state, and of organized religion fails to produce firm foundations for any such cathartic climaxes.

XI. CONCLUSION

This study is not intended to be comprehensive. Its focus is on the
Four Plays for Dancers and their posited relationships with the
Japanese Noh drama. The core of the book, accordingly, lies in the
comparative chapters. In these, point for point the features that
serve to give drama its formal structure have been examined, so
that the differences between classical Noh and Yeats's *Four Plays
for Dancers* can emerge as well as the affinities. This exercise was
undertaken in no kind of flat-footed assumption that drama can be
understood solely by analysis : on the contrary, it was done in the
full and prior awareness that theatre, of its very nature, is a magical
process, whereby through performance language and action create
in the audience something new, some startling perception or set of
feelings. The comparative exercise was persisted in — relentlessly
— because it has never been done before, and it is a necessary step
in the full understanding of the relationship between Yeats and
Noh.

It is *only* a step, however. The wider implications of this study
extend past 1921 (when *Four Plays for Dancers* was published) to
1939 (when *The Death of Cuchulain* was finished). Much happened
to Yeats as playwright in between, as several existing studies of
Yeats's plays have well shown. Yet it is not possible to understand
these later plays, from *The Resurrection* on, without realizing to
what extent they represent a pragmatic abandonment of the
Japanese model. To be sure, elements remain: haphazard use of
masks, use of music and dance, and use of symbolic setting, to
name just a few. But these later plays are eclectic, ironic, and combative where the *Four Plays for Dancers* were more purely
theatrical. The later plays fill more and more with bitterness : a
harsh criticism of the ignobility and brutality of modern values. Of
course, they have their own place in Yeats's canon and in the
history of modern theatre and drama: *The Words Upon the
Window-pane* will always have its band of followers so long as
there are readers of the biographies of Swift and Yeats alike;
Purgatory, in its strange combination of longing and horror will
continue to fascinate all for whom modern tragedy is not dead;

117

while *The Herne's Egg* and *The Death of Cuchulain,* even more than *A Full Moon in March,* will tease and tempt readers, performers, and directors with texts that challenge conventional notions of personality, truth, moral value and heroism in exciting theatrical styles.

A study and/or a series of productions of these later plays would establish clearly how far Yeats moved away from the Noh and used the theatre to express his individual tragic vision. To a considerable degree he abandoned the selflessness implicit in the Noh in order to make a space for his personal, if indirect, statements on the dissolution of western civilization. What the gains and losses were, however remain to be freshly assessed.

*

The Cat and the Moon, written in 1917, was not included in *Four Plays for Dancers.*[1] It is sadly missed. Whether or not those four plays would work together on stage in an evening's programme, they need relief. The atmosphere generated by four tragic tales is too intense, the mood evoked by the Musicians too insistently elegiac, to assure an audience's pleasure. Even if divided by an interval, the four plays would, in performance, perhaps be uncomfortably cathartic. If *The Cat and the Moon* were included, however, say at the opening of the second part of the programme (Yeats himself suggested it might be played in between *At the Hawk's Well* and *The Dreaming of the Bones,*[2] forgetting, it would appear, that *The Only Jealousy of Emer* occupies that space) it would go some way towards providing the relaxation and restoration necessary for a vital theatrical response. But the omission of *The Cat and the Moon* is indicative of Yeats's vulnerability as dramatist. That play has all the right ingredients for the Noh form of farce, the *kyogen* : a grotesque quality in the characterization of Lame Man and Blind Beggar (suggested in their masks), a visit to a holy well (allowing a lively combination of parody and simple faith), use of the supernatural in a naive but direct form, and in the end a dance which is theatrically effective because it establishes the magical transformation on which drama ultimately depends :

The Lame Beggar begins to dance, at first clumsily, moving about with his stick, then he throws away the stick and dances more and more quickly. Whenever he strikes the ground strongly with his lame foot the cymbals clash. He goes out dancing . . . [3]

Throwing away the stick is the ultimate risk of the playwright; it is walking the tighrope without a safety net. As dramatist, Yeats did not do this often enough, yet it is a gesture essential to the successful presentation of his dance plays. What it amounts to, in this case, is the burying of philosophical subtext in joyous physical action. Reading Yeats's notes to *The Cat and the Moon* one would have to think that the farce was an essay in metaphysics, whereas the energy of the play, its linguistic and physical rumbustiousness, is what communicates to the audience and carries the images which absorb and sustain interest.

One worries that if Yeats did not realize what he had got when he wrote *The Cat and the Moon* perhaps he insufficiently was aware of what he was attempting in *Four Plays for Dancers*. As is apparent from the comparative analyses undertaken in the earlier chapters of this book, there is a lack of finish in the plays, a failure to follow up inspirations and to complete the promise inherent in the material. In particular, the lack of consideration given to the dance itself, its nature, timing, and relation to the style of each play, is disappointing. So, too, is the seeming indifference to unity of design : the ideas on mask, scenery, costume and staging never actually cohere into a realized *praxis*. Of course, lack of a theatre in which to try out ideas with actors and designers must mitigate this particular criticism; Yeats's alienation from the Abbey Theatre during the second decade of this century paralyzed his efforts to create a new dramatic style. Yet one could wish he had determined more to find the right theatre, and saved us all those dreary notes about how weary he was quarrying his own stone and so forth. His attitude towards these dance plays was, it must be said, too aristocratic, too amateur, to achieve their full potential.

*

What remains, even though the experiment was in many respects a failure, is the strange adventure on Yeats's part to find in his drama common ground with a form from the other side of the world, antithetical to western culture, alien in language and altogether different in style and conventions. What Yeats perceived, albeit through a glass darkly, was undoubtedly a set of narrative procedures and a use of signs and symbols which transcended both place and language. As Jan Kott has said of the Noh :

Of all the kinds of writing, this system of theatrical signs is closest to calligraphy . . . A sign becomes more important than its meaning, a medium more important than its message.[4]

It is clear to Kott that here is the essence of what attracted Yeats, and not only Yeats, working in a debased theatre of realism.

Theatre at its most vital celebrates not timebound actuality but the timeless, key situations in human experience. Images on a stage, consequently, form a special language and manifest the universality of theatre. They may explain why Yeats — even though he lacked persistence in this area — could find and create for audiences mutual understanding in those plays modelled on Japanese Noh.

The *Four Plays for Dancers* stands out as a marvellous discovery of the richness of Japanese classical theatre. Yeats's very genius, however, ensured that his admiration for the Noh had to give way to a form subjectively responsive to his personal, home-made philosophy. Consequently, his encounter with the Japanese drama in translation, coupled with his concentrated efforts to write in that form, compose an emblem of Yeatsian heroic failure. It is none the less admirable for that.

NOTE ON *TAKAHIME,* A NOH
ADAPTATION OF *AT THE*
HAWK'S WELL

At the Hawk's Well was adapted in the Noh theatre by Mario
Yokomichi, first as *Takano-I* and then as *Takahime.* The first adaptation is structurally close to Noh plays but unlike Noh in its
essence. The second adaptation is somewhere between a Noh play
and Yeats's play. The difficulty in adapting this play only proves
the point made in this conclusion of Yeats's heroic failure to adapt
Noh plays. *Takahime* is not really included in the repertoire of the
Noh theatre, but is occasionally performed by actors who are searching for further possibilities for the development of their theatre.

Characters in *Takahime* including Cuchulain as a young prince
of a country called Hashi, the Guardian of the Well as a Mountain
Spirit in the shape of a young girl, and an Old Man as a ghost.
Yokomichi recognised the Old Man as the lead, and created the Old
Man's ghost according to Noh traditions.

Yokomichi follows Noh tradition in other ways, for example in
his use of two prompters and stage hands. He is also similar on
choosing a flute player and three drummers. He differs, however,
in allowing his five Rocks to leave the stage, and thereafter their
part is taken by eight chorus figures. In creating these five speaking
and singing rocks, the playwright is original.

The performance of *Takahime* starts by fading all the lights in
both the auditorium and the stage. In absolute darkness, the musicians play a short sequence on a flute and two drums. Then the
stage is half lighted, but the auditorium is left dark. These lighting
arrangements are different from Yeats's lighting arrangements
which used the permanent light of a huge chandelier.

The first four Noh musicians appear across the bridge and sit at
the far back of the main stage. Two prompters and stage hands
carry in a miniature set of a mountain, which symbolises Zelkova
Wood, and then they sit at the back right-hand side facing the
audience. The Young Girl enters at the same time and moves to the
left side of the stage.

Scene I

Musicians play a short piece with a flute and two drums. This short piece of music sets an appropriate atmosphere on the stage. Then the First Rock starts singing;

> The fountain is dried up
> The fountain is dried up
> Cold winds blow through Zelkova Wood.

This opening song follows the Noh tradition of three lines all together, the first repeated. Here Yokomichi only adapted the essence of the first sequence of song by the First Musician in *At the Hawk's Well*. His adaptation is free, however, when the rocks converse to describe Cuchulain climbing the hill and his predicted unsuccessful attempt to get the miraculous water, his loss of youth and consequent death. This scene ends with lines taken directly from the translation of *At the Hawk's Well*:

> The boughs of the hazel shake,
> The sun goes down in the west.

Scene II

Yokomichi dropped eighteen lines of the original text, and began this scene by the first Rock's announcement of the Old Man's arrival: 'Look an old man is climbing up hither.' This is repeated by the second Rock, following the Noh tradition: 'Indeed, an old man is climbing up hither.' In his original text, the Old Man has watched for water at the well for fifty years, but in Yokomichi's adaptation it is more exaggerated:

> First Rock: Fifty years.
> Third and Fourth Rock: No, a hundred years.
> First, Second and Fifth Rock: No, a thousand years.

The first musician's speech about the Old Man making a fire and the following songs by all the musicians are faithfully adapted in Yokomichi's text.

Scene III

The Old Man's first speech and the following conversation between

him and Cuchulain are close to Yeats's original text, although a few
lines have been edited from the original referring to 'woman':
'. . . . shedding of men's blood and for the love of woman.' and
'Nor beautiful woman to be carried.' He only simplified a few lines,
such as The Old Man's speech. 'No. Go from this accursed place.
This place belongs to me, girl there, and those others, Deceivers of
men,' simply into,'No, this well belongs to me.' Yokomichi adds
three lines immediately after this, to be spoken by all the rocks
denying the Old Man's claim. 'No, this well belongs to the girl. The
well belongs to the girl, To the girl who is the mountain spirit.'

After the Old Man's long speech starting with 'One whom the
dancers cheat. I came like you', Yokomichi changed the original
text, and made this character announce that he is the Ghost of the
Old Man who died there. Cuchulain's response to this is unlike
Noh. He does not show any sympathy, but simply says, 'Strange,
you are a living soul. None the less, I shall wait here.'

Scene IV

This scene begins with a hawk cry. Yokomichi at first did not
accept Yeats's plot here, made Cuchulain believe it was a hawk cry,
and omitted several lines from the latter's speech. Yokomichi's text
reads as follows:

> Cuchulain: Listen, a hawk cries.
> Where is this hawk cry coming from?
> Old Man: No, that is not a hawk.
> Cuchulain: Yes, It is a hawk cry.
> When I reached from the shore to the rocky
> mountain and started climbing the sharp cliff, I
> saw a hawk, it has a sharp golden beak.
> Old Man: (*sings*) That hawk is the mountain spirit . . .

The Woman of the Sidhe is changed into the mountain spirit. At
this point Yokomichi cut short the Old man's speech, and altered
the following thirty-four lines to create mounting pressure on
Cuchulain to leave the island and stress his determination to stay
on.

> All Rocks: (*sing*) Cuchulain cannot escape, either.
> Old Man: Leave this island. Now.

Cuchulain: Old man, you try to deceive me.
           The evil spirit tried to frighten me.
           I am a prince of Hashi, I am not moving.
           (*Young girl moves violently.*)
Cuchulain: Hawk cry.
           The Hawk cries again.
           No, it is the young girl's voice.
           The young girl is making the hawk cries.
Old Man: (*sings*) The young girl is the Hawk.
           She is the mountain spirit.
All Rocks: (*sing*) Young girl moves her body and spreads
           her sleeves. She rubs her hands and shakes her
           hips.
Old Man: Leave this island Cuchulain.

Yokomichi also omitted the dispute between Cuchulain and the
Old Man over the water:

Cuchulain: (*sings*) It is not only the Old Man who has waited
           for the water. There is no difference in waiting,
           whether it is for a thousand years or a day. We
           shall share and drink it together.

Scene V

In Yokomichi's stage direction the Old Man goes into the miniature
mountain like a dream walker, after the Guardian of the Well
throws off her cloak and rises. This gives the actor performing the
role of the Old Man a chance to change masks before his later
appearance.

The mounting tension in Yokomichi's text is created by the
chorus singing repeatedly 'aashiya, ooshiya'. This short piece can
produce a terrifying and mysterious atmosphere.

The Guardian of the Well starts dancing to the music of a flute
and three drums in Yokomichi's version. The Guardian and
Cuchulain fight to fierce music, until Cuchulain falls to the ground,
exhausted, and falls asleep, instead of Yeats's 'drops his sword as
if in a dream and goes out.'

Yokomichi created a few lines to conclude this scene.

All Rocks: (*sing*) Poor Cuchulain,
           If he had not searched for the water,
           If he had not chased the hawk,
           He could have lived with his family,
           He could have had parties with his friends,

And he could have had an easy life.
Poor Cuchulain.

Scene VI

This is the climactic section of the play, and Yokomichi broke Yeats's
First Musician's speech, starting with 'I have heard water splash: it
comes . . .' into nine short phrases to increase the dramatic effect. In
Japanese drama, unlike European drama, repetitions of short phrases
sung sharply can create a strong tension. The following translation will
probably sound odd to European readers:

> First Rock: The time has come.
> All Rocks: The time has come.
> First Rock: When the water wells out.
> All Rocks: Water wells out.
> First Rock: Water.
> All Rocks: Water, Water.

Yokomichi, instead of letting the Guardian of the Well go out, makes
her scoop up the water from the well, and continue to dance. The Guardian goes out when the cloth covering the mountain is taken off, revealing the ghost of the Old Man. From this point Yokomichi ceases to
follow Yeats's text.

All the Rocks go out, and re-appear as a chorus and sit at the left hand
side of the stage.

Scene VII

Yokomichi omitted the scene of Cuchulain's re-appearing after his
chase of the Hawk/Young Girl, and his announcement of his determination to face a battle with Aoife. This scholar concentrated,
instead, on the Old Man. The Japanese adaptation starts with the Old
Man still singing inside the miniature mountain set:

> Old Man: (*sings*) Cuchulain, have you taken the water from
> the well?
> If the water had welled up for you,
> My grudge would have increased,
> Since I have waited unsuccessfully for a hundred
> years.
> On the edge of the well dried leaves are blown about
> by the storm,
> Blowing the tree tops.

The Old Man comes out of the miniature mountain and goes around the stage, accompanied by the piece of music called 'tachi-mawari'. This is unlike Yeats's text, where the Old Man 'creeps up to the well'. The chorus comes on stage to represent elements of the Old Man's feelings. This and the following scenes concentrate on the Old Man's sufferings amd misery.

> Old Man: (*sings*) The perpetual bewitchment.
>   (*The Old Man starts moving to a slow rhythmical tune called* oonori.)
>   The cursed threads.
> Chorus: (*sings*) The cursed threads,
>   Spread over the Old Man,
>   Binding his body tight,
>   He cannot leave the place,
>   Being tied to a boulder of rock,
>   He has become the ghost of the mountain.

Scene VIII

This final sequence can be called 'kiri' and should be sung smoothly and rhythmically, and the lead, the Old Man acts and dances using traditional, symbolic Noh gestures to reinforce the feelings and ideas explained by the chorus. The whole translation of the *kiri* piece is as follows:

> Chorus: (*sings*) The result of seeking the water,
>   The result of seeking the water,
>   His sufferings are endless,
>   His white hair has grown to his shoulders.
>   Ruthless winds from the mountains send down,
>   Heat in Summer, and snow in Winter.
>   Drinking rain water, eating wild birds,
>   He quenched his hunger,
>   Just like the savage monkeys.
>   His dream was never realised,
>   Even when the time came,
>   His dream was never realised.
>   Even when the time came,
>   The curse weakened his arms and his legs,
>   And made him fall,
>   Raging against the ruthless hawk.
> Old Man: Trapped in a delusion.
> Chorus: It is a delusion.
>   Though you think it a delusion,
>   You cannot give up the obsession.
>   Hard to leave the well.

Hard to leave the well.
Thunderous voice rings out among the trees and
rocks,
But the figure is disappearing,
with the storm over the mountain.
With the storm,
the figure had disappeared toward the lines of
mountains.
Zalkov wood alone is left.
Zalkov wood stands still.

*(The Old Man goes out. Cuchulain rises from
sleep, and stamps to conclude the piece of music,
and finishes the performance. Cuchulain leaves.
The prompter and stage hands go out carrying
the mountain props, and then, finally, the musicians and chorus exit.)*

The negative feelings that finally overwhelm the chief character,
the Old Man (although he has no heroic qualities), link this
Japanese version of *At The Hawk's Well* with European tragedies
in a general sense, as their heroes' concluding sufferings can never
be fully atoned for, and put right within their protagonists'
lifetimes. Indeed *Takahime* is less religious, more tragic than
Yeats's original play.

Japanese Noh plays are usually far more positive in their plots,
which do not seek to limit their action to any one dimension or
timespan, as they profit from the greater possibilities of an
optimistic reincarnational framework. In Noh plays, which are an
explanation and demonstration of Japanese religious beliefs, the
protagonist is usually saved by divine intervention, as in the form
of a local deity or through the caring prayers of an itinerant monk.
Souls in various forms of torment, whether physically alive, as in
the case of Princess Rokujo, or otherwise, as when guests are
evoked, are helped in their spiritual evolution.

ACTING IN *THE DREAMING OF THE BONES*

COLLEEN HANRAHAN

By producing both the Noh play *Nishikigi* and the Yeats play *The Dreaming of the Bones*, our small company at University College, Dublin was able to become attuned to the Noh principles and techniques through the direction of Professor Masaru Sekine. Our performance first of *Nishikigi* provided us with an experiential base to try to recreate the authentic acting skills Yeats might have desired for *The Dreaming of the Bones*. A phase of analysis seemed to follow naturally upon this series of catalytic experiences. That analysis was directed towards assessing how our acting employed the Noh and how strategies impacted upon our characterization of the roles in *The Dreaming of the Bones*.

The following selection of the major Noh features as they were experienced in the play are examined for their influence on character formation: (1) mask; (2) *yugen*; (3) physical restraint; (4) travel song; (5) rhythmic incantation. Fenollosa shows a similar array of Noh features to appear as facets of the total unified impression:

The beauty and power of the Noh lie in the concentration. All elements — costume, motion, verse, and music — unite to produce a single clarified impression.[1]

The crystalline unity of a Noh performance is its own transparent, yet almost impenetrable, barrier to the dissection of its elements.

(1) Mask

Although we used masks with great effect in *Nishikigi* for the ghost lovers, we did not use masks for Diarmuid and Dervorgilla in *The Dreaming of the Bones*. Even though Yeats noted that his shades were to be masked, I believe that we did not diverge from the original interpretation because masks are only a representation of the supreme reality encompassed in the actor's role. The absence of masks in *The Dreaming of the Bones* can be reconciled with Noh and with Yeats's own intentions for the play if we consider his views on the mask.

Yeats wrote: 'Style, personality — deliberately adopted and therefore a mask — is the only escape from the hot-faced bargainers and the money changers.'[2] Mask according to Yeats was an affected style or pose adopted to unify the dialectic of opposites surging within us.[3] Every living human wears a mask and in this light Yeats observed that we are not too different from the actors on the stage.

There is a relation between discipline and the theatrical sense. If we cannot imagine ourselves as different from what we are and assume that second self, we cannot impose a discipline upon ourselves, though we may accept one from others. Active virtue as distinguished from the passive acceptance of a current code is therefore theatrically consciously dramatic, the wearing of a mask . . . One constantly notices in very active natures a tendency to pose, or if the pose has become a second self a preoccupation with the effect they are producing.[4]

The phenomenon of internalizing the mask is integral to manifesting the forces in man and offering existential ground for each one to change his way of life.

Masaru Sekine explored this possibility of internalizing characters by having Diarmuid and Dervorgilla in the Yeats play develop the parts without the use of masks. Even in the Noh the mask and the actor are two separate entities, both having to adapt to the reality of the part. Sekine was explicitly trying to encourage the powers of concentration in our actors so that they might perform with mask-like intensity. Before a mask is placed on a Noh actor, he himself must seek release from his own personality.[5] In our rehearsals Masaru Sekine trained all actors to seek their antithetical selves. That internal search is consistent with the Yeats doctrine of mask.

By blocking off the distraction of the individual characteristics of the actors, the masks in *Nishikigi* helped the audience to perceive the ghostly pair as universal forces. This effect was also intended for Diarmuid and Dervorgilla without the use of masks. Such an expectation can be justified in that the organic foundation of Yeats's doctrine of mask extends beyond the actual use of the device of the mask itself. Our evening's production, beginning with *Nishikigi* using masks, permitted the audience to assimilate and respond to the mask imagery and then to catch, by association, the similar treatment in the roles of the ghost lovers without masks in *The Dream-*

ing of the Bones. This strategy seemed to have accomplished our aims for Yeats. An Irish woman in the audience (Mrs. Rachel Burrows), who had produced almost all of Yeats's plays at some time, mentioned to me that it was good not to have used masks in *The Dreaming of the Bones* because the characters of the evening's production were well suited to fall spontaneously into their roles. In particular, Professor Chris Murray, in the role of Diarmuid, she noted, with his silver hair, stately mien, and his resonant expression was well suited to Yeats's Celtic verse.

To a large extent, however, dance replaced the need of masks in our production. The ritual dance of Diarmuid and Dervorgilla choreographed by Masaru Sekine, making heightened use of gesture to create gaps in reality, helped the actors to slip into their ghostly roles naturally. Sekine's ritualistic wheel dance sequence, with its languid spoke-like movements, was somewhat reminiscent of Yeats's gyres in the cycles of the great wheel of time. The movements imaged the parallel between the doomed age represented by the dancing lovers and the new antithetical yet regenerative one embodied in the unyielding posture of the young man.

(2) Yugen: *Symbolic reflection*

The costumes of the ghosts served to join the linguistic symbolism of the play with a visual dimension of symbol and to enhance the mood created. The dreamers, those passionate shades, are cloaked in radiant, sumptuous costumes symbolic of the power of their longing that seems to fill the valley to overflowing. *Yugen*, or beauty in its darker side of *hie*, emanates from their forms, a beauty marred by sorrow. In our production Dervorgilla wore a robe of glistening bronze gold and Diarmuid was mantled in green-blue highlighted by gold.

These particular costume hues help to create a mood, especially since they reflect the visual images of the play, correlating with the jade and agate symbolism in the first musician's song:

> That all the valley fills
> With those fantastic dreams.
> They overflow the hills,
> So passionate is a shade,
> Like wine that fills to the top
> A grey-green cup of jade,
> Or maybe an agate cup.[6]

and with its repetition in the following speech. The imagination of the audience can out pick onstage the likeness of the agate and the jade to the gem-like costumes of Diarmuid and Dervorgilla. The ghostly lovers are vessels like the formation of the hills and the wine cup; their customes help to make that association and keep them from being seen as real people.

(3) Physical restraint in the sense of Tai-Yu

The power in a Noh performance lies in knowing how much rhythmic stress to place in bodily energy. The ultimate goal is a supremely controlled and relaxed appearance which has the potential of creating a kind of reverie in the audience. Thus 'mind' acting renders a dreamlike movement encouraging a mood of quiet contemplation. In our production Masaru Sekine had the ghost lovers in *The Dreaming of the Bones* move like gliding emanations. This technique paralleled that of the Noh actor:

He chants his lines as he glides to and fro, the stamping of his stockinged feet on the resonant pinewood floor of the stage combining with the piercing notes of the transverse rhythmic accompaniment to his highly stylized movements.[7]

In *Nishikigi* the controlled 'downhill-skier' posture in movement seemed clipped in rehearsals without *kimono*, but once viewed in costume it became strikingly transformed. The draping folds of the *kimonos* seemed to bestow the actors' movements with a flowing easy slide and dignified noble demeanour. It was the mental process of dominating and controlling the physical output that made the acting graceful.

Miriam Purtill, who portrayed *Tsure* in *Nishikigi*, complained of constant headaches during rehearsals. Sekine explained to her that this was a natural result in acting a Noh play as energy is deliberately restrained to about seventy per cent of its natural power.[8] The withholding of bodily energy causes mind to dominate the scene with almost an hypnotic effect. Under the enveloping influence of controlled energy, the audience falls into the dreamlike world of reverie.

We know that Yeats admired bodily control and the intensity an extended pose created on stage. The fascination Yeats had with the Sarah Bernhardt and Edouard De Max version of *Phèdre*[9] shows that Yeats was impressed as early as 1902 with the notion of the power of the mind to evoke even more powerful images on stage in these statuesquely held poses. We tried to recreate this concept and soften it by using the delicately flowing rhythms of the Noh. For instance, as Dervorgilla I moved quite slowly and for the first half of the play held an entranced pose while I watched the other two characters engaged in dialogue. This restrained repose may have made the audience tune in more effectively when I suddenly came to life to begin my speech. I found that this energy-retention technique certainly drew our already close audience further towards us. The boundaries between audience and actor seemed to dissolve. This pause for a statuesque pose was hard to maintain, but I could feel the emanations of energy that rebounded from the audience in that small room. It seemed to me that the controlled energy of the performance set a force field about the audience and the actors. I believe that this restrained kinetic atmosphere created 'a more profound psychological effect' within our audience.

(4) Travel song: The convention of michiyuki

Our theatrical production leaned more towards the Noh when interpreting Yeats's travel song. The Noh convention of *michiyuki*, or travel song, is

a short piece of song by the *waki* or the *shite* describing the changing landscapes while he is travelling. While singing this piece the actor does not walk about. This theatrical convention enables an actor to travel hundreds of miles in a short time without moving.[12]

The journey of the travel song may be long, but

the audience are expected to imagine that he is travelling while singing, although he does not move at all. At the end of the song he announces that he has arrived . . . [at his destination].[13]

In the context of the Noh play the travel song is simply a musical narrative technique working with all other aspects in the play to elucidate meaning.

A central motif in *The Dreaming of the Bones* is the travel song, for Yeats followed the Noh dramatic concept of having the symbolic landscape evoked in song. His travel song also portrays the shifting moods in the consciousness of the Young Man. This psychological landscape of the song parallels the physical terrain described in the accompanying passages of blank verse. The first stage of the journey, passing places of mourning with an owl crying overhead, symbolizes the fleeting passage of life and leads into the song of the heart's response to the fears of life. The climb of the journey, then, by hedge and thorns near the place of death with its 'tomb-nested owl' and the song takes up the conflicts in choice as the heart would seek to escape death. Finally, the ascent brings the traveller to a high place beyond 'briar and thorn', beyond the claims of life and death, and the song reaches a climax in the fervour of 'the dreaming bones'. Thus, each stage of the physical journey has a parallel in song that speaks to the heart. The progress of the physical journey acts as a generative force upon the flow of consciousness to reach a plateau in the full surge of conscious energy. The progressive texturing of the symbols allows the actor and audience to slip easily away from the physical journey into the journey of soul.

Our production applied the authentic Noh theatrical convention of *michiyuki*, which calls for the actor to remain still until the travel speeches and songs are delivered. Having the actors remain stationary and in an attitude of dream-like suspension can lead an audience into a state of receptivity. Though Yeats's specific acting directions are for the actors to 'go around the stage once' at the beginning of each of the three divisions of the journey, our actors remained like statues, distantly removed. The divisions of the travel song in our production were marked by the dreamy rich notes of the flute. Assuming the Noh convention of *michiyuki* for the travel song seemed more appropriate than physical action to initiate Yeats's goal of bringing the audience to a state of reverie.

Thematically, Yeats's travel song marshals its symbols and ascending musical force for an incursion into the spiritual realm. The musician's speeches in blank verse and meditative, iambic measure set up the symbolic message that is to be driven home by the sharp melody of the trimeter lines of the music. Overwhelmingly, Yeats's aim in the travel song is to attain the trance effect in the depths of consciousness. I found in our production Theresa Wright's delivery of both the musician's songs and speeches had a trance-inducing effect on our audience. Her still posture also seemed to heighten the impact of the words. Thus, using the Noh *michiyuki* approach, we were able to recreate the atmosphere necessary to show the landscape as symbolic of spiritual life more effectively and to make Yeats's travel song approach the archetypal mode of journey.

(5) Incantation

The mood of Yeats's play is all-encompassing; the travel song and lyrics, with their refrain, create an energy field from which the characters seem to emerge. This rhythmic quality is conducive to the dreamy aura that the characters must emanate. In our production of *The Dreaming of the Bones* the travel song had a strong effect on our audience. The way in which we treated it created a wave-like energy response from the audience as the enfolded meaning[14] of the play was compactly unfolded in symbol, much as the mimetic folding and unfolding of the cloth at the beginning and conclusion of the play.[15] We used the original score of music composed in 1917 by Walter Morse Rummel for the travel song and had a flautist accompany our singer providing those mind-stirring notes in the interludes between the speeches and songs.

The refrain of the travel song,

> Red bird of March, begin to crow!
> Up with the neck and clap the wing,
> Red cock and crow![16]

has musical directions that call for a *forte*, roughly plucked delivery whose overall effect should be 'very rhythmic and strong'.[17] The massing of short vowels and the quick pace of the phrasing of this refrain issue in an almost strident sound. In sharp contrast to the refrain, the music of the accompanying description of the journey is 'weirdly expressive without, however, covering the voice,[18] and the musical introduction is rendered 'dreamingly, always in [the] background'.[19] Yeats's travel song has a surge of energy provided by the refrain after each of the melodic stanzas. The pattern of this repetitive incantation is useful to propel psychic movement in the audience by means of its upbeat tempo. The dreamlike, delicate strains of the music score of the travel song act, then, like a receding, calming force from this wave swell.

The refrain is picked up again as the final lines to the closing lyric of the play. This lyric is slower and more deeply expressive in its sad plaintiveness than the travel song, but the wave-like motion in rhythm is still present. In the middle of this last song, the melody swings up with the words

> Those crazy fingers play
> A wandering airy music;
> Our luck is withered away,[20]

and declines again, returning to the former sadly expressive mood. Towards the last refrain, however, the song becomes 'more vigorous and alive'.[21] The wave-like pattern of rhythm surges forward with the lines . . .

> My heart ran wild when it heard
> The curlew cry before the dawn[22]

and begins its urgent descent graduating into calm with . . .

> And the eddying cat-headed bird;
> But now the night is gone.[23]

The music from this point ascends into the rough, energetic strains of the refrain, only this time the crashing waves of the last line of the play quietly linger, becoming slower and softer in the music until it goes out 'like a sigh'.[24]

To achieve a more effective impact on our audience at University College at the conclusion of *The Dreaming of the Bones*, we plunged the room into total darkness as the last strains of the music fade out like a sigh. The audience was left momentarily cut off from everything else to be free to ponder on the import of the last words of the refrain.

The music Yeats chose to accompany and to express his play illustrates, by its culminating wavelike momentum of consistently rising and abating levels, his intentions for a parallel receptivity in the consciousness of the audience. It is the creative force that mobilizes the mind of the audience to reorganize and perceive the moment in time that his play is reflecting. Discovery arises in a state of reverie, a languid dreaminess.[25] Prior to that stage there has to be some level of perturbation of all the images. The wave analogy approximates this psychic movement towards reaching and experiencing that moment of moments, by its languid recessions and pivotal crescendos.

This petitionary call to action of the refrain is an exciting energetic force. The incantory line is the resounding cry of the play with all action returning cyclically to it. The red cock of March may be associated with the denial of Christ by one of his followers just as the impulses of the young man embodied by Diarmuid and Dervorgilla are to be denied. The fierce bird imagery also relates to the Cuchulain cycle with its aggressiveness. All of these associations — the regrowth of spring, the Cuchulain cycle and the Christ cycle — have to do with the coming of a new order. This hortatory refrain appeals to the regenerative forces to assume control. Both the music and the hard consonants provoke an active soul-stirring response from the audience. The refrain interrupts the low and gentle reflectiveness inspired by its preceding verse. Its echo rises above the undercurrents of the dreamy trance-inspiring melody of the songs. The orchestration of the music of this play shows an intricacy of tone and power that brilliantly illustrates Yeats's stratas of meaning.

An interesting change in the refrain occurs in the last lyric of the play. The subject is now plural, red cock*s*, and the form is an assertion that the birds are a-crow.

The strong March birds a-crow.
Stretch neck and clap the wing,
Red cocks, and crow![26]

There is an inevitability that things will take their course. This subtle change in refrain indicates a disequilibrium in the contemplative
manner of the play and also a slight tipping of the scales towards
revolutionary symbolism. *The Dreaming of the Bones* is a play
where Yeats openly rehearses the revolutionary history of
Ireland.[27] These finely crafted changes in the refrain of the travel
song, as well as the orchestration of the music in the play, reflect
the care Yeats takes 'in handling such radioactive material'.[28]

MUSIC IN TRANSLATION:
YEATS; POUND; RUMMEL; DULAC

PETER DAVIDSON

I

This essay examines the music which Yeats approved for publication with two of his Plays for Dancers: *At the Hawk's Well* and *The Dreaming of the Bones*. It attempts an evaluation of the relation which this music bears to the music of the Japanese Noh.

The process by which Yeats discovered the form and convention of his Plays for Dancers is well known: Ezra Pound introduced him, in the winter of 1913, to the draft translations from the Japanese drama amongst the papers of Ernest Fenollosa. What might also be stressed is that Pound seems to have been a strong influence on the choice of composers and the form of music for the plays. By 1913, Pound had already formed strong musical theories, not the considered thoughts of the nineteenth-thirties which saw him as a discriminating champion of the revival of early European music, but rather a half-formed aesthetic based on a random acquaintance with certain aspects of the music of the past — Provençal song (although it is unlikely that Pound could have arrived at any real understanding of this from the study of the original manuscripts), the Elizabethan love-song, the *Parlar-cantando* of Henry Lawes — which he felt to have importance for the music and poetry of the future. Yeats seems to have deferred to Pound on musical questions throughout his career — even to the extent of allowing Pound to wish the pseudo-Futurist compositions of his talentless protegé, Georges Antheil, on the 1929 Abbey production of *Fighting the Waves*.[1]

The explanation for this lack of musical direction in Yeats himself appears to be in the fact that he had a very limited musical perception — a physical condition rather than any lack of discrimination — and that this disability rendered him prone to take the musical advice of others, often against the one musical instinct which he possessed — an intuitive appreciation of Irish folk-song. In the preface to the publication of *At the Hawk's Well* in the March 1917 issue of *Harper's Bazaar*, Yeats wrote,

Music where there are no satisfying audible words bores me . . . for I have no ear or only a primitive one.

Where Yeats appears to have chosen dramatic music without taking advice, he seems consistently (and always with effect) to have selected those simple forms of *song* (as opposed to any sort of aesthetic *Parlar-cantando*), to which his ear and his instinct led him. Edward Malins[2] gives the instances of the Victorian hymn in *The Words Upon the Window-pane* (1930) and the nursery-song in *Purgatory* (1939). In the early plays Irish folk-songs are used; the funeral dirge 'Do not make a great keening' in *Cathleen Ni Houlihan* produces even on the printed page a simple but total effect of desolation with its rootless turn of tune ascending five tones with a dramatic twist to a sharpened dominant. These examples are all *song* in the conventional sense of word-setting which has elements of musical organization independent of the word-dominated musical recitation.

In the years preceding the composition of the Plays for Dancers, however, Yeats had turned increasingly to the study of the kind of musical delivery of words where the purely musical element is minimal, pitch rhythm and musical shape arising solely from the pattern of speech.

My ears are only comfortable when the singer sings as if more speech had taken fire, when he appears to have passed into song almost imperceptibly.[3]

It is to this mode that the recitations of Florence Farr belong: a kind of *sprechstimme*, a formalized rise and fall of spoken tone, following the contours of the verse. Yeats's own reading was of this kind, as though he had compensated for his limited ability to perceive conventional musical tone by the substitution of a verbal tone and pattern. The effect and manner of Yeats's recitation is recollected by Pound in the *Pisan Cantos*.[4]

> so that I recalled the noise in the chimney
> as it were the wind in the chimney
>   but was in reality Uncle William
> downstairs composing
> that had made a great Peeeeacock
>   in the proide of his oiye
>   had made a great peeeeeeecock in the . . .

made a great peacock
  in the proide of his oyee
proide of his oy-ee
as indeed he had and perdurable

'Wind in the chimney' catches the tone of incantation, but Pound's repetitions also convey Yeats's awareness of the pitches of spoken words, his experimentation with a rising pitch in the word 'eye'.

It must be questioned whether this mode of heightened recitation can be considered properly as music — in musical terms the pitches are random and musical aesthetics pay no part in determining the shape of the vocal line.

Yeats's rejection of the art-music of the earlier part of the twentieth century is unsurprising:

I have written the little songs of the chorus to please myself, confident that singer and composer, when the time came for performance, would certainly make it impossible for the audience to know what the words were.[5]

The styles of word-setting which were current before the composition of the Plays for Dancers, would not have appealed to Yeats, with his affinity for folk song, his inability to enjoy more complex music, and his belief that the simplest variations of vocal pitch sufficed to 'set' a poem. In the late-romantic music of the early twentieth century words are easily lost, both through the imposition of metrically antipathetic rhythmic patterns and the composition of the sonorities of an 'accompaniment' which is rarely subordinate. With the exception of occasional performances of earlier music by Yeats's and Pound's friends the Dolmetsch family, little vocal music can have been heard in London at the time which could have satisfied either poet by clarity or sensitivity in word-setting. Pound's musical criticism, written in the years 1917–1921 for the periodical *The New Age*, also indicates another difficulty which would have tended to turn both poets away from conventional song-writing: the standards of performance and style of the period. Again and again Pound complains of perverse and slipshod articulation, of the practice of singing art-songs in translations of abysmal quality.[6]

Given these conditions and the musical affinities which Yeats had shown up to the time when he began to study the Noh texts in Pound's possession, one may assume that he would be interested by the idea of making a new dramatic music in the image of the Japanese original.

At this point arises the difficulty which must stand as the focus of this essay: Yeats had few means of either hearing or studying

Japanese music and no composer of any great ability came forward to re-invent it for the western stage in the way in which Pound and Yeats had been able to re-invent in their poetic versions and adaptations of the Noh.

Yeats had the *general* idea that a chanting voice accompanied by flute, harp, drum and gong would provide the music for his plays:

the voice must be freed from this competition [the orchestra] and find itself among little instruments, only heard at their best perhaps when we are close about them.[7]

but he had little *specific* indication as to how the music worked in the Noh, although Fenollosa's notes, throughout, stress its importance. He seems to have been unaware that the Noh play is sung throughout (although at points where the music reinforces prose speech the song is a musically — minimal chant).

they sing as much as they speak, and there is a chorus which describes the scene.[8]

Neither Yeats nor Pound could obtain any satisfactory knowledge of Noh music, but it is possible to itemize the information which they did possess.

Apart from specific enquiry and material contained in Fenollosa's notes, there seems to have been little information generally available in London at the time.[9] Rather confusingly, Edmund Dulac, the illustrator and amateur musician, is credited with interest in European and Oriental folk music and with having made Polynesian bamboo nose-flutes,[10] but if he had information to offer it is surprising that Pound was forced to seek information from Japanese acquaintances and that he admitted in *The New Age* April 15, 1920:

I have never been able to determine how far various alleged oriental melodies, as concocted for example by Borodine, have been mis-written by our notation of how far the writing is sound and *would* indicate the right tune and rhythm to a performer who knew the right manner of presentation.[11]

Was it perhaps Dulac who had shown him the transcriptions of which he wrote in *The Egoist* of August 1917,

We pride ourselves on having exact transcriptions of Arabic and Japanese and Zulu and Malay music . . .[12]

and had he come by 1920 to the conclusion that these specimens remained un-knowable without interpreters trained in their respective musical traditions?

In Fenollosa's notes on the Noh, the section of music is cryptic and uninformative in the extreme, the discussion of rhythm and metre may be rendered comprehensible only by reference to a Japanese source[13] and one must conclude that Pound misinterpreted what Fenollosa can only have partially understood.

It is significant that Pound's footnote to this passage comes as near as Pound ever comes to admitting incomprehension, and hastens to suggest that some sort of parallel must be drawn with Pound's favoured achievements in European metric:

This looks like a sort of syncopation. I don't know enough about music to consider it musically with any fulness, but it offers to the student of metric most interesting parallels, or if not parallels, suggestions for comparison with sapphics and with some of the troubadour measures . . . the chief trouble being that Professor Fenollosa's notes at this point are not absolutely lucid.[14]

Information might have come from the Japanese dancer Michio Ito, who danced in the first performance of *At the Hawk's Well*, but he was trained in modern schools in Japan and Paris and his knowledge of the Noh came only from books and from performances which he had seen in childhood. His friend the painter Tami Konmé (one of whose paintings long remained amongst Pound's household gods) may have been able to supply some more concrete idea of Noh performance in that he claimed to have danced in his childhood a small role in the play *Hagoromo*.[15] He may be identified with the 'pleasant' young man from Japan who played a large bamboo flute and who visited Pound after 1915, but from these contacts and from the dramatist Nijuichi Kayano (who gave a recitation to Yeats with Tami Konmé) neither Yeats nor Pound could have gained any real idea of Noh music in performance.[16]

At the end of this investigation we are left, at least, with a useful clearing of the ground: with exceptions, music was not at the centre of Yeats's interests. Yeats and Pound could have obtained only the most general idea of Noh music. The composers whom they chose had only the idea of a chanting chorus accompanied by flute, drums and gong on which to build their settings.

*

It does not advance our understanding of Yeats's poetic drama to give any full musical analysis either of Dulac's music for *At the Hawk's Well* or Rummel's for *The Dreaming of the Bones*. Neither composition is particularly distinguished either as word-setting or as music in its own right.

Dulac scores for a singer doubling harp, flute and drum and gong.[17] The scale utilized has 'exotic' overtones neither quite pentatonic nor whole-tone but with suggestions of both. If Dulac's music has any merit greater than Rummel's it is that of comparative simplicity: the harp remains steady, underlining the progression of the music with step-movements of block chords; the flute offers an occasional decorating descant to the voice, but moves usually in parallel with it; the dance is built up very simply from the repetition of short sequences which appear with increasing quantities of decoration as the movement progresses.

The music would appear to be performable if uninspired, moving only to any purely musical interest at the end of the dance when a gong-roll forms a pedal for a sequence of repeating downward figurations on the harp which answer the mention of water in the text without over-painting the words. The last phrase of the closing song is as simple as a pentatonic folk-tune rising to fade on an inconclusive F sharp (the sixth of the implied scale of A)

One need look no further than this two-bar phrase to find the chief weakness of these Dulac settings as far as Yeats's aesthetic is concerned: a lack of sensitivity to the duration of verbal sounds as opposed to their stress. In this example 'who but an idiot' is hurried over in two beats, two equal triplets, six notes of equal duration, while praise (a sound shortened by the closed vowels) has a beat and a half and the stress of the third beat of the bar on it. In the same way a regular pattern is imposed on the four lines which begin 'the boughs of the hazel shake' with an oddly cramping effect.

Walter Morse Rummel did not compose his music at Yeats's suggestion, but presumably at the instigation of Pound whom he had known since 1908, and with whom he had collaborated on realizations of Troubadour songs (1913) and whose poems he had set to music (1913).[18] He was a pupil of Debussy and a successful if controversial concert pianist. He remained on the continent throughout the war, so he probably made his setting (dated 1917) without having the opportunity to discuss matters with Yeats or Pound in person. It is unlikely that Yeats had heard the music when he allowed it to be printed in conjunction with his play and indeed I have found no record that it has ever been performed.

Rummel's pretentious note to the music can be translated as stating his intention of composing not to satisfy any musical aesthetic but simply to bring out the music inherent in the words regardless of musical effect.

Music of tone and music of speech are distinct from each other.
Here my sole object has been to find some tone formula which will enhance and bring out a music underlying the words. The process is therefore directly opposed to that of tone music creation, which from the formless directly creates its tone form, whereas I seek to derive a formless overflow from that already formed.

He scores for singer doubling zither, flute, a one-stringed bass with a sympathetic string and a drum. The music is notated in extraordinary detail, dynamic and interpretative directions being given for every second note, to no great effect. Edward Malins rightly dismisses the music as 'water-gruel Debussy'[19] and points out the superimposition of regular musical phrases on irregular verbal phrases and misplaced stresses within phrases. For all Rummel's claim that he is simply writing the music which lies in the words, he resorts to musical clichés to depict apprehension in the opening song of the play — the horror-film alternation of phrases built on the chords:

which destroys any notion of dignity or ritual. Even granted that he is inconsistent with his declared aim of avoiding music expressive in conventional musical terms he fails to make any intelligent reading of the closing song, setting the words 'But now the night is gone' in a limp fall of regret which runs counter to the vitality of the stanza which ends the play on the triumphant cock-crow. Rummel's closing phrase is the last quotation which will be needed to demonstrate both the music's unsuitability for singing and its lack of sympathy with its text.

By accident, one phrase of Rummel's music does indeed resemble, in its flat and even line, the 'strong' form of Noh singing:

but this coincidence is the only actual musical resemblance between his music and the music of the Noh.

In conclusion, it may be suggested that the inferior music written for these two Plays for Dancers was the result of an imperfect act of translation: an attempt to write *Japonaiserie* with no knowledge of the original.

All that was known was the simple fact of singer, flute and drum. This combination is found also in Irish folk-music, and the creative solution to the composition of music for these plays might have been to have re-invented the music in Irish terms to match the poet's use of Irish material within the Noh form.

In doing this the music might truly match the words provided by Yeats, who moved, throughout his career as a writer of words for music, closer to the vigour and directness of popular song.

ENIGMATIC INFLUENCES: YEATS, BECKETT AND NOH

KATHARINE WORTH

In a recent production of *Waiting for Godot* at the National Theatre, London (opened 25 November 1987) the atmosphere suddenly changed when Vladimir and Estragon moved into the following sequence of dialogue:

VLADIMIR: We have our reasons.
ESTRAGON: All the dead voices.
VLADIMIR: They make a noise like wings.
ESTRAGON: Like leaves.
VLADIMIR: Like sand.
ESTRAGON: Like leaves.
              Silence.
VLADIMIR: They all speak together.
ESTRAGON: Each one to itself.
              Silence.
VLADIMIR: Rather they whisper.
ESTRAGON: They rustle.
VLADIMIR: They murmur.
ESTRAGON: They rustle.
              Silence.
VLADIMIR: What do they say?
ESTRAGON: They talk about their lives.
VLADIMIR: To have lived is not enough for them.
ESTRAGON: They have to talk about it.
VLADIMIR: To be dead is not enough for them.
ESTRAGON: It is not sufficient.

The passage was separated from the rest of the dialogue by the more intense and musical delivery given to it by Alec McCowen and John Alderton in the roles of the two friends. The phrases which Beckett has divided by silences had a broken, anxious effect. The actors changed tone: one of them walked away, turned his back to the audience for a moment; there was a sense of emotion welling

145

up, pushing its way through the under-stated, wry, often impish style they preserved for the most part. Yet the phrasing was musical, highly controlled and stylized. Clearly the actors were suggesting that something strange and special is happening here. The dead are invading the stage: the atmosphere is pervaded by the rustle of ghostly presences. The country road at evening, which is also the cage or net in which Vladimir and Estragon are trapped, opens up briefly to allow a glimpse of some other region. We are on the border line between the living and the dead.

The word 'presences' which this scene brings irresistibly to mind links Beckett with Yeats whose drama is devoted to just such epiphanies. From *The Shadowy Waters* to *Purgatory* and *The Death of Cuchulain* his stage is commonly laid out as that kind of border country: an ambiguous zone of being where encounters are to be experienced with gods and ghosts and messages are to be received in the world normally thought of as 'real' from the other world which Yeats ardently struggled to bring into being. As Beckett's run-down pair hear murmurs and rustles from the land of the dead, so too Yeats's Cuchulain, in characteristically more heroic vein, hears singing which has not yet sounded from the ghostly shape he sees waiting to embody him after his death, and, earlier, warns his mistress not to speak loudly about this approaching death: 'Who knows what ears listen behind the door?' Eithne takes the word 'door' in its mundane sense but for Yeats it was also an image of the closeness — and shut-off nature — of the immaterial world. Bishop Berkeley's writings, he said, make us feel that 'eternity is always at our heels or hidden from our eyes by the thickness of a door'.[1]

This dream-like territory is the great province of Noh. Its stage is above all a place where earthly characters go through Yeats's imaginary door into the region which has been there all the time except that they did not recognize it. Many of the Noh plays turn on the moment of recognition: something which had seemed part of ordinary reality is suddenly revealed as belonging to the supernatural order which enfolds it. The old couple tidying the ground under an ancient pine tree and talking to a priest about the symbolism of the 'double pine' (in *Takasago*), will finally manifest themselves as the spirits of the pines. Or some simple, routine operation of real life will provide the basis for a fantastic vision, as in *Himuro*, when an account of the business of preserving ice for the emperor's household culminates in the spectacular revelation that the old man explaining the operation is the god of ice himself. To see, as I did recently, a performance of *Himuro* in Tokyo and then later by chance to be shown an ancient ice house in a palace garden in Kyoto was to be struck anew by the remarkable transitions the Noh makes between the necessary and mundane details of life and the supernatural.

Sometimes the apparitions themselves will be of the human rather than the inhuman world. Indistinguishable at first from the flesh and blood characters they encounter, they emerge from the limbo where they are wandering, to tell the story of their earthly lives. They still live in that life, painfully attached to it by some powerful emotion, whether of love or hate. Of the lovers in *Nishikigi* or the desolate Rokujo in *Nonomiya* it might be said, as Vladimir and Estragon say in the passage quoted at the start of this essay, 'To have lived is not enough for them. They have to talk about it.'

To pursue this line alone is to see affinities between the Noh and the theatre of Yeats and Beckett come flooding in. They come unsought for those familiar in some degree with these dramatic oeuvres. Perhaps it should be said that, so far as Noh is concerned, for most westerners this will mean acquaintance with the plays in translation and — it is to be hoped — in performance. It should be enough, alien and exotic though the convention may be: the two playwrights under discussion had much less!

At this point it is necessary to pause and consider whether the comparisons which thrust themselves upon one from the plays themselves have any backing from acknowledgements of influence made by the playwrights. So far as Yeats is concerned there is no problem. He acknowledged in the most excited way the impact made on him by the Noh, and pretty well everything he said on the matter — in the essay, on 'Certain Noble Plays of Japan',[2] and elsewhere — has been exhaustively discussed and analysed.[3] It is not in dispute that his acquaintance with Noh was slight. Never having seen a full performance, only demonstrations by individual performers like Ito, and depending on the Fenellosa translations, he could not but have had an incomplete view of the way Noh functioned as a theatrical entity. But that is really beside the point. He was not setting out to write a treatise nor to attempt to reconstruct the so-alien form in the unlikely settings — London drawing rooms, rooms in his own house in Merrion Square — where his dance plays were performed.

The dance plays drew inspiration from what he knew of Noh but the inspiration did not send him in a totally new direction. He had been experimenting with total theatre techniques for a drama with a supernatural dimension since he used music and a spell-binding dance in *The Land of Heart's Desire* in 1894 and *Where There is Nothing* in 1904.[4] The Japanese showed him the way to a bolder, more total stylization: 'more formal faces', that is, masks; and 'a chorus that has no part in the action' (*E&I*, p. 226). In that way Noh helped him in 'inventing', as he claimed, a new form. But he took only what he needed: if he had a narrowly angled view of the source from which he drew, it was enough. The barest hints were always enough to impel his strong, searching imagination, but only in directions it had elected for itself. He continually draws our attention to the way he is assimilating the inspiration into his own mythology, as when he summarizes the classical situation of Noh as 'the meeting with ghost, god, or goddess at some holy place or much-legended tomb' and goes on to reflect that this reminds him of Irish legend and belief. He was travelling in the 'creative circle' that Okifumi Komesu speaks of in his subtly argued essay on *At the Hawk's Well* and *Taka no Izumi*, the Noh play re-created by Mario Yokomichi from Yeats's play. Both writers, Komesu points out, were reacting at once 'receptively and destructively' to the aesthetic forms on which they drew, and this was inevitable. Every artist is rooted in his own culture even in the act of seeming to break from it; the 'break' is really an act of renewal. Komesu finds only 'dim and distorted adumbrations of Noh' on Yeats's canvas but concludes that although 'direct and simple-minded comparison' between the two forms yields little critical insight, yet comparisons (of another sort) demand to be made.[5]

This is surely right. To speak of Yeats and the Noh or Beckett and the Noh, is to speak always of difference as well as of certain likenesses. It is the differences, the extraordinary renewals and refreshments of dramatic tradition, that excite and hold us, after all. In extending the comparison with Noh from Yeats to Beckett it would certainly be necessary to avoid direct, line-for-line comparisons such as Komesu warns against, for Beckett provides us with no tempting and dangerous evidence of specific influence comparable to that in Yeats's dance plays.

What grounds do we have, then, for linking his theatre with the Noh? Above all else, there are the perhaps coincidental but nevertheless striking affinities and likenesses to be observed in the plays themselves, as in the passage from *Waiting for Godot* with which I began. This is the heart of the matter. There is also the line of connection which encourages those of us with Yeats's plays deeply in mind to imagine Beckett's sharing in the admiration of one whom he so much admires. Particular features of the plays encourage us to think of his joining with Yeats in dramatic explorations — far

removed from the conventional mode of their own western tradition — which take them both into the domain of Noh. Or perhaps
one should say, a domain which breathes something of the same
air, since even Yeats, for all his admiration, did not really enter it.
It is at the point where material and immaterial meet that we can
see most clearly the triple thread binding these otherwise unlike
dramas. When I wrote on the affinities between Yeats and Beckett
some years ago I suggested, among other things, that Beckett's
plays were ghost plays in Yeats's sense of a ghost as a 'clinging
presence, an emanation from some obscure region of consciousness
or a mysterious continuation of mind outside body'.[6] It is this line
of thought, I believe, that leads most clearly into the Noh — and
is being pursued from the other side of the cultural space by
Japanese scholars such as Yasunari Takahashi.[7]

It does not seem necessary to dwell at any length on the connec-
tions between Yeats and Beckett which make it natural to consider
the two playwrights together in the present context. These have
already, I believe, been sufficiently established and are generally
recognized. How indeed could they not be when Beckett himself
has highlighted the powerful place Yeats holds in his imagination?
He gives him a voice in his own plays, summoning him up in an
allusion, a snatch of verse — 'The wind in the reeds' in *Waiting for
Godot*, 'I call to the eye of the mind' in *Happy Days*. In the most
spectacular instance, . . . *but the clouds* . . ., the detached voice
of the persona crouched over a table (as it were a writer at work)
describes the endless attempts made by the other persona moving
about on the television screen to animate an image, make the lips
of a spectral woman move and utter sounds that can be heard.
When we do at last hear the sounds in full they are the closing lines
from 'The Tower', Yeats's valedictory, his 'making' of his soul. In
later work again, Beckett continues to move close to Yeats, as in
Quad (1982), a dance play in which four silent figures 'complete
their courses' through permutations of pattern and colour, creating
without words (but with the aid of light and percussion) a forceful
image of compulsive drives that must be obeyed: it becomes clear
that they will never move into the centre but must always swerve
to avoid it. Echoes here, one might say, of the mute Hawk Woman
drawing Cuchulain away from the well in *At the Hawk's Well*, the
play to which Beckett has indeed paid special tribute in a rare comment of the kind. He would give the whole of Shaw, he said (alas,
poor Shaw), 'for 'a sup of the Hawk's Well, or the Saints', or a
whiff of Juno, to go no further'.[8]

With *At the Hawk's Well* we return to the ambience of Noh, for this was the play which in 1916 launched Yeats's new form of dance drama, ('distinguished, indirect and symbolic') with the help, as he said, of Japanese plays 'translated by Ernest Fenollosa and finished by Ezra Pound'. *At the Hawk's Well* is undoubtedly one of the plays that means most to Beckett, along with *Purgatory*, an out-and-out ghost play which echoes Noh in its austere focus on the encounter between the Old Man and the 'earth-bound shell' of his dead mother. So it could be argued that Beckett achieves connection with Noh through Yeats. Perhaps no more specific link will be found: Beckett has not spoken of any special interest in Noh, has indeed said in answer to enquiries that he is not familiar with it (though this does not preclude the possibility, given Beckett's wide-ranging erudition, of his knowing something about it).

Yet for those who love Beckett's plays, especially perhaps those who come to him with Yeats in mind, acquaintance with the Noh is liable to produce a spontaneous and irresistible sense of a line of affinity stretching from that ancient drama to the great living Irish playwright. The affinities are to do with substance as well as form — though in fact, in these brief, intensely concentrated, poetic plays, the two can scarcely be divided and it might be better to speak of the total nature of the dramatic experience. Beckett's theatre, like that of Yeats and Noh, is a theatre of evocation. The characteristic process is movement towards revelation of some truth, some 'shape' of things that has hitherto been concealed or cloudy. In the Noh, which has a huge range of topics, revelations may be presented in supernatural or in purely human terms, as in those several plays which concern discovery of a lost member of a family (*Kashiwazaki* is one such). The boundary between the two states is dissolved in Noh without awkwardness. A play which is centred on love and grief in human life may easily take a super-natural turn, as it does in the moving *Sumidagawa* when the mother praying by the grave of her young son (whose fate she has just discovered) is allowed a moment of communion with the dead. The boy's voice is heard, he appears briefly on stage, as he was in life, then departs for ever. For westerners this is one of the easiest of the plays to feel at home with, touching familiar springs of feeling (as well as being known through Britten's operatic adaptation in *Curlew River*).

Many of Beckett's plays go into that world of loss — and offer revelations of some spiritual restorative beyond it, though in enigmatic form. *Ohio Impromptu* in its fifteen-minute length creates the same profound sense of grief as *Sumidagawa* and brings a similarly mysterious comfort. The white-haired man who reads

from a book the story of a man sent to comfort someone bereaved
is reading to a mute listener who is his look-alike and who shares
(by knocking on the table) in the editing and therefore the making
of the story. So perhaps the play invites us to see the consolation
as coming entirely from within, does not open up into a dimension
where the voice of the loved one is 'really' heard, the living image
seen. Yet the Reader creates through the story (and hypnotic
rhythm) a powerful sense of just such another dimension:

One night as he sat trembling head in hands from head to foot a man appeared to him and said, I have been sent by — and here he named the dear
name — to comfort you. Then drawing a worn volume from the pocket
of his long black coat he sat and read till dawn. Then disappeared without
a word.

We cannot but feel ourselves in the presence of a mystery here,
and in a region very near to Noh, it seems to me. Beckett's 'visitation' is internalized, of course, in a way foreign to Noh: in stage
terms his play is very enclosed and private, while a play like
Sumidagawa is open and public. All the people of the village are
to be thought of as sharing in the bereaved mother's experience
(though by stage convention the effect is made through chorus and
narrative rather than realistically). Religious differences too make
themselves felt, though perhaps not so drastically as we might ex-
pect. The spiritual manifestation that occurs in *Sumidagawa* rests
on a basis of Buddhist belief: Beckett's is a context of modern,
agnostic questioning. Yet the divide cannot be absolute or we
should hardly be able to respond with similar feeling — as I believe
we can — to both plays. Beckett's may be the more enigmatic but
the Noh form has its own ambiguities. It would be possible, after
all, to interpret the vision experienced by the bereaved mother as
a projection from her own consciousness at a moment of great emotional intensity. And, conversely, possible to see Beckett's Reader
and Listener as elements in a psychic experience that has tapped
some ethereal source: 'unspoken words' lie behind those that are
spoken and they have been brought from far away, beyond
thought:

What thoughts who knows. Thoughts, no, not thoughts. Profounds of
mind. Buried in who knows what profounds of mind. Of mindlessness.

When the Reader closes the 'sad tale', he and the Listener for the
first time exchange a strange look: it is 'Unblinking. Expressionless.'
Like the curious mirroring of story and stage image and the sense
of being somehow out of time which it engenders, that unblinking
look takes us a long way out of the normal daylight world. It calls

to mind the 'unfaltering, unmoistened eyes' of Yeats's Hawk
Woman, eyes dreaded by the Old Man because they 'are not of this
world'. With that comparison we move in another direction,
towards the 'god' Noh (Kami Noh). Just before going on, though,
it might be noted that Yeats, much more overtly romantic than
Beckett, yet had his own sort of interest in relating other-worldly
revelations to ordinary human need, which is the distinguishing
feature of *Ohio Impromptu* and *Sumidagawa*. *The Words upon the
Window-Pane* lifts off into its fearful evocation of the dead Swift
from the deliberately mundane base of a Dublin spiritualist séance,
with its mixed bag of pathetic and not so pathetic seekers, and a
medium whose uncanny performance leaves uneasily open the
question all in the play are pursuing: is there a world other than
the material one?

Scepticism about these possibilities is as much a feature of Yeats's
metaphysical explorations as his willingness to believe. This makes
for an interesting tension in the plays. Something similar could be
said of Beckett. Scepticism or even disbelief is the ground on which
mystical patterns are traced: they remain, even when undermined
with an ironic word or a disconcerting change of tone. So, in *Foot-
falls*, May suddenly gives a comical new turn to the ghostly play
when she addresses the audience directly in a pleasant reader's
voice: 'Old Mrs Winter, whom the reader will remember . . .' Yet
even if we smile and see it all for a moment as fiction, she retains
her awesome power to convince us that she is in some more
mysterious way the 'semblance' she has described as if it had a
separate existence: 'Faint, though by no means invisible, in a certain light.'

Scepticism and humour (the last pervasive and often comical as
well as ironic in Beckett's theatre) decidedly separate both the
modern playwrights from Noh, which seems always to be more
purely tragic (or celebratory). It is all the more remarkable that
despite their modern ironies and changes of tone they should be
able to approach so closely in their different ways to Noh in its
most un-modern aspect, when it is summoning up gods and spirits.
The evocation has to be worked for by the characters in the modern
plays. They are on their own, individuals in a world with no supporting background of religious belief such as allows the divine an
easier entry to the Noh stage. Often a manifestation occurs there
simply as a reward for listening to the telling of a story, as in
Takasago, though it can also come about as a result of an active
human demand for full revelation. In *Hagoromo*, for instance, the
goddess dances for a simple but persistent, deeply curious fisher-

man, who came by accident on her cloak of feathers, and used it
to keep her with him. She cannot return to heaven without it but
eventually he receives payment for its restoration which comes in
the form of a dance, the conventional mode for expression of the
spirit world — and in stage terms a magnificent apotheosis.

For Yeats, in *The Only Jealousy of Emer*, the same sort of spectacular revelation is made possible when his human character,
Cuchulain, is *in extremis*, hovering between life and death. His
Ghost then acquires a power similar to the fisherman's. He is
visited by a goddess who needs him as much as he needs her
('Because I long I am not complete'). She dances for him — and between them — her dance and his words — they create a vision of
transcendental beauty.

> Who is it stands before me there
> Shedding such light from limb and hair
> As when the moon, complete at last
> With every labouring crescent past,
> And lonely with extreme delight,
> Flings out upon the fifteenth night?

Yeats's hero is equally hubristic as the Noh fisherman: he wants to
possess the goddess herself, in her metalic otherness. It is only the
intervention of his wife which saves him from his desire: the play
implies that it would be his death. There are psychological under-
tones here, of a very complicated kind, which separate the 'dance'
experience from any Noh prototype. Yet something of the impersonal remains — closely related (as it is also in Beckett's plays) to
the creativity of the artist and his interest in that creativity as a
subject for his drama.

The characters of Beckett's stage who wait for signals from an
unseen world have lower expectations. They start from a bleaker
position, a world which is often in the 'shades of grey' ironically
described by the invisible narrator's voice in *Ghost Trio*. The light
is 'faint, omnipresent. No visible source.' 'Faint' is a key word. The
mute figure on the screen, crouched on a pallet, clutches a cassette
and from time to time music is heard. The strains of Beethoven's
Fifth Piano Trio (The Ghost) are also faint, holding out no more
than a muted promise of escape into some transcendental experience. The figure is listening intently for another sound. 'He will
now think he hears her', says the voice and we see the movements
appropriate to this state, the sharp lifting of the head, the tense
pose. He listens at the door, opens the window. All actions draw
a negative. Door and window close of themselves: nothing has
been revealed. Does this mean, as some suppose, that Beckett is

denying the possibility of breaking out of the grey room, of hearing sounds existing in some enigmatic other dimension; is this a bleak, modernist variation on the theme of visitation?

It would be possible to think this and still feel a link with Yeats and Noh, since the silent figure who listens so hard for the unheard sound is able to convey to us, with the aid of Beethoven's ethereal music, that his longing is for something inexpressible. If it were to occur, this would be no ordinary visit but a visitation, an equivalent, perhaps, though in suitably Beckettian 'shades of grey', to Yeats's metallic goddess or the more benign angelic visitant of *Hagoromo*. For some, the vision in *Ghost Trio* is not totally negative, however. We do not hear 'her' but there is a glimpse of a world outside the grey room when the window opens a second time to reveal 'Rain falling in dim light' and through the open door is seen a corridor (admittedly grey like the room: 'grey rectangle between grey walls') stretching into darkness. Finally there is indeed a manifestation. Suddenly, after the 'Ghost' music has been heard once more and the man settled on his pallet, as if resigned to frustration, we hear a sound most startling in this context of faintest promise: a knock on the door. It is repeated, the door creaks slowly open, and something phenomenal appears:

Cut to near shot of small boy full length in corridor before open door. Dressed in black oilskin with hood glistening with rain. White face raised to invisible F. 5 seconds. Boy shakes head faintly. Face still, raised. 5 seconds. Boy shakes head again . . .

We may, as before, take this as a total negative. Or it may make a suggestion, faint as always, that there is some existence in another dimension to which the Boy has access, though for some reason it is not open — or perhaps not yet open — to the man. The Boy unequivocally shakes his head and Beckett is known to prefer him not to smile, as he did, angelically, in the first production by the BBC (17 April 1977). Even that enigmatic promise was apparently going too far.

Whatever our interpretation may be — it depends to some extent on temperament — one fact is clear. A play written for television which engages us in questions of that nature marks itself out as a rare work indeed and one in a rare tradition: Peter Brook has called it the 'holy theatre'. He has also said, more recently (Platform Lecture, National Theatre, 27 April 1988), that a striking feature of Japanese acting, as he has encountered it in his International Group working in Paris, is the ability to represent ghosts, phantoms, immaterial beings on stage in a realistic way. Where western actors would have to think about how to make choices from various techniques and apply them artificially, a Japanese actor could do it naturally, because such concepts were still part of his culture, whether or not he subscribed to any religious belief. It is just this naturalness, this refusal to mark out a rigid dividing line between the material and the immaterial which distinguishes Beckett's theatre and links it with Noh.

The Boy who appears in *Ghost Trio* is not the only such character on Beckett's stage. A Boy brings the message from Godot which keeps Vladimir and Estragon perpetually cheated and perpetually ready to go on waiting. The youthful messenger from another world, a figure familiar in Noh, has to answer Vladimir's tormented questions about such things as the colour of Godot's beard. 'I think it's white, sir,' he says. This is one of the moments when, as Takahashi comments, the play could seem almost like an unintentional parody of a 'Kami Noh' ('god' Noh) — though at the same time it could be taken as an unorthodox version of a true one, because Godot is after all what keeps the play in being. He certainly is no less a force for being absent. And however unreliable the messenger — he has no memory for faces — the existence of the Boy, with clouds of biblical imagery hanging about him, means that the great, unspoken question about the existence of God can never be eliminated from the play. It is the other way round in *Endgame*, where again a Boy appears; though only to be reported on by Clov. The 'small boy' seen through the 'earth' window never succeeds in getting into Hamm's room. 'If he exists . . .' is all Hamm has to say of him: no epiphany is to be expected here.

Beckett's is also, supremely, a theatre of memory. Here again it comes very close to Noh, as Poh Sim Plowright demonstrated in the delicate collage she created for the BBC, *Days that are Gone* (BBC, Third Programme, 1985). The title is a quotation from the Noh play, *Sekidera Komachi*, in which an old lady holds a conversation about poetry with priests and a child who is studying at the Sekidera Temple. She then reveals that she herself is the famous poet and former beauty, Ono no Komachi. Now her days go by in loneliness. 'Oh how I long,' she cries in pain, 'for the days that are gone.' The poignancy of the lines reflects the mood the play retains to the end: the old woman returns to her lonely hut when the temple festival is over at break of dawn. Before then, however, she has performed a dance, following on from the dance given by the child. There is a suggestion of something consoling and uplifting in this outpouring of spirit in art, with old succeeding young in a creative act. In her interweaving of such phrases and cadences from the Noh

with lines from Beckett's plays, Poh Sim Plowright brought out
vividly the subtle balance achieved in both theatres between the
sorrows of human experience and the fragile moments of spiritual
attainment that are, amazingly, drawn out of it by recall of the
past. As happens in *Sekidera Komachi* or in the poignant *Matsukaze*, with its fisher girls faithful to a lost love, so in Beckett's *That
Time*, the evocation of his own past by the Listener creates a state
of feeling which transcends the regret, unsatisfied longings and
other shadows attendant on such 'retrospectives'. Like the withered
Komachi, Beckett's old man is in a state of physical decay: in the
otherwise total darkness of the stage we see 'as if from above' his
old white face and long, flaring white hair and hear his laboured
breathing. He is listening to his own voice telling of 'days that are
gone' and the narrative is suffused with nostalgia and some pain:

was your mother ah for God's sake all gone long ago all dust the lot you
the last huddled up on the slab in the old green greatcoat with your arms
around you whose else . . .

Yet he has been able to weave out of the life material a story with
meaning, the kind of meaning art bestows on life. Three voices, his
own yet not his own (for they have somehow been projected outside him) create an exquisite pattern of sound and imagery, far
removed from the physical capacity of the man who no longer finds
it easy even to breathe. It might not seem too far-fetched to think
of this creative achievement, so intimately linked to the Listener's
sense of time's dilapidations, as the equivalent of Komachi's
dance.

The telling of a story to a listener whose listening becomes part of a
mysterious transforming process: this could be a description of Noh.
It would also be a way to describe the characteristic Beckettian process, though, of course a great and obvious difference between the
two forms is the internalizing practised by Beckett. Teller and listener
are not easily separated in his theatre. A succession of solitary figures
holds his stage, sometimes represented only by their organs of
cerebration or verbal communication: Winnie's head or the heads in
the urns of *Play*, Mouth floating in the dark, like the Listener in *That
Time*. Increasingly fierce and concentrated use of stage light and dark
highlights the solitariness and devices like the tape recorder
emphasize the inwardness. Many of his characters are listening to
their own recorded voices, a strange phenomenon which might seem
to place the action irretrievably in the private world of the mind — and
thus separate it crucially from Noh. Yet there are counter currents. The
concern to make the story true, to get at 'the right one', as Voice

desperately repeats in *Cascando*, is felt as a powerful driving force. This is a moral concern not so dissimilar from the eagerness to hear the truth of a story in Noh. That similarity is not obscured, I think, by Beckett's more modern concern with metatheatrical effects. He often focuses on the writing process itself, probing into its ambiguities: the two stories in *Eh Joe*, the dream-like merging of 'real life' and obvious fiction in *Embers*, the mirroring of one story in another in *Ohio Impromptu*, the bafflement of the Opener in *Cascando* when confronting his control over music as well as words ('Is that mine too?'). The modern note is never more sharply struck than in *Play*, with its use of the theatre apparatus, the spotlight, to draw ironic attention to the 'play' by which the sense of identity is achieved — and lost ('Am I as much as being seen?'). Yet it is also a play about a purgatory such as those in Noh where lovers endlessly re-live the traumas of their earthly existence. Beckett takes us more directly, even violently, into the 'replay' by his extraordinary repetition of the whole action.

It is appropriate to conclude with differences since these are legion, but even in thinking of the ways in which Beckett is unique, one is reminded of ways in which he seems to draw near to a drama he may hardly know. *Waiting for Godot* showed this at the start, not only in ways already mentioned but in its infinitely slow rhythm, its direct involvement of the audience in the sense of time almost at a stop. This was a new experience for western audiences, though familiar to those of Noh. In the brief, intense plays of a later phase, comedy thins down and rhythms become more hypnotic, often elegiac, as in *Rockaby*, where the woman in the rocking chair draws us into her own space with her soft, inexorable murmuring, in tune with the rhythm of the chair that moves her through life. It comes in the end to seem like a great force such as is understood to animate a pine or the murmur of grass in a Noh play when the spirits reveal themselves.

Echoes multiply. We might think of those many old men on Beckett's stage, their long white hair streaming, telling and listening to stories which reach out far beyond their own lives, into some almost unimaginable 'void'. Or the extreme stylization, in its own 'poor' mode as fantastic and significant as the elaborate costumes and symbolic properties of the Noh stage. The hypnotic black and white patterning of *Ohio Impromptu* is one of many such examples. Yeats shares ('up to a point', as the narrator in *Company* says) in these explorations. He has his Old Men — perhaps more consciously derived from those ubiquitous figures of Noh — as well as his goddesses. He brought on to the modern stage the 'dreaming back' in which his and Beckett's characters engage (and which is provided by Yeats too with a metatheatrical context, as in the ironic framing of *The Death of Cuchulain*). He pays tribute to Noh with some devices that Beckett would not use. (Masks, for instance, are deliberately excluded from possible methods of representing the faces in *Play*.) But the effect Beckett aims at by different means — 'faces so lost to age and aspect as to seem almost part of urns' — is not so far from the 'more formal faces' that Yeats desired for his stage, and found models for in Noh. The reason for the stylization is in all three cases the same: to create an appearance for something that is beyond appearances.

Finally, it seems as if Beckett is in some ways closer to Noh than Yeats. His is a drama of images rather than plot (Yeats's plots are important) and he supremely creates the slow rhythm and 'twilight' effect which is associated in Noh with the sought-after *yugen*. Yet we cannot say that he responded to influences reaching out from that distant source, only that he is close in spirit to the modern playwright who above all others did so respond. It is a tale of strangely ghostly influence and it leaves us with an enigma; just such a one as often provides subject matter for these dramas, that are so different and yet approach each other in such fascinating ways.

NOTES

I 'LIKE AN OLD TALE STILL': YEATS'S FOUR PLAYS FOR DANCERS

1 See the section, 'The Praise of Old Wives' Tales', in *Discoveries* (1906), followed by the comment: 'I come back always to this thought. There is something of an old wives' tale in fine literature. The makers of it are like an old peasant telling stories of the great famine or the hangings of '98 or from his own memories. He has felt something in the depth of his mind and he wants to make it as visible and powerful to our senses as possible.' W. B. Yeats, *Essays and Introductions* (London and New York: Macmillan, 1961), p. 276.

2 James Joyce, *A Portrait of the Artist as a Young Man* (Harmondsworth: Penguin, 1960), p. 226. Cf. Seamus O'Sullivan, *The Rose and Bottle and Other Essays* (Dublin: Talbot Press, 1946), pp. 118–21.

2a *The Variorum Edition of the Plays of W. B. Yeats*, eds. Russell K. Alspach and Catharine Alspach (Basingstoke and London: Macmillan, 1966), p. 167.

3 'The Plays of W. B. Yeats', *Threshold* No. 19 (Autumn 1965), ed. Roger McHugh, p. 4.

4 'Samhain: 1905', in *Explorations* (London: Macmillan, 1962), p. 196.

5 'Samhain: 1904: First Principles', in *Explorations*, p. 153.

6 'The Circus Animals' Desertion', in *Collected Poems* (London: Macmillan, 1950, 1963), p. 392.

7 Leonard E. Nathan, *The Tragic Drama of William Butler Yeats: Figures in a Dance* (New York: Columbia University Press, 1965), p. 171.

8 'The six [history] plays, that are but one play, have, when played one after another, something extravagant and superhuman, something almost mythological.' See *Essays and Introductions*, p. 109.

9 Philip Edwards, *Threshold of a Nation* (Cambridge: Cambridge University Press, 1979), p. 207. Cf. Peter Ure, *Yeats and Anglo-Irish Literature* (Liverpool: Liverpool University Press, 1974), pp. 203–24 ('W. B. Yeats and the Shakespearian Moment').

10 Ezra Pound and Ernest Fenollosa, Introduction, *'Noh', or Accomplishment: A Study of the Classical Stage of Japan* (New York: Knopf, 1917), pp. 11–12.

11 'The Freedom of the Theatre', reprinted by James W. Flannery, *W. B. Yeats and the Idea of a Theatre* (New Haven and London: Yale University Press, 1976), p. 326.

12 *Ibid.*, p. 327.

13 Quoted by James W. Flannery, 'W. B. Yeats, Gordon Craig and the

Visual Arts of the Theatre', in *Yeats and the Theatre*, eds. Robert
O'Driscoll and Lorna Reynolds (London and Toronto: Macmillan,
1975), pp. 83–4.

14   See Shotaro Oshima, 'Yeats and the Japanese Theatre', in *Threshold, op.
cit.*, p. 92. See also Liam Miller, *The Noble Drama of W. B. Yeats*
(Dublin: Dolmen Press, 1977), p. 194; and Masaru Sekine, *Ze-Ami and
His Theories of Noh Drama* (Gerrards Cross: Colin Smythe, 1985), p. 20.

15   *Essays and Introductions*, p. 222.

16   Quoted James W. Flannery, 'W. B. Yeats, Gordon Craig and the
Visual Arts of the Theatre', p. 97.

17   Introduction, *Certain Noble Plays of Japan* (Dublin: Cuala Press,
1916), p. ii; also *Essays and Introductions*, p. 221.

17a See Helen Caldwell, *Michio Ito : The Dancer and His Dances*
(Berkeley : University of California Press, 1977), pp. 37-54.

18   Liam Miller, *The Noble Drama of W. B. Yeats*, p. 220.

19   *The Variorum Edition of the Plays of W. B. Yeats*, p. 399. All subsequent quotations from *At the Hawk's Well* refer to this edition, from
which page numbers will be given parenthetically.

20   In his preface to *Four Plays for Dancers* (London: Macmillan, 1921),
Yeats said he knew but vaguely what he wanted but 'I do not want
any existing form of stage dancing' (p.v). See *Variorum*, p. 1304.

21   It is worth recalling also that the successful revival of *On Baile's
Strand* in London in 1915 had prompted Yeats's interest in completing
his 'heroic cycle'. See *The Letters of W. B. Yeats*, ed. Allan Wade
(London: Hart-Davis, 1954), p. 595.

22   *Variorum*, p. 529. All subsequent quotations from *The Only Jealousy
of Emer* refer to this edition, from which page numbers will be given
parenthetically.

23   *Variorum*, p. 764. All subsequent quotations from *The Dreaming of
the Bones*, unless otherwise indicated, refer to this edition, from which
page numbers will be given parenthetically.

24   Wade(ed.), *Letters*, p. 626. The date was 11 June 1917.

25   *The Noble Drama of W. B. Yeats*, p. 240.

26   Introduction to *Fighting the Waves*, in *Variorum*, p. 569.

27   Wade(ed.), *Letters*, p. 645. The date was 14 January 1918.

28   Peter Ure, *Yeats the Playwright* (London: Routledge and Kegan Paul,
1963), p. 113.

29   *The Drama of W. B. Yeats: Irish Myth and the Japanese No* (New
Haven and London: Yale University Press, 1976), p. 155.

30   *Essays and Introductions*, p. 137.

31   *Variorum*, p. 781. All subsequent quotations from *Calvary* refer to
this edition, from which page numbers will be given parenthetically.

32   *Complete Works of Oscar Wilde*, with an introduction by Vyvyan
Holland (London and Glasgow: Collins, 1966), p. 864. Cf. Liam
Miller, p. 253. Another source of *Calvary* is possibly Yeats's own 'The
Tables of the Law', in *Mythologies* (London: Macmillan, 1959), pp.
305–6.

33 *Variorum*, p. 1140.
34 *Variorum*, p. 950.
35 *Inishfallen, Fare Thee Well* (London: Pan Books, 1972), pp. 270–71.
36 *The Dramatic Imagination of W. B. Yeats* (Dublin: Gill and Macmillan; New York: Barnes and Noble, 1978).
37 'The Fascination of What's Difficult', *Collected Poems*, p. 104. Lennox Robinson, a practical man of the theatre and no lover of 'academic' drama, put on record his high regard for Yeats as a playwright in 'The Man and the Dramatist', *Scattering Branches*, ed. Stephen Gwynn (London: Macmillan, 1940), pp. 66–114.
38 'The Irish Dramatic Movement', *Autobiographies* (London: Macmillan, 1955), pp. 559–72.
39 *Four Plays for Dancers*, p. 86; *Variorum*, p. 415.
40 T. S. Eliot, 'Yeats', in *On Poetry and Poets* (London: Faber and Faber, 1957), p. 260.
41 Note on *At the Hawk's Well*, in *Four Plays for Dancers*, p. 86; *Variorum*, p. 415.
42 *Yeats and the Noh* (New York and Tokyo: Weatherhill, 1974), pp. 97, 107.
43 'Yeats and the Noh', in *The Dolmen Press Yeats Centenary Papers VI*, ed. Liam Miller (Dublin: Dolmen; London: Oxford University Press, 1968), p. 151. Cf. Okifumi Komesu, *The Double Perspective of Yeats's Aesthetic* (Gerrards Cross: Colin Smythe; Totowa: Barnes and Noble, 1984), pp. 122–32.
44 Wade (ed.), *Letters*, p. 917. The date was 20 October 1938.

II. WHAT IS NOH?

1 This is a poem by the seventy-fifth Emperor, Sutoku-in, and was included in a *waka* anthology, *Shikashu*, edited by Akisuke Fujiwara between 1151–54 A.D., at the request of Sutoku-in.
2 *Ze-Ami & Zenchiku*, edited by Akira Omote (Tokyo: Iwanami, 1974), pp. 34–5.
3 *Ibid.*, p. 55.
4 *Ze-Ami and His Theories of Noh Drama*, p. 98.

III THEMES

1 Richard Ellmann, *Yeats: The Man and the Masks* (New York: Macmillan, 1948; 2nd edition, London: Faber and Faber, 1961), p. 218.
2 Ezra Pound, and Ernest Fenollosa, *'Noh' or Accomplishment, a Study of the Classical Stage of Japan* (London: Macmillan, 1916; New York: Knopf, 1917).
3 W. B. Yeats, 'Introduction,' *Certain Noble Plays of Japan* (Dundrum: The Cuala Press, 1916), p. 2.

4   See Jan Kott, 'Noh, or about Signs', *The Theater of Essence and Other Essays* (Evanston: Northwestern University Press, 1984), pp. 109–16.
5   W. B. Yeats, *Explorations* (London: Macmillan, 1962), p. 257.
6   *Ibid.*, p. 258, italics added.
7   See Richard Taylor, 'Assimilation and Accomplishment: Nō Drama and an Unpublished Source for *At the Hawk's Well'*, in *Yeats and the Theatre*, eds. Robert O'Driscoll and Lorna Reynolds (London and Toronto: Macmillan, 1975), p. 158.
8   Quoted by Ellmann, *Yeats: The Man and the Masks*, p. 219. Cf. *Autobiographies*, p. 106.
9   *Two Plays for Dancers* (Dundrum: Cuala Press, 1919), p. 35.
10   *The Variorum Edition of the Plays of W. B. Yeats*, p. 566.
11   Dante Alighieri, *The Divine Comedy*, trans. Henry Wadsworth Longfellow (3 vols., Boston: Ticknor and Fields, 1867), III, p. 18.

IV CHARACTERIZATION

1   Richard Taylor, *The Drama of W.B. Yeats: Irish Myth and the Japanese Nō* (New Haven and London: Yale University Press, 1976), p. 129.
2   Curtis Baker Bradford, *Yeats at Work* (Carbondale and Edwardsville: Southern Illinois University Press, 1965), p. 190.
3   W. B. Yeats, *Explorations*, p. 68.
4   See Herbert J. Levine, *Yeats's Daimonic Renewal* (Ann Arbor: UMI Research Press, 1977), pp. 87–105. The autobiographical line taken over *The Only Jealousy of Emer* here is rather embarrassing; it is difficult to accept that the play is 'about' Yeats's marriage and subsequent emotional adjustments.
5   Okifumi Komesu, *The Double Perspective of Yeats's Aesthetic* (Gerrards Cross: Colin Smythe; Totowa, N.J.: Barnes & Noble, 1984), p. 171.
6   *Ibid.*, pp. 173, 176.
7   A. S. Knowland, *W. B. Yeats: Dramatist of Vision* (Gerrards Cross: Colin Smythe; Totowa, N.J.; Barnes & Noble, 1983), p. 160.
8   Karen Dorn, *Players and Painted Stage: The Theatre of W. B. Yeats* (Brighton: Harvester Press; Totowa, N.J.: Barnes & Noble, 1984), p. 52.

V PLOTS AND FUNCTIONS OF MUSICIANS

1   *The Yeats We Knew*, ed. Francis MacManus (Cork: Mercier Press, 1965), p. 14.
2   Lady Gregory, *Our Irish Theatre* (Gerrards Cross: Colin Smythe, 1972), pp. 100–2.
3   W. B. Yeats, *The Letters of W. B. Yeats*, ed. Allan Wade (London: Hart-Davis, 1954), p. 741.

4   There is as yet no general study of the sources of Yeats's plays comparable to Geoffrey Bullough's monumental study of Shakespeare, *Narrative and Dramatic Sources of Shakespeare*. For the *Four Plays for Dancers*, the best guides include Birgit Bjersby, *The Interpretation of the Cuchulain Legend in the Works of W. B. Yeats*, and F. A. C. Wilson, *Yeats's Iconography*. For a convenient and reliable guide, however, the reader should consult A. Norman Jeffares and A. S. Knowland, *A Commentary on the Collected Plays of W. B. Yeats*.
5   W. B. Yeats, *Essays and Introductions*, p. 230.
6   'Assimilation and Accomplishment: Nō Drama and an Unpublished Source for *At the Hawk's Well*', p. 153.
7   William B. Worthen, 'The Discipline of the Theatrical Sense: *At the Hawk's Well* and the Rhetoric of the Stage', *Modern Drama* 30: 1 (March 1987), p. 92.
8   For a comparison between *Nishikigi* and *The Dreaming of the Bones*, see David Clark's essay in *Theatre and Nationalism in Twentieth Century Ireland*, ed. Robert O'Driscoll (Toronto: University of Toronto Press, 1971).
9   *Variorum*, p. 763, italics added.
10   Okifumi Komesu, *The Double Perspective of Yeats's Aesthetic*, p. 155.

VI CONCEPTS OF MASKS

1   See James W. Flannery, 'W. B. Yeats, Gordon Craig and the Visual Arts of the Theatre', in *Yeats and the Theatre*, eds. Robert O'Driscoll and Lorna Reynolds, p. 95.
2   Liam Miller, *The Noble Drama of W. B. Yeats* (Dublin: Dolmen Press, 1977), p. 212.
3   Karen Dorn, 'Dialogue into Movement: W. B. Yeats's Theatre Collaboration with Gordon Craig', in *Yeats and the Theatre*, p. 109.
4   W. B. Yeats, *Memoirs*, ed. Denis Donoghue (London: Macmillan, 1972), p. 151.
5   *Ibid.*, p. 153.
6   A. Norman Jeffares, *W. B. Yeats: Man and Poet* (London: Routledge and Kegan Paul, 1949; New York: Barnes & Noble, 1966), p. 159.
7   *Memoirs*, p. 191.
8   *Autobiographies*, p. 189.
9   Cf. *Memoirs*, p. 259, n.2.
10   See *Mythologies*, pp. 325–42.
11   *Mythologies*, p. 337.
12   *Essays and Introductions*, p. 226.
13   *Four Plays for Dancers*, p. 86; *Variorum*, p. 416.
14   Liam Miller, *The Noble Drama of W. B. Yeats*, p. 212.
15   See Helen Caldwell, *Michio Ito : The Dancer and His Dances* (Berkeley: University of California Press, (1977), pp. 45–8.

16 *Variorum*, p. 1305.
17 A. S. Knowland, *W. B. Yeats: Dramatist of Vision*, p. 111.
18 *Explorations*, p. 38, n.1.
19 Wade (ed.), *Letters*, p. 669.
20 *Four Plays for Dancers*, pp. 86–7; *Variorum*, p. 416.
21 See *'Noh' or Accomplishment: A Study of the Classical Stage of Japan* (New York: Knopf, 1917), p.115.
22 *Players and Painted Stage*, p. 45.

VII STAGE PROPS AND COSTUMES

1   *Explorations*, p. 177.
2   *Ibid.*, p. 178.
3   *Ibid.*, p. 179.
4   *At the Hawk's Well*, in *Variorum*, p. 398..
5   *Essays and Introductions*, p. 222.
6   *The Drama of W. B. Yeats*, p. 160.
7   *Essays and Introductions*, p. 169
8   *Explorations*, p. 109.
9   *Essays and Introductions*, p. 148.
10 *Variorum*, p. 644.
11 Flannery, *W. B. Yeats and the Idea of a Theatre*, p. 250.
12 Miller, *The Noble Drama of W. B. Yeats*, p. 215.
13 Wade (ed.), *Letters*, p. 587. Yeats to Charles Ricketts, 11 June 1914.
14 *W. B. Yeats and the Idea of a Theatre*, pp. 260–1.
15 Helen Caldwell, *Michio Ito: The Dancer and his Dances*, p. 48.
16 *Ibid.*, p. 163, n. 47.

VIII DANCING AND ACTING

1   *Essays and Introductions*, p. 231.
2   *Ibid.*
3   See Taylor, *The Drama of W. B. Yeats*, p. 112. Cf. Caldwell, *Michio Ito*, pp. 38–44.
4   *Four Plays for Dancers*, p. 88. *Variorum*, p. 417.
5   *Essays and Introductions*, p. 224.
6   P.v; *Variorum*, pp. 1304–5.
7   Dorn, *Players and Painted Stage*, p. 84.
8   Richard Taylor, 'Assimilation and Accomplishment: Nō Drama and an Unpublished Source for *At the Hawk's Well*', p. 155.
9   *Variorum*, p. 554.
10 *Ibid.*, p. 567.
11 *Ibid.*, p. 777.
12 *Players and Painted Stage*, p. 112, n. 48.
13 Katharine Worth, *The Irish Drama of Europe from Yeats to Beckett* (London: Athlone Press; New Jersey: Humanities Press, 1978), p. 179.
14 *Essays and Introductions*, p. 528.

15 *Explorations*, pp. 86–7.
16 *Ibid.*, p. 172.
17 *Ibid.*, p. 173.
18 *Ibid.*, p. 173.
19 *Essays and Introductions*, p. 529.
20 Phyllis Hartnoll ed., *The Oxford Companion to the Theatre*, 4th edition, corrected (Oxford: Oxford University Press, 1985), p. 809. In *The Death of Cuchulain*, an Old Man 'looking like something out of mythology', who directs the play, describes himself as possibly the son of Talma, who was 'so old that his friends and acquaintances still read Virgil and Homer' (*Collected Plays*, p. 693). In this ironic passage Talma represents the classical, aristocratic ideal in the theatre.
21 *Autobiographies*, p. 524.
22 *Explorations*, p. 249.
23 *Essays and Introductions*, p. 232.
24 Sekine, *Ze-Ami and His Theories of Noh Drama*, p. 98.
25 *Four Plays for Dancers*, pp. 87–8; *Variorum*, p. 416.
26 Reg Skene, *The Cuchulain Plays of W. B. Yeats: A Study* (New York: Columbia University Press, 1974), p. 107.
27 *Four Plays for Dancers*, p.v; *Variorum*, p. 1304.
28 Wade (ed.), *Letters*, p. 609.
29 *Ibid.*, p. 611.
30 *Variorum*, p. 416. The second performance was on 4 April, in Lady Islington's drawing room, attended by three hundred fashionable people.
31 *Explorations*, p. 256.
32 *Ze-Ami and His Theories of Noh Drama*, pp. 90–1.
33 *Ibid.*, p. 90.
34 *Explorations*, pp. 176–77.
35 *W. B. Yeats: Dramatist of Vision*, p. 155.
36 Sekine, *Ze-Ami and His Theories of Noh Drama*, p. 82.

IX POETRY AND IMAGERY

1 *Ze-Ami & Zenchiku*, eds. Omote, Akira & Shuichi Kato, in *Nihon Shiso Taike*: vol. 26 (Tokyo: Iwanami Shoten, 1974), p. 134.
2 *Explorations*, p. 210.
3 *Essays and Introductions*, pp. 234–5. We should recall that as early as 1900 Yeats said that 'poetry moves us because of its symbolism', *Essays and Introductions*, p. 163.
4 *Yeats: The Man and the Masks*, p. 219.
4a Henrik Ibsen, *Brand*, trans. Michael Meyer (London: Eyre Methuen, 1967), p. 112.
5 *The Dramatic Works of James Sheridan Knowles*, 3 vols (London: Edward Moxon, 1841–1843), I, p. 170. It is not known whether Yeats

knew Knowles's plays, but as an expatriate Irish writer of poetic drama Knowles could well have been attractive to Yeats.

6 *Variorum*, pp. 555–7, italics added.
7 Ezra Pound and Ernest Fenollosa, *The Classic Theatre of Japan* (New York: New Directions, 1959), p.76.
8 ibid.
9 *Variorum*, 763, italics added.
10 *Variorum*, pp. 774–5, italics added.
11 John Montague, *Poisoned Lands* (London: MacGibbon and Kee, 1961), p. 48.
12 *Variorum*, p. 790.
13 *Players and Painted Stage*, p. 53.

X RITUALS

1 *Explorations*, p. 129, italics added.
2 *W. B. Yeats and T. Sturge Moore: Their Correspondence 1901–1937*, ed. Ursula Bridge (London: Routledge and Kegan Paul, 1953), p. 156. The date was 31 July 1929, when *Fighting the Waves* was being staged at the Abbey.
3 *Essays and Introductions*, p. 294.
4 Thomas Kinsella, 'Mirror in February', *Selected Poems 1956–1968* (Dublin: Dolmen Press, 1973), p. 61.
5 Cf. John Rees Moore, 'Yeats was convinced that religion, not morality, was the true basis for drama.' *Masks of Love and Death* (Ithaca and London: Cornell University Press, 1971), p. 18.

XI CONCLUSION

1 W. B. Yeats, 'Notes on *The Cat and the Moon*, in Variorum, p. 805.
2 In his notes to the first edition (Cuala Press, 1924), Yeats said: 'I wrote this play with the intention of including it in "Four Plays for Dancers", but did not do so as it was in a different mood.' See *Variorum*, p. 805. Understandably John Rees Moore discusses *The Cat and the Moon* as if it were, indeed, one of the 'plays for dancers': see *Masks of Love and Death*, pp. 243–8.
3 *Variorum*, p.804. Liam Miller has noticed that the musical in-struments mentioned in the text do *not* include cymbals, 'and these, therefore, must have been introduced as a detail of the first production of the play in 1926.' See Miller, *The Noble Drama of W. B. Yeats*, p. 252. However, 'cymbals' could well be what Yeats wrote, just as in the first edition of *At the Hawk's Well* the Musicians cry out 'and clash their cymbals' (*The Wild Swans at Coole, Other Verses and a Play in Verse*, p. 39), *a stage direction which became simply 'strike gong'* in *Four Plays for Dancers* (p. 21). The gong, one fancies, was Dulac's idea, while Yeats's preference may have been for cymbals.

4   Kott, 'Noh, or about Signs', *The Theater of Essence and Other Essays*
     (Evanston: Northwestern University Press, 1984), p. 112.

ACTING IN *THE DREAMING OF THE BONES*

Colleen Hanrahan

1   Ernest Fenollosa and Ezra Pound, *The Classic Noh Theatre of Japan*
     (New York: New Directions, 1959), p. 69.
2   William Butler Yeats, *Autobiographies* (London: Macmillan, 1980), p.
     401.
3   James Flannery, *W. B. Yeats and the Idea of a Theatre* (London: Yale
     University Press, 1976), p. 14.
4   W. B. Yeats, *Autobiographies*, p. 469.
5   Richard Taylor, *The Drama of W. B. Yeats, Irish Myth and the
     Japanese No* (London: Yale University Press, 1976), p. 104.
6   W. B. Yeats, *Collected Plays*, p. 434.
7   Phyllis Hartnoll, *The Theatre, A Concise History* (London: Thames
     and Hudson, 1980), p. 230.
8   See Masaru Sekine, *Ze-Ami and His Theories of Noh Drama*
     (Gerrards Cross: Colin Smythe, 1985), p. 93.
9   Richard Taylor, *The Drama of W. B. Yeats, Irish Myth and the
     Japanese No*, p. 5.
10 Masaru Sekine, *Ze-Ami and His Theories of Noh Drama*, p. 94.
11 *Ibid.*, p. 95.
12 *Ibid.*, p. 163.
13 *Ibid.*, p. 53.
14 David Bohm, *Wholeness and the Implicate Order* (London: Ark
     Paperbacks, 1983), p. 177.
15 W. B. Yeats, *Four Plays for Dancers* (New York: Macmillan, 1921),
     p. 53. Here Yeats requests a 'song for the folding and unfolding of the
     cloth'.
16 *Ibid.*, pp. 115–16.
17 *Ibid.*, p. 117.
18 *Ibid.*, p. 114.
19 *Ibid.*
20 *Ibid.*, pp. 122–23.
21 *Ibid.*, p. 123.
22 *Ibid.*, pp. 123–24.
23 *Ibid.*, pp. 124.
24 *Ibid.*, p. 125.
25 W. B. Yeats, *Essays and Introductions*, p. 159.
26 W. B. Yeats, *Four Plays for Dancers*, pp. 124–25.
27 Augustine Martin, 'Kinesis Stasis, Revolution in Yeatsean Drama',
     The Yeats Society of Japan Bulletin, No. 5, Oct., 1984, p. 90.
28 *Ibid.*

MUSIC IN TRANSLATION: YEATS; POUND; RUMMEL; DULAC

Peter Davidson

1 Edward Malins, *Yeats and Music* (Dublin: Dolmen Press, 1968), pp. 499–500.
2 *Ibid.*, pp. 493–5.
3 'Certain Noble Plays of Japan', *Essays and Introductions* (London: Macmillan, 1961), p. 223.
4 *The Cantos of Ezra Pound* (London: Faber, 1975), pp. 533–4. Canto *LXXXIII*.
5 Note to *Calvary, Variorum Edition of the Plays of W. B. Yeats*, eds. Russell K. Alspach and Caroline Alspach (London: Macmillan, 1966), p. 789.
6 *Ezra Pound and Music*, ed. R. Murray Schafer (London: Faber and Faber, 1978), pp. 57–241.
7 'Certain Noble Plays of Japan', *Essays and Introductions* (London: Macmillan, 1961), p. 223.
8 *Ibid.*, p. 236.
9 It does appear, however, that a Kabuki company had played at the Criterion Theatre in London in 1907, and their music was particularly noted in Max Beerbohm's review. *Around Theatres, The Bodley Head Max Beerbohm*, ed. David Cecil (London: Bodley Head, 1970), pp. 357–60.
10 Schafer, *op. cit.*, p. 490.
11 *Ibid.*, p. 224.
12 'Arnold Dolmetsch', *ibid.*, p. 49.
13 *Ze-Ami and His Theories of Noh Drama*, p. 77.
14 *The Translations of Ezra Pound*, intro. Hugh Kenner (London and Boston: Faber and Faber, 1970), p. 225.
15 Yet *Hagoromo* has no *kogata* or small role, the only parts being *waki*: Fisherman, *waki-tsure*: fishermen and *shite*: Ten-min.
16 Cf. Noel Stock, *The Life of Ezra Pound* (London: Routledge and Kegan Paul, 1970), pp. 185–6; Richard Taylor, *The Drama of W. B. Yeats* (New Haven and London: Yale University Press, 1976), pp. 111–14.
17 A combination which with a western flute and the strong resonance of the zither would produce an effect vastly different from the scoring of Noh music.
     The music to which reference is made may be found in *Plays and Controversies* (London: Macmillan, 1923), pp. 420–53.
18 Schafer, *op. cit.*, pp. 504–5.
19 Malins, *op. cit.*, p. 504.

ENIGMATIC INFLUENCES: YEATS, BECKETT AND NOH

Katharine Worth

1 'Bishop Berkeley' in *Essays and Introductions* (London: Macmillan, 1961), p. 403.
2 *Op. cit.*, pp. 221–37.
3 Among the many who have written on the subject, Richard Taylor draws interesting comparisons in his *The Drama of W. B. Yeats: Irish Myth and the Japanese No* (New Haven and London: Yale University Press, 1976).
4 The dates are those of the first productions.
5 '*At the Hawk's Well* and *Taka No Izumi* in a "Creative Circle" ', in *Yeats Annual*, ed. Warwick Gould (London: Macmillan, 1987).
6 In Katharine Worth, *The Irish Drama of Europe from Yeats to Beckett* (London: Athlone Press, 1978), p. 253.
7 Yasunari Takahashi, 'The Ghost Trio: Beckett, Yeats and Noh', in *Cambridge Review*, vol. 107, December 1986, pp. 172–6.
8 Beckett's comment is recorded in the Shaw Centenary programme, Gaiety Theatre, 1956, and quoted in the catalogue, *Samuel Beckett: an Exhibition held at Reading University Library May to July 1971*, 1971.

SELECT BIBLIOGRAPHY

Yeats's Works

Autobiographies (London: Macmillan, 1955).
The Collected Plays of W. B. Yeats (London: Macmillan, 1952).
The Collected Poems of W. B. Yeats (Second edition, London: Macmillan, 1950).
Essays and Introductions (London: Macmillan, 1961).
Explorations (London: Macmillan, 1962).
Four Plays for Dancers (London: Macmillan, 1921).
The Letters of W. B. Yeats, ed. Allan Wade (London: Hart-Davis, 1954).
Letters to W. B. Yeats, eds. Richard J. Finneran, George Mills Harper, and William M. Murphy, 2 vols (London and Basingstoke: Macmillan, 1977).
Memoirs, ed. Denis Donoghue (London: Macmillan, 1972).
Mythologies (London: Macmillan, 1959).
Two Plays for Dancers (Dundrum: Cuala Press, 1919).
Uncollected Prose by W. B. Yeats, collected and edited by John P. Frayne. Vol. I: First Reviews and Articles 1886–1896 (London: Macmillan, 1970).
Uncollected Prose by W. B. Yeats, collected and edited by John P. Frayne and Colton Johnson. Vol. 2: Reviews, Articles and other Miscellaneous Prose 1897–1939 (London and Basingstoke: Macmillan, 1975).
The Variorum Edition of the Plays of W. B. Yeats, eds. Russell K. Alspach and Catherine Alspach (Basingstoke and London: Macmillan, 1966).
A Vision (London: Macmillan, 1937).
The Wild Swans at Coole, Other Verses and Play in Verse [At the Hawk's Well]. (Dundrum: Cuala Press, 1917).
W. B. Yeats and T. Sturge Moore: Their Correspondence 1901–1937, ed. Ursula Bridge (London: Routledge and Kegan Paul, 1953).
Note: Unless stated otherwise, all quotations from Yeats's plays are from *The Variorum Edition of the Plays of W. B. Yeats*, abbreviated in the text as *Variorum*.

Critical and Secondary Works

Bjersby, Birgit, *The Interpretation of the Cuchulain Legend in the Works of W. B. Yeats* (Upsala: Lundequistska, 1950).

Select Bibliography 171

Bramsbäck, Birgit, *Folklore and W. B. Yeats: The Function of Folklore Elements in Three Early Plays*. (Uppsala: Uppsala University, 1984).

Bushrui, S. B., *Yeats's Verse Plays: The Revisions, 1900–1910* (Oxford: Clarendon Press, 1965.

Bradbrook, M. C., 'Yeats and the Noh Drama of Japan', *Aspects of Dramatic Form in the English and the Irish Renaissance. The Collected Papers of Muriel Bradbrook*, vol. 3 (Brighton: Harvester Press; Totowa, N.J.: Barnes & Noble, 1983).

Bradford, Curtis Baker, *Yeats at Work* (Carbondale and Edwardsville: Southern Illinois University Press, 1965).

——, *The Writing of the 'Player Queen': Manuscripts of W. B. Yeats, Transcribed, Edited, and with a Commentary by C. B. Bradford* (De Kalb: Northern Illinois University Press, 1977).

Bradley, Anthony, *William Butler Yeats*, World Dramatists Series (New York: Ungar, 1979).

Caldwell, Helen, *Michio Ito: The Dancer and His Dances* (Berkeley: Uinversity of California Press, 1977).

Certain Noble Plays of Japan, from the Manuscripts of Ernest Fenollosa, Chosen and finished by Ezra Pound, with an Introduction by William Butler Yeats (Dundrum: Cuala Press, 1916).

Chiba, Yoko, 'Ezra Pound's Versions of Fenollosa's Noh Manuscripts and Yeats's Unpublished "Suggestions & Corrections" ', *Yeats Annual* No. 4, ed. Warwick Gould (Basingstoke and London: Macmillan, 1986).

Clark, David R., *W. B. Yeats and the Theatre of Desolate Reality* (Dublin: Dolmen Press, 1965).

Clarke, Brenna Katz and Harold Ferrar, *The Dublin Drama League 1918–1941.* (Dublin: Dolman Press, 1979).

Dorn, Karen, 'Dialogue into Movement: W. B. Yeats's Theatre Collaboration with Gordon Craig', *Yeats and the Theatre*, eds. Robert O'Driscoll and Lorna Reynolds (Toronto and London: Macmillan, 1975).

——, *Players and Painted Stage: The Theatre of W. B. Yeats* (Brighton: Harvester Press; Totowa, N.J.: Barnes & Noble, 1984).

Ellis-Fermor, Una, *The Irish Dramatic Movement* (London: Methuen, 1939; second edition, 1954).

Ellmann, Richard, *The Identity of Yeats* (New York: Oxford University Press, 1964).

——, *Yeats: The Man and the Masks* (New York: Macmillan, 1948; second edition, London: Faber and Faber, 1961).

Fay, Frank, *Towards a National Theatre: The Dramatic Criticism of Frank J. Fay*, edited by Robert Hogan (Dublin: Dolmen Press, 1970).

Edwards, Philip, *Threshold of a Nation: A Study in English and Irish Drama* (Cambridge: Cambridge University Press, 1979).

Eliot, T. S., *On Poetry and Poets* (London: Faber and Faber, 1957).

Flannery, James W., *W. B. Yeats and the Idea of a Theatre: The Early Abbey Theatre in Theory and Practice* (New Haven: Yale University Press, 1976).

——, 'W. B. Yeats, Gordon Craig and the Visual Arts of the Theatre', *Yeats and the Theatre*, eds. Robert O'Driscoll and Lorna Reynolds (London and Toronto: Macmillan, 1975).

Friedman, Barton R., *Adventures in the Deeps of the Mind: The Cuchulain Cycle of W. B. Yeats* (Princeton: Princeton University Press, 1977).
Good, Maeve, *W. B. Yeats and the Creation of a Tragic Universe* (London: Macmillan, 1987).
Gregory, Lady Augusta, *Our Irish Theatre: A Chapter of Autobiography* (London: Putnams; third edition, revised and enlarged, Gerrards Cross: Colin Smythe, 1972).
Gwynn, Stephen (editor), *Scattering Branches: Tributes to the Memory of W. B. Yeats* (London: Macmillan, 1940).
Hartnoll, Phyllis, *The Oxford Companion to the Theatre*, Fourth edition (Oxford: Oxford University Press, 1983, 1985).
Hogan, Robert and James Kilroy, *The Irish Literary Theatre*, Vol. 1 in *The Modern Irish Drama: A Documentary History* (Dublin: Dolmen Press, 1975).
Hunt, Hugh, *The Abbey: Ireland's National Theatre 1904–1979* (Dublin: Gill and Macmillan, 1979).
Jeffares, A. Norman, *W. B. Yeats: Man and Poet* (London: Routledge and Kegan Paul, 1949; New York: Barnes & Noble, 1966).
——, and A. S. Knowland (editors), *A Commentary on the Collected Plays of W. B. Yeats* (London: Macmillan, 1975).
——, *W. B. Yeats: The Critical Heritage* (London: Routledge and Kegan Paul, 1977).
——, *W. B. Yeats: A New Biography* (London: Century Hutchinson, 1988).
Kermode, Frank, *Romantic Image* (London and Glasgow: Collins/Fontana, 1971).
Knowland, A. S., *W. B. Yeats: Dramatist of Vision* (Gerrards Cross: Colin Smythe; Totowa, N.J.: Barnes & Noble, 1983).
Komesu, Okifumi, *The Double Perspective of Yeats's Aesthetic* (Gerrards Cross: Colin Smythe; Totowa, N.J.: Barnes & Noble, 1984).
——, *At the Hawk's Well* and *Taka No Izumi* in a "Creative Circle" ', *Yeats Annual* No. 5, ed. Warwick Gould (Basingstoke: Macmillan, 1987).
Kott, Jan, *The Theater of Essence and Other Essays* (Evanston: Northwestern University Press, 1984).
Levine, Herbert J., *Yeats's Daimonic Renewal* (Ann Arbor: UMI Research Press, 1977).
McHugh, Roger (editor), *Threshold*, XIX (Autumn 1965). A special issue on the drama of W. B. Yeats.
Martin, Heather C., *W. B. Yeats: Metaphysician as Dramatist* (Waterloo, Ont.: Wilfrid Laurier University Press; Gerrards Cross: Colin Smythe, 1986).
Mikhail, E. H. (editor), *The Abbey Theatre: Interviews and Recollections* (Basingstoke and London: Macmillan, 1988).
——, *W. B. Yeats: Interviews and Recollections*, 2 vols (London and Basingstoke: Macmillan, 1977).
Miller, Liam (editor), *The Dolmen Press Centenary Papers VI* (Dublin: Dolmen Press; London: Oxford University Press, 1968).

——, *The Noble Drama of W. B. Yeats* (Dublin: Dolmen Press, 1977).

Moore, John Rees, *Masks of Love and Death: Yeats as Dramatist* (Ithaca: Cornell University Press, 1971).

Moore, Virginia, *The Unicorn: William Butler Yeats' Search for Reality* (London: Macmillan, 1952).

Nathan, Leonard E., *The Tragic Drama of William Butler Yeats: Figures in a Dance* (New York: Columbia University Press, 1965).

O'Casey, Sean, *Autobiographies*, 2 vols (London: Mácmillan, 1963).

O'Driscoll, Robert (editor), *Theatre and Nationalism in Twentieth Century Ireland* (Toronto: University of Toronto Press, 1971).

——, and Lorna Reynolds (editors), *Yeats and the Theatre* (London and Toronto: Macmillan, 1975).

Oshima, Shotaro, *W. B. Yeats and Japan* (Tokyo: Hokuseido Press, 1965).

Parkin, Andrew, *The Dramatic Imagination of W. B. Yeats* (Dublin: Gill and Macmillan: New York: Barnes & Noble, 1978).

Qamber, Akhtar, *Yeats and the Noh*, (New York: Weatherhill, 1974).

Robinson, Lennox, 'The Man and the Dramatist', *Scattering Branches: Tributes to the Memory of W. B. Yeats*, ed. Stephen Gwynn (London: Macmillan, 1940).

——, *Curtain Up: An Autobiography* (London: Michael Joseph, 1942).

Saddlemyer, Ann (editor), *Theatre Business: The Correspondence of the First Abbey Theatre Directors: William Butler Yeats, Lady Gregory and J. M. Synge* (Gerrards Cross: Colin Smythe, 1982).

——, 'Yeats and the Noh', *Irish Writers and the Theatre*, ed. Masaru Sekine (Gerrards Cross: Colin Smythe; Totowa, N.J.: Barnes & Noble, 1986).

Sidnell, Michael J., George P. Mayhew, David R. Clark (editors), *Druid Craft: The Writings of 'The Shadowy Waters'* (Amherst: University of Massachusetts Press, 1971).

Skelton, Robin and Ann Saddlemyer (editors), *The World of W. B. Yeats: Essays in Perspective* (Victoria: University of Victoria; Dublin: Dolmen Press, 1965).

Skene, Reg, *The Cuchulain Plays of W. B. Yeats: A Study* (New York: Columbia University Press, 1974).

Taylor, Richard, 'Assimilation and Accomplishment: Nō Drama and an Unpublished Source for *At the Hawk's Well*', *Yeats and the Theatre*, eds. Robert O'Driscoll and Lorna Reynolds (Toronto and London: Macmillan, 1975).

——, *The Drama of W. B. Yeats: Irish Myth and the Japanese Nō* (New Haven and London: Yale University Press, 1976).

——, *A Reader's Guide to the Plays of W. B. Yeats* (London and Basingstoke: Macmillan; Dublin: Gill and Macmillan, 1984).

Thompson, William I., *The Imagination of an Insurrection, Dublin, Easter 1916: A Study of an Ideological Movement* (New York: Oxford University Press, 1969).

Ure, Peter, *Yeats the Playwright: A Commentary on Character and Design in the Major Plays* (London: Routledge and Kegan Paul; New York: Barnes and Noble, 1963).

——, *Yeats and Anglo-Irish Literature: Critical Essays by Peter Ure*, edited by C. J. Rawson (New York: Barnes & Noble, 1974).

Vendler, Helen Hennessy, *Yeats's 'Vision' and the Later Plays* (Cambridge, Mass.: Harvard University Press, 1963).

Wilson, F. A. C., *W. B. Yeats and Tradition* (London: Methuen; New York: Macmillan, 1958).

——, *Yeats's Iconography* (London: Gollancz, 1960).

Worth, Katharine, *The Irish Drama of Europe from Yeats to Beckett* (London: Athlone Press; New Jersey: Humanities Press, 1978).

Worthen, William B., 'The Discipline of the Theatrical Sense: *At the Hawk's Well* and the Rhetoric of the Stage', *Modern Drama* 30: 1 (March 1987).

Zwerdling, Alex, *Yeats and the Heroic Ideal* (New York: New York University Press, 1965).

The Noh Texts

Ze-Ami & Zenchiku, eds. Omote, Akira & Shuichi Kato, in *Nihon Shiso Taike: vol. 26 (Tokyo: Iwanami Shoten, 1974)*.

Nogakuronshu, ed. Nishio, Minoru, in *Nihon Koten bungaku taikei*, vol. 65 (Tokyo: Iwanami Shoten, 1961).

Zeami jurokubushu hyoshaku, ed. Nose Asaji (Tokyo: Iwanami Shoten, 1966).

Translations of Ze-Ami

Izutsu, Toshiko and Izutsu, Toyo, *The Theory of Beauty in the Classical Aesthetics of Japan* (The Hague: Martinius Nijhoff, 1981).

Nogami, Toyoichiro, *Zeami and his Theories on Noh*, translated by Ryozo Matsumoto (Tokyo: Hinoki, 1955).

Rimer, J. Thomas and Yamazaki Masakazu, *On the Art of No Drama. The Major Treatises of Zeami* (Princeton, N.J.: Princeton University Press, 1984).

Sakurai, Shuichi and others, *Zeami's Kadensho* (Kyoto: Sumiya — Shinobe Publishing Institute, 1968).

Critical and Secondary

Hoff, Frank and Willis Flint, eds., 'The Life Structure of Noh', adapted from the Japanese of Yokomichi Mario, *Concerned Theatre Japan* 2, Spring 1973, 209–56.

Inoura, Yoshinobu, *A History of Japanese Theatre I, Noh and Kyogen* (Tokyo: Kokusai Bunka Shinkokai, 1971).

Inoura, Yoshinobu and Kawatake, Toshio, *The Traditional Theatre of Japan* (Tokyo: The Japan Foundation, 1981). This is a one-volume edition containing *A History of Japanese Theatre, I and II.*

Keene, Donald, *No, the Classical Theatre of Japan* (Palo Alto and Toyko: Kodansha International, 1966).

Keene, Donald, *Twenty Plays of the No Theatre* (New York: Columbia University Press, 1970).

Komparu, Kunio, *The Noh Theatre Principles and Perspectives* (New York, Tokyo, Kyoto: Weatherhill and Tankosha, 1983).

McKinnon, Richard N., 'Zeami on the Art of Training', *Harvard Journal of Asiatic Studies*, 16 June 1953, 200–24.

Nakamura, Yasuo, *Noh. The Classical Theatre Performing Arts of Japan* (New York, Tokyo and Kyoto: Weatherhill and Tankosha, 1971).

Nogami, Toyoichiro, *Ze-Ami and his Theories on Noh* (Tokyo: Hinoki, 1955).

O'Neill, P. G., *Early No Drama, Its Background Character and Development* (London: Lund Humphries, 1958).

Pilgrim, Richard, 'Some Aspects of *Kokoro* in Zeami', *Monumenta Nipponica, 31, Autumn 1976, 251–274.*

Pound, Ezra and Ernest Fenollosa, *'Noh' or Accomplishment: A Study of the Classical Stage of Japan* (London: Macmillan, 1916; New York: Knopf, 1917). Reprinted as *The Classic Noh Theatre of Japan* (New York: New Directions, 1959).

Raz, Jacob, 'The Actor and His Audience: Zeami's Views on the Audience of the Noh', *Monumenta Nipponica, 31, Autumn 1976, 251–74.*

Sekine, Masaru, *Ze-Ami and his Theories of Noh Drama* (Gerrards Cross: Colin Smythe Ltd, 1985).

Sieffest, René, *La Tradition Secrète du No,* (Paris: Gallimard, 1960).

Watsuji, Tetsuro, 'Japanese Ethical Thought in the Noh Plays of the Murmachi Period', translated by David Dilworth, *Monumenta Nipponica, 24, 4, 1960, 467–98.*

Yamazaki, Masakazu, 'The Aesthetics of Transformation: Zeami's Dramatic Theories', translated by Susan Matisoff, *Journal of Japanese Studies 7,* Summer 1981, 215–58.

Books in Japanese

Goto, Hajime, *Noh no Keisei to Ze-Ami* (Tokyo: Mokujisha, 1966).

Goto, Hajime, *Nohgaku no Kigen* (Tokyo: Mokujisha, vol. I, 1975, vol. II, 1980).

Goto, Hajime, *Noh to Nihon Bunka* (Tokyo: Mokujisha, 1980).

Kanai, Kiyomitsu, *Noh no Kenkyu* (Tokyo: Ofusna, 1969).

Matsuda, Tamotsu, *Ze-Ami to Noh no Kenkyu* (Tokyo: Shindokusha, 1972).

Nishi, Issho, *Ze-Ami Kenkyu* (Tokyo: Sarubia Press, 1967).

Nose, Asaji, *Nohgaku Genryu-Ko* (Tokyo: Iwanami-Shoten, 1938).

Omote, Akira, *Nohgaku-Shi Shinko* (Tokyo: Wanya-Shoten, 1979).

Onishi, Yoshinori, *Yogen to Aware* (Tokyo: Iwanami-Shoten, 1939).

Shoda, Shojiro, *Nohgaku Daijiten* (Tokyo: Kikkawa-Kobunkan, 1907).

Toita, Michizo, *No-Gei-Ron* (Tokyo: Keisoshobo, 1965).

BIOGRAPHICAL NOTES

PETER DAVIDSON was born in Scotland and studied English and related literatures at the Universities of Cambridge and York, taking his Ph.D. at Cambridge. He has published numerous articles and two books of poems, and is preparing *The Penguin Book of Cavalier Verse* and a complete edition of *The Poems of Sir Richard Fanshawe* for the Clarendon press. He is active as a composer: his cantata 'The Banks of Italy' was performed in the official programme of the 1988 Edinburgh Festival, and his second opera, *Faelanus ad Matutinam*, was performed in August 1989. He is a temporary lecturer in English at the University of St Andrews.

COLLEEN HANRAHAN completed an honours arts degree at Saint Mary's University, Nova Scotia, where she was an active member of the drama society, appearing in the Faith Ward production of *The Man Who Came to Dinner*. At L'Université Ste. Anne, Nova Scotia, she was involved in producing and acting in French dramatic works. She obtained a Master's degree in Anglo-Irish Literature with first-class honours from University College, Dublin, and is currently working on her Ph.D. While at UCD she acted in Masaru Sekine's productions of *The Dreaming of the Bones* and of *Nishikigi*.

AUGUSTINE MARTIN was born in Ballinamore, Co. Leitrim, and was educated at the Cistercian College, Roscrea, and University College, Dublin, where he gained his Ph.D.. After returning to the Cistercian College to teach for some years, he took up an appointment at UCD, where he later became Professor of Anglo-Irish Literature and Drama. Among his publications are *James Stephens; A Critical Study* (1977), *Anglo-Irish Literature: A History* (1981), *The Genius of Irish Prose* (1985), critical biography of W. B. Yeats (1983, revd. 1990), and has edited *The Collected Poems of W. B. Yeats* (1990) and a short story anthology, *'Forgiveness' and Other Stories* (1990). He is presently under contract to write the official biography of Patrick Kavanagh.

He has been Director of the Yeats International Summer School in Sligo, Chairman of the Board of the Irish National Theatre, and a Senator in Seanad Eireann. He is founder and Director of the James Joyce Annual Summer School at Newman House, University College, Dublin.

He has lectured in universities in North America, Europe, the Lebanon, India, Japan and Singapore. A well-known broadcaster, he has devised and presented some fifty programmes for Telefis Scoile (Irish Educational Television).

CHRISTOPHER MURRAY was an undergraduate at University College, Galway, and subsequently took his Ph.D. at Yale University. He is currently a statutory lecturer in the Department of English at University College, Dublin. He is author of *Robert William Elliston, Manager* (1975), has edited a restoration comedy, *St. Stephen's Green*, by William Philips (1980), was guest editor of the special issue of *Irish University Review* on Sean O'Casey (1980), and his *Selected Plays of Lennox Robinson* was published in 1982. He was written numerous articles on Irish theatre and drama, and contributed to the latest edition of *The Oxford Companion to the Theatre*. He was secretary of the International Association for the Study of Anglo-Irish Literature (1973–76), and is currently editor of *Irish University Review*. He is working on a biography of the nineteenth-century playwright James Sheridan Knowles.

MASARU SEKINE, a trained Noh actor, is a graduate of Waseda University, Tokyo. As a British Council Scholar, he studied at the Universities of Manchester and Stirling. He was a Research Curator at the Theatre Museum, Tokyo, and lecturer in English and Drama, before becoming an Associate Professor at Waseda University, when he is now a Professor of English. He was a Japan Foundation Visiting Professor of Japanese Culture at University College, Dublin. He has written on various aspects of modern drama and translated plays. He founded IASAIL-JAPAN (the Japanese branch of the International Association for the Study of Anglo-Irish Literature). He is author of *Ze Ami and His Theories of Noh Drama* (1985), and has edited *Irish Writers and Society at Large* (1985), *Irish Writers and the Theatre* (1986) and (with Okitumi Komesu) *Irish Writers and Politics* (1990).

KATHARINE WORTH is Emeritus Professor of Drama and Theatre Studies in the University of London and currently Visiting Professor at King's College, London. She is author of *Revolutions in Modern English Drama* (1973), *The Irish Drama from Yeats to Beckett* (1978), *Oscar Wilde* (1983), *Maeterlinck's Plays in Performance* (1985) and of many essays on modern drama in journals and symposia. She edited *Beckett the Shape Changer* (1975) and her critical edition of Yeats's *Where There is Nothing* and *The Unicorn from the Stars* by Yeats and Lady Gregory was published in 1987. Her study of *Waiting for Godot* and *Happy Days* has just been published.

In collaboration with David Clark she has produced new versions of Beckett's television play, *Eh Joe*, and his radio plays, *Words and Music*, *Embers* and *Cascando*. Her adaptation of *Company* has been performed in London, Belfast and New York since its first presentation at the 1987 Edinburgh Festival.

INDEX

Noh plays are indexed by name, not under author. Entries on W. B. Yeats are restricted to his works.